Design Secrets:
Layout

50 Real-Life Projects Uncovered

Design Secrets:
Layout

50 Real-Life Projects Uncovered

GLOUCESTER MASSACHUSETTS

ROCKPORT
PUBLISHERS

Rodney J. Moore

First published in the United States of America by
Rockport Publishers, Inc.
33 Commercial Street
Gloucester, Massachusetts 01930-5089
Telephone: (978) 282-9590
Fax: (978) 283-2742
www.rockpub.com

Library of Congress Cataloging-in-Publication Data
Moore, Rodney J.
    Design secrets—layout: 50 real-life projects uncovered / Rodney J. Moore
        p.   cm.—(Design secrets)
    ISBN 1-59253-091-5 (hardcover)
    1. Advertising copy. 2. Advertising layout and typography. I. Title II. Series
  HF5825.M66 2004
  659.1'32—dc22   2004011016
                                              CIP

ISBN 1-59253-091-5

10 9 8 7 6 5 4 3 2 1

Layout and Production: *tabula rasa* graphic design
Cover Design: Madison Design & Advertising, Inc.
Copy Editor: Pamela Elizian
Proofreader: Matt Blanchard

Printed in China

Thank you to my family and friends for their unwavering support, most of all Kyna. A big thank you to the design firms and designers who gave their time, energy, and work to this project. And lastly, thank you to Kristin, Pamela, Rochelle, and all of the folks at Rockport.

contents

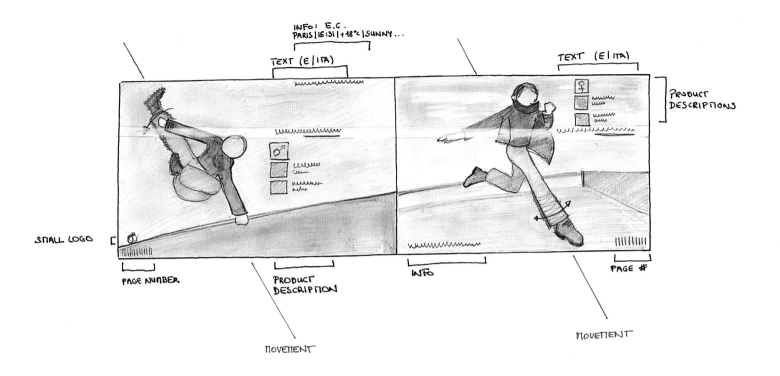

INFO: E.C.
PARIS | 15:31 | +18°C | SUNNY...

TEXT (E | ITA)

TEXT (E | ITA)

PRODUCT
DESCRIPTIONS

SMALL LOGO

PAGE NUMBER

PRODUCT
DESCRIPTION

INFO

PAGE #

MOVEMENT

MOVEMENT

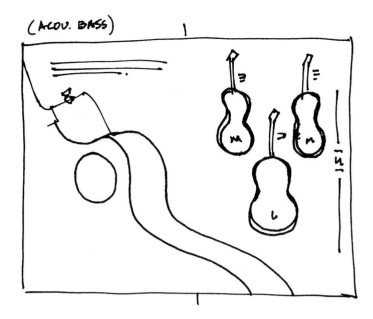

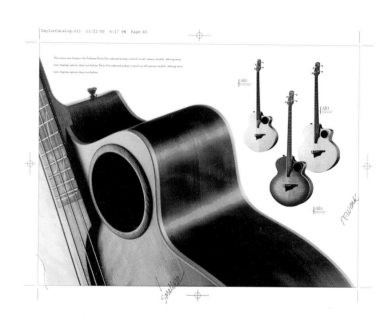

introduction

Layout is, at its very core, about the creative process. I admit, that's what intrigues me the most about design in general. More specifically, how do creative ideas evolve into an end result? What does the process look like? The truth is: design is personal. Each designer or artist approaches a job or project differently. A designer brings his own personality, experience, education, imagination, and preferences to each piece.

As a copywriter, I often have the privilege of working with many talented artists and designers. This collaborative process is something I always enjoy because the better I understand how designers work, the better I can work with them. As I gathered projects for this book, the difficult task was not only choosing from a wide range of material, but also selecting items that I thought would appeal to a diverse audience. I chose two types of projects: pieces that were created for recognizable brands and projects that are simply unique no matter the brand or organization.

Design Secrets: Layout covers 50 different design projects from sketch phase to finished piece. It's a peek over the shoulder of designers—a rare glimpse into their creative world and their interpretation of how to solve problems. This glimpse is valuable only if you look for inspiration to bring to your own work. There are no secret formulas to follow here. What you will find is inspiration and professional tips throughout the text. Most of the secrets shared by designers are personal and conventional, however, when taken together, they could be a rough guide to layout for new and experienced designers alike.

I hope that within these pages you will find plenty of encouragement and creative sparks. Perhaps you will even uncover a new insight or approach to problem solving you never considered before. Ultimately, after reading *Design Secrets: Layout,* I hope you will arrive at this overall conclusion: keep learning, exploring, and taking risks.

AIGA Design Camp How do you design invitations and attendance materials for a designers' camp? Ask Derek Sussner of Sussner Design Company in Minneapolis, Minnesota.

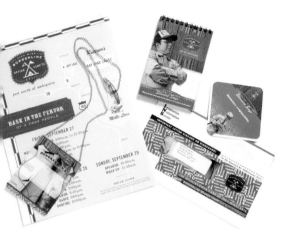

After changing the theme from "No Boundaries" to "Borderline Design Camp," Sussner and company became inspired to create a character and organization specifically for the camp.

Sussner had both cochaired the annual student event (Portfolio 1-ON-1) in 1997 and designed the event materials. He also served on the AIGA Minnesota Board of Directors. Given his background with AIGA, Sussner was asked by one of the board members to take on the AIGA Design Camp materials. He agreed—his first step was to modify the camp's theme of "No Boundaries," the tagline at that time for Ford trucks, to "Borderline Design Camp."

Sussner and company proceeded to develop the overall look of the materials by dissecting the word *borderline*, looking for inspiration in the definition. All five designers and a copywriter were involved in the initial concept and development stages. Each designer then executed a piece or two, with Sussner acting as the creative director.

The group found inspiration in a movie called *Canadian Bacon* starring John Candy and Stephen Wright. Other inspiration came from the INS and its staid government forms.

To pull off the concept of the mock INS (the Imagination Nurturization Service), Sussner created a mascot, Stewart, to play the INS agent. He allowed Stewart to choose the font for the invitation and conference materials. Turns out it was Sussner Design's collective least-favorite font, Cooper Black—but it was perfect for the mock INS group.

A character guide was created to ensure that all aspects of the project adhered to what Stewart would want. Sussner even had a friend take pictures of a custodian's office at a nearby school. Finally, the team trekked to the local Army-Navy surplus store and picked out Stewart's uniform. "After we set up Stewart's character, it was relatively easy to extend the idea into the various collateral materials," Sussner says. "Each designer had the liberty to add a bit of themselves. (It is, after all, 'Stew'.) One designer added a typeface, another a background texture, and another a shape or printing technique."

The team hit a roadblock when Sussner decided to use PMS 354 on one of the envelopes for the invitation materials. Pantone denied the request to use the color reference, so he used the equivalent as a CMYK breakdown.

Sussner knew from the beginning that Stewart would have to be a professional actor because none of his staff could pull off the act. However, he did use an unsuspecting designer as a stand-in for the early materials. "Brent, one of our designers, dressed up and stood in for a preliminary photo shoot so we would have some shots to use when first presenting the concept to AIGA," says Sussner. "He made me promise that we wouldn't use his photos for the real 'Stew.' He didn't want to be known in designer circles as 'that Stew guy.' We became so used to seeing Brent as

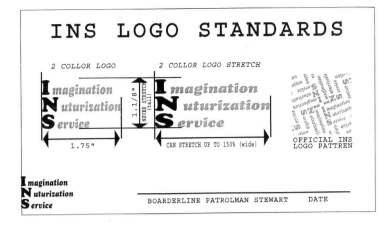

INS LOGO STANDARDS

2 COLLOR LOGO 2 COLLOR LOGO STRETCH

Imagination
Nuturization
Service

1.75"

1-1/8"
NEVER STRETCH (tall)

Imagination
Nuturization
Service

CAN STRETCH UP TO 150% (wide)

OFFICIAL INS
LOGO PATTREN

Imagination
Nuturization
Service

BOARDERLINE PATROLMAN STEWART   DATE

Imagination **N**uturization **S**ervice

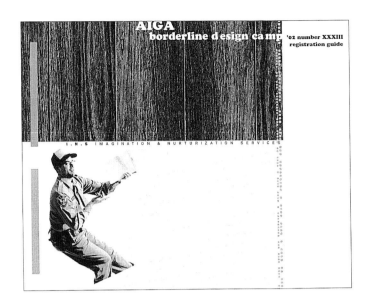

◇ "What Would Stewart Do?" became the concept for the design camp materials.

◇ Sussner was inspired by actual Immigration and Naturalization Service forms. He tried to capture the staid government-form appearance throughout the materials, even creating his own version of the INS— the Imagination Nurturization Service.

◇ This early mockup of the conference materials shows a stand-in for the character of Stewart.

emboss

◇ During a preliminary photo shoot, Sussner had one of his designers stand in for the character of Stewart so he could present the concept to AIGA. He later reluctantly replaced the designer with an actor.

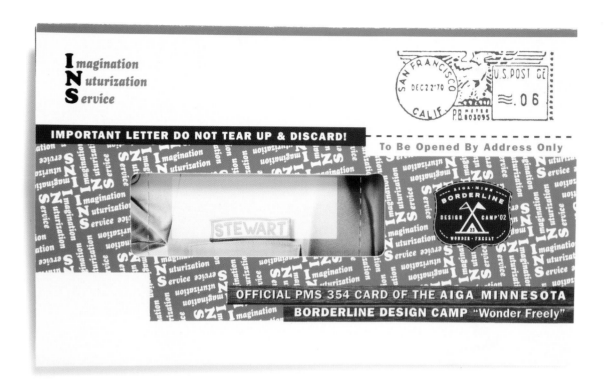

Stew with all the comps we were doing, it was hard to change our perception of who Stew was, even after we cast the actor."

Sussner says his overall approach to design is instinctual rather than methodical. "What works well for me is to fill up the bucket in my mind," Sussner says. "First, I'll review the business objectives, audience, key ideas, competitors, and so on. Then I like to brainstorm with word associations, tone, or definitions. I prefer to develop concepts with copywriters because they have a great ability to think of ideas and meaning, instead of just a visually cool layout. Then I look for the all-important concept or big-picture idea from which the piece or pieces can grow. After a trip to the bookstore to look at typefaces, I'll let everything incubate for a day, overnight, or sometimes just an hour or so. When there's enough stuff in the bucket, the execution just starts to spill out of it. I like to look for the one thing that everything else will revolve around—an icon, image, word—and build on that."

In total, Sussner Design spent 757 hours on the project, all of which were pro bono. But Sussner is happy to have designed a project for his peers. He says it's a challenge that doesn't come along very often, but when it does, he can't pass it up.

The poster mailer containing registration materials included a tipped-on tongue-in-cheek registration form.

Amica Mature Lifestyles is Canada's preeminent provider of **select accommodation and services** to mature adults. Amica operates nineteen senior **independent living** apartments,

Because the brochure had to explain a partnership, dossier told the stories of both companies, mirroring each against the other by presenting the stories on either side of the brochure.

retirement communities, and skilled-nursing residences in four provinces. Amica had successfully completed a rebranding campaign, including a name change from Ishtar to Amica, and tapped Vancouver-based dossiercreativeinc., who had worked with Amica for several years, to help them through their rebranding.

On the heels of a $15-million joint venture with the building developer Daniel Group, Amica realized that a communications piece was required to explain the merger to potential investors. The piece needed to communicate the superiority of the two companies in their fields and what their capabilities would be after the merger. It also needed to show the attention to detail, hand-craftsmanship, and personal attention and care that is evident in each of Amica's residences.

"The brochure was designed to tell the story of two companies coming together to provide the best in mature-lifestyle living," says art director Don Chisholm. "The brochure opens to a two-fold accordion-style page with the story of Amica Mature Lifestyles, detailed with photos, illustrations, and copy throughout the front side of the brochure. The story of Daniel Group is on the opposite side. The design and layout needed to portray the partnership's story, which we believed was unique and powerful. The stories of Amica and Daniel Group needed to be separate but holistic, creating an overall cohesive story of the two companies coming together. We needed to tell two stories within one brochure, each mirroring the other. The accordion-style fold represented the inner meshing of the two different concepts."

Chisholm says that Amica had no predetermined idea for the brochure. He was given an objective and began brainstorming how to go about achieving the objective. "The number-one goal was to get attention, but it wasn't supposed to be a heavy-read piece—it was more of a visual-impact piece. By playing around with ideas: we could put it in a box, wrap it, have it in a shrink-wrap sleeve, bag it—all kinds of different things. The accordion fold grew out of the idea to communicate one message on one side and another on the other side, without creating two stories that were too different as far as the image and the feel. The "aha!" moment was really the cover—to go with that thick cover material and bookend it was cool and different.

"There are two soft messages there as you go from front to back cover, and when you go from the back to the front again, as you rotate the piece, it would tell a slightly different story. They are very soft stories because it's being narrated by somebody with Amica, so they are really using the piece almost as a guidebook or reference point to have a conversation with someone. That's how it was designed. It wasn't designed for someone to sit and read the piece for a lot of information.

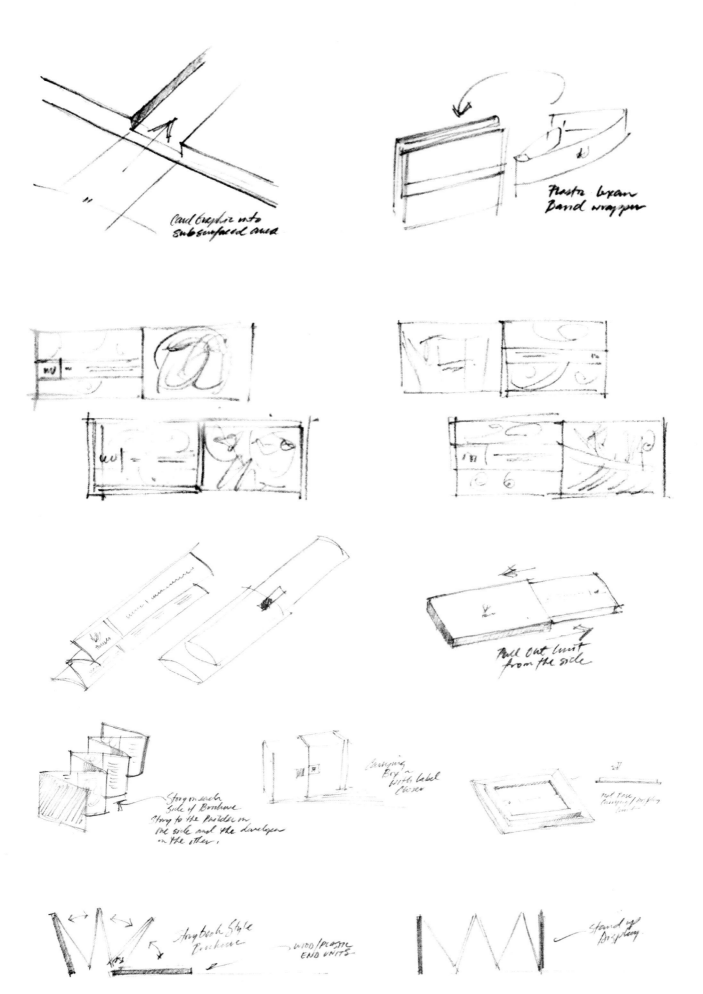

Dossier sketched out several ways for the brochure to be constructed. They explored many options but eventually settled on the accordion-fold pages.

"We provided the client with only one mechanical process for how the piece would go together, and it was approved," says Chisholm. "We created two concept layouts of how the design could fold out in the brochure. When one of the directions was chosen, we finalized it and provided it within the time frame allotted us. We provided alternative options for the outer carrier piece, from bands to boxes. We ended up with a Lexan band wrap, individually hand-bound for each piece.

"The patterns were largely found in an archive. We found a few that had the right feel, but we couldn't get enough patterns so we created a couple of our own. This was a little bit of a chore because they were old archival patterns, so we had to clean them and prepare them properly to be produced. A lot of the images were shots that we had already taken; others we got through stock photography."

One of the challenges of the brochure was the unusual binding and accordion-style fold for the inside pages. Amica had difficulty explaining the fold to the printer, and the printer had difficulty executing the fold properly. "Every project always has at least one challenge for the designers. For this particular project, the binding proved to be more challenging than initially anticipated. Accuracy in the binding was vital, but it was difficult to bind the accordion fold to 1/16"- (1.6 mm-) thick cintra stock covers so that as the pages folded the covers would meet perfectly. For Amica and Daniel, this sort of attention to detail is paramount. It is the foundation upon which both companies built their tradition of providing superior service to their clients."

Chisholm says that because AMICA is a publicly traded company, there is an expectation of a conservative mindset; however, the brochure set out to shatter this perception by separating AMICA from the competition. The overall design concept accomplishes this with its unorthodox approach. In fact, because the brochure is designed to open much like a traditional book, senior executives would often present the document in person, and when they would actually fold it over so the story was continuous, it would work like gangbusters.

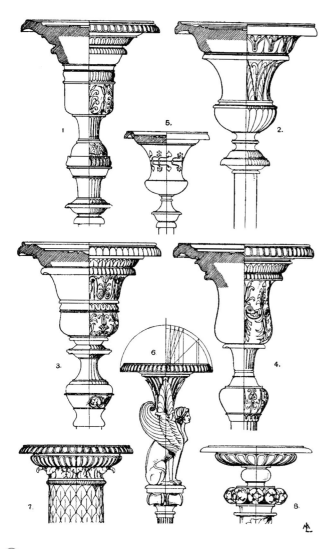

Dossier chose elegant columns and ornamental patterns found in an archive. Some were actually created for the backgrounds of pages with a text overlay.

5-6   Wellness & Vitality

7-8   design expertise

11-12   the mature lifestyles market

The final spreads of the AMICA brochure feature a balance of story and image selection for both AMICA and the Daniel Group.

The APIM, or Portuguese Knitwear Association, is an association of **entrepreneurs** that includes companies that produce **fabrics and yarn,** clothing and knitwear, dyeing, printing and finishing, trimmings, **lacework, and embroideries.**

The APIM, or Portuguese Knitwear Association, asked local design firm SETEZEROUM to put together a technical essay that would actually get read. The end result is a manual called *Textile Fibers: Characteristics, Care, and Applications.*

A key factor of their competitiveness is a better knowledge of the raw materials they use. APIM approached local design firm SETEZEROUM about putting together a technical essay that would actually get read. Setezeroum had been working with APIM as graphic design consultants for almost two years.

"We were APIM's regular consultant on graphic design. One afternoon while we were discussing our progress project for them, the research manager asked me how I felt about technical essays," says Jose Manuel Da Silva. "My answer was, 'Most of them are dull. They don't encourage you to read them.' One week later, they called me to talk about how I could make a technical essay more desirable to read."

"The main idea was to present a different kind of technical manual (essay) for the textile engineers," Da Silva says, "not something as conservative and austere as technical books used to be, but with a fresh and appealing look, keeping the technical data, text, images, icons, and technical tables simple and attractive, even for the nontechnical reader."

Da Silva originally wanted to use rubber on the covers, but costs prohibited this approach. Instead, he chose to use plastic that could be embossed with a logo. "The green swirl was the first solution for the page background of the frosted PVC cover, when the project included only washing cares or conditions of the different materials. It was set aside when the client decided that the project would have more technical amplitude. That's when I chose a clean background for the frosted PVC cover.

"There were only a few sketches from the main chapter's pages, just to provide an overview of it," Da Silva says. "In this case, we had to work on the layouts virtually at the same time we got the material from the client—time was short.

"During the early stage of the project, the book theme covered only washing conditions—a more practical and simple approach from the client's standpoint. One of the options for the cover was a picture with the pages reflecting only washing care signs. As soon as they saw the first sketches they started to broaden the contents of the textile manual. The changes of the layout started when I realized that my early approach allowed them to work on the run for a much wider spectrum. That gave me room to apply a richer layout using color, images, icons, and technical tables."

Da Silva says the biggest challenge in the project was trying to achieve what the client wanted but not diverging from his own standards. "Trying to achieve the client's aims without compromising our values and beliefs in a simple design sometimes is a

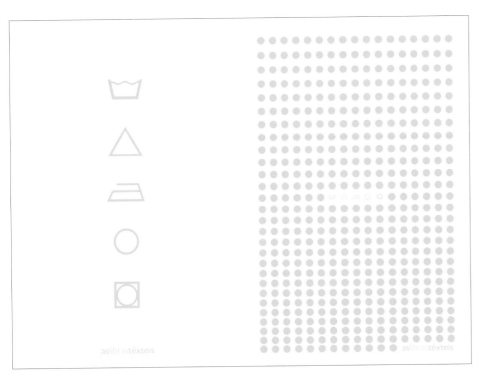

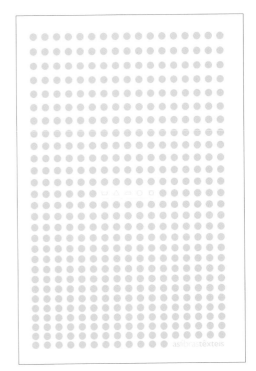

Early options for the front and back covers included the universal symbols of fabric care: washing, bleach, ironing, dry cleaning, and dryer.

secagem

Lorem ipsum dolor sit amet, consectetuer adipiscing elit, sed diam nonummy nibh euismod tincidunt ut laoreet dolore magna aliquam erat volutpat. Ut wisi enim ad minim veniam, quis nostrud exerci tation ullamcorper suscipit lobortis nisl ut aliquip ex ea commodo consequat. Duis autem vel eum iriure dolor in hendrerit in vulputate velit esse molestie consequat, vel illum dolore eu feugiat nulla facilisis at vero eros et accumsan et iusto odio dignissim qui blandit praesent luptatum zzril delenit augue duis dolore te feugait nulla facilisi. Lorem ipsum dolor sit amet, consectetuer adipiscing elit, sed diam nonummy nibh euismod tincidunt ut laoreet dolore magna aliquam erat volutpat. Ut wisi enim ad minim veniam, quis nostrud exerci tation ullamcorper suscipit lobortis nisl ut aliquip ex ea commodo consequat. Duis autem vel eum iriure dolor in hendrerit in vulputate velit esse molestie consequat, vel illum dolore eu feugiat nulla facilisis at vero eros et accumsan et iusto odio dignissim qui blandit praesent luptatum zzril delenit augue

7

This alternate opening page sequence had to be adjusted because of the changing aspects of the manual's content.

This was the first solution for the background image behind the frosted PVD cover. However, when the client broadened the technical amplitude of the manual, SETEZEROUM chose a simpler solution.

demanding job," says Da Silva. "It was challenging describing an idea to people who are used to having a professional detachment from design; they know only one way to look at numbers and technical charts.

"The first issue was the color. It was hard to persuade the technical team responsible for the textile research to use colorful pages instead of a dull and regular one-color document," Da Silva says. "The second issue was the size and the spiral-wire finishing. The major issue was the page layout design. When we explained how we intended to set up text, images, icons, and technical tables using practical examples, they gave us the freedom to express ourselves.

"I'm not particularly inspired by anybody's work," says Da Silva. "There are designers that I admire, but I never try to follow. I find inspiration by observing our environment—music, video clips, films, architecture, art, design magazines, design books, street posters, outdoors, websites. Then, if I find something that catches

my attention, I try to pick up on how it's done. I try to understand the solutions that apply to a particular piece. That helps me respond when I analyze a project or a client's needs.

"For me, one of the secrets of design is that there are classic rules for a layout, those we learn at design school, but those rules can be shaped and broken. That is our mission as designers, knowing exactly when and how to shape or break the rules," Da Silva says.

"There are other secrets, such as to constantly grow in your quality of work, you must have strong convictions and be aware of trends. Trends are important to broaden your horizon, but are inimitable sometimes, and most of them are brief. We must understand it like that, and then we might make a work so unique that we create a rule of our own."

Although there might not be a rule in the APIM Textile Fiber manual, SETEZEROUM did get recognition in *HOW Magazine*'s International Design Annual.

Two early comps of the chapter openings served as templates for the remaining chapters. In the final design, the text headers were not as bold and the chapter symbols were taken directly from the headers.

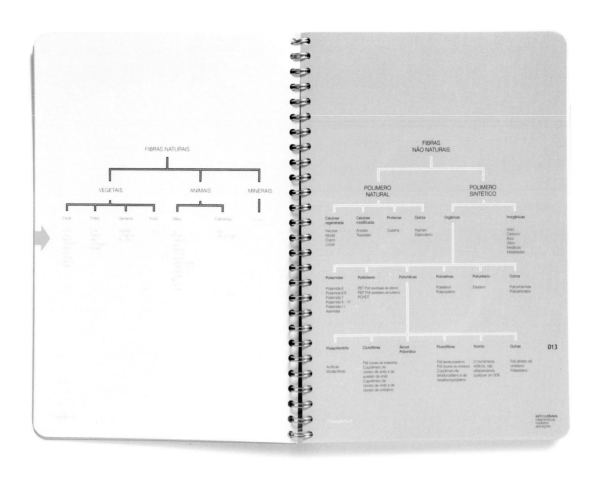

The final design of the manual incorporates more use of color than traditional manuals, which typically featured only one color.

AptarGroup, Inc., operates in the packaging components industry, which includes the development, manufacturing, and sale of consumer product dispensing systems, such as pumps, closures, and aerosol valves.

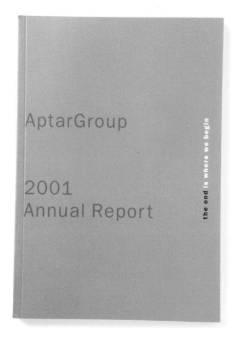

AptarGroup

2001
Annual Report

the end is where we begin

Because AptarGroup's principal product lines are pumps, closures, and aerosol valves, it made sense to tell their story in reverse, beginning with the end consumer and ending—or beginning, depending on where you start reading—with the employees.

Chicago-based SamataMason has been designing AptarGroup's annual report since AptarGroup become a publicly traded company in 1993. During those ten years, SamataMason has developed a deep knowledge of the company's strategic direction and diverse product offerings. Occasionally, this kind of history and level of understanding can make designing something original more of a challenge.

Fortunately, SamataMason found their inspiration for the 2001 annual report early on, during a meeting with the CEO. "We've been doing the annual report for ten years, and it's always about educating the market and people about who the company is and what their innovations are," says partner and art director Kevin Krueger. "Well, the year we did this report, they wanted to focus on everything. So, we thought, what's the best way to package everything so that it flows like a story and works together? When they started talking about how it really begins with the end product—that's where the idea came from. It's not like a new story, but for them to put it down in words and pictures to explain the process and who they are, it's new for them.

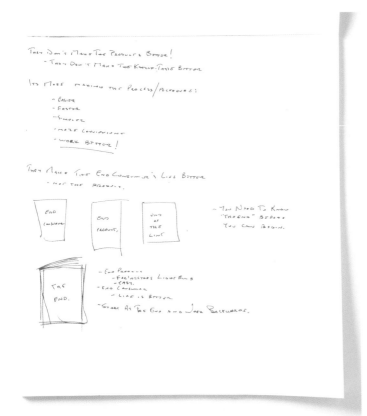

⊘ Early notes from client meetings provided the motivation for structuring the report around the concept of "The End." Sketches showed how the report could look with this theme.

"We were working with this idea of 'the end,'" says Krueger. "So we started thinking about the end product, the end consumer, the end result, the end of year reporting, and the end of the day. We needed to tie everything together. We began writing the message and sketching out a possible pacing for the book. How could we take everything and make it communicate on all levels?

"That was the biggest challenge—trying to organize it and build it in a way so that it communicated on different levels for different people. Annual reports nowadays have such a diverse audience. It's not just individual and institutional shareholders; it's for recruiting, marketing, and public relations. Companies use annual reports to their fullest because there's a lot of benefit to it.

"There was another direction that we were exploring to tie in the story and trace the product. AptarGroup works so hard to develop these products that are invisible to the consumer. This strategy makes them successful, because if they are invisible, then they are doing their job well. We considered this direction, but it seemed too technical and too boring. We knew what the client's objectives and strategies were, even though the other report would be considerably longer and more costly. The previous year's book was 70 pages, whereas this one was 120."

Krueger says the first big comp was used to determine whether the pacing worked and the size was right. He says the process is basically taking their notes and putting it into sketches. Krueger also likes to use this early stage to find the exact message or messages to communicate in the report.

"In some ways, this was one of those projects that just clicked," Krueger says. "I started writing down some notes about this end-product notion and tried to find the story in that. In some of the early sketches we were looking for ways to show a grid of consumers, just to get the idea across. Then we needed to show the product, but how many? We could show several because AptarGroup produces lots of small products. Then we needed to show employees; well, how do they interact with it? They're really the beginning of the process, but in our report concepts, they're the end of the process." Essentially, SamataMason flipped the traditional company narrative on its head by ending with the employees rather than beginning with them.

"In the end, it was a strong idea that lived through a lot of adverse conditions," Krueger says. "You can sketch out the pacing of what comes first and how that would intersect with other ideas. It was always that first concept, but until you get it in your hands as the reader, you can't understand how these messages work together. When we did the next iteration, the design was still pretty close to what we originally had in mind, but it just seemed to be on a higher level."

It seems many agreed, including the client. "Our client was thrilled with the report," Krueger says. "The challenge we go into every year is, 'how are we going to make a better book than we did the year before?'. The bar is always lifted. Employees loved it and they loved being included."

Krueger's track record with the publication in design competitions was also very good. In fact, of the competitions into which it was entered, the AptarGroup annual report won nine out of ten times, including the AR100 Show, AIGA's 365 Annual Design Competition, *STEP Inside Design*'s Annual 100, and the Applied Arts Awards Annual.

The first thumbnail comps of the report showed a more technical and scaled-down version of how to treat AptarGroup's products.

The report began to take shape with the first rough comp, which showed image and copy placement with the client's changes and initial approval.

With the second comp, images had begun to get more definitive. However, stock photos were still used in back of the report.

This third and final comp was sent to AptarGroup for final approval of all images and type placement. At this stage only minor adjustments were made before the last approval was given via a PDF file to the client.

the end is where it begins
AptarGroup 2001 Annual Report

ArjoWiggins, the Anglo-French fine papers conglomerate, has been a client of **Toronto-based Viva Dolan** for 12 years. Buoyed by the **success of their fine paper line** in North America, ArjoWiggins asked Viva Dolan to **help launch five additional products** into this market for a total of six.

The final swatchbook had a fictitious or tongue-in-cheek affinity that appealed more to the audience and gave Viva Dolan a higher degree of creative latitude.

Viva Dolan Communications & Design recommended that they consolidate all six brands under a new umbrella called Curious Collection and make each paper line an aspect of the new brand. Doing so would allow their resources to be used to build one strong brand rather than, in effect, splitting the pie six ways. ArjoWiggins agreed with the strategy, and the Curious Collection was officially launched.

With the subsequent success of the Curious Collection in the North American market, ArjoWiggins was inspired to employ the same strategy in Europe and elsewhere around the globe. They asked Viva Dolan, as the originators of the idea and the brand's name, to assist in their strategy. In this second iteration of the European version, the brand has now been consolidated to four lines: Curious Translucents, Curious Touch, Curious Particles, and Curious Metallics.

"The creative problem, beginning with the first North American version, has been to ensure that whereas each line of paper is unmistakably part of the Curious Collection system, each must also be differentiated according to its unique physical characteristics," says art director and principal Frank Viva.

During the initial approval process, ArjoWiggins had some reservations about a few of the earlier pitches from Viva Dolan, especially the mobile direction. "They felt it might be too North American for our primarily European audience," says Viva. "We argued that Europeans are avid consumers of American pop culture. Still, they felt the solution didn't look as though it had been created for a high-end European company with roots dating back hundreds of years."

ArjoWiggins wasn't entirely comfortable with the mobile direction, so Viva Dolan set out to create a more fictitious-looking package. "The final idea didn't arise from any single inspiration," Viva says. "It was distilled from a long list of potential solutions and arrived at by weighing the relative merits of each from the perspective of creative latitude, cost, and suitability for the audience.

"In earlier versions, we used patterns and personalities to achieve the goal of unity," says Viva. "In this version, after considering a number of ideas, we decided that fictitious (tongue-in-cheek) packaging would be appealing to our design audience and offer a high degree of creative latitude. The other, interrelated challenge was to group the system physically in some sort of container, to underline that this should be seen as a single resource/toolbox for fine text and cover papers.

"The most challenging aspect of this project was that we'd not only set for ourselves the problem of designing four swatchbooks, a slipcase, and an overview booklet, we also had to create four full-blown 3-D consumer packages as well," says Viva. "The other challenging aspect was that the products had to be produced for twenty international markets in twelve languages using seven printers in four countries."

To manage this daunting task, Viva Dolan designed an approval process that was entirely Web-based and segmented by markets. There was a separate team for France, Switzerland, and so on. "Our simple and effective solution was to centralize all of the content for approval on a password-protected part of our Web server," says production manager Hiram Pines. "In conjunction with this, we persuaded our clients to use Acrobat's editing and annotation tools to communicate their comments and corrections to us."

"We don't have a single way of approaching a design problem," Viva says. "It varies according to the specific challenges of the project. In this case, it was very structured because of the complexity and number of people involved. In other cases it's very fluid.

"In my experience, brainstorming with the design team is very useful, provided that the problem we have to solve as a group is well defined," Viva says. "A well-defined problem leaves as much room as possible for experimentation in the expression of a solution but with a clear understanding of the project goals. Of course, collaboration also engenders a positive team spirit. The relative complexity of this project did impose some creative constraints, but that was all part of the fun."

That fun came through loud and clear because the Curious Collection piece won several recognitions in top design annuals such as *STEP Inside Design, Applied Arts Magazine,* and *HOW Magazine.*

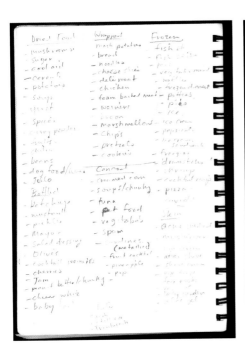

Early brainstorming produced a list of items to associate with each of the different paper lines. The list was later pared down to just a handful.

Viva Dolan initially developed a creative approach to packaging the paper. Ideas included simulated TV dinners and cookie boxes.

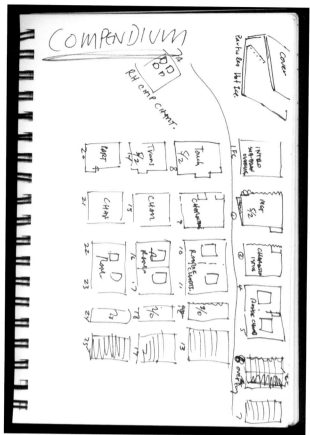

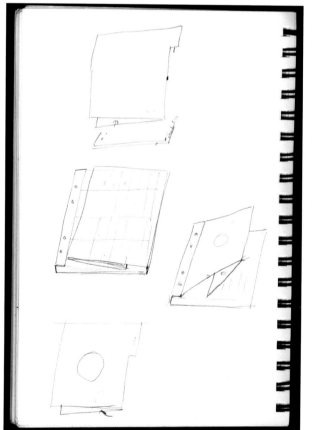

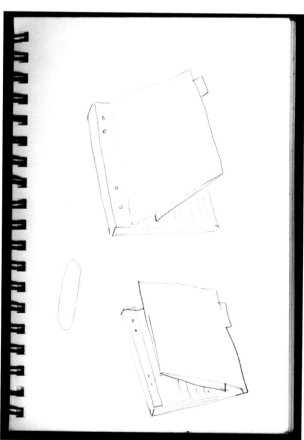

 Concepts for the swatchbook construction included a fold-out cover and a mixture of enclosures.

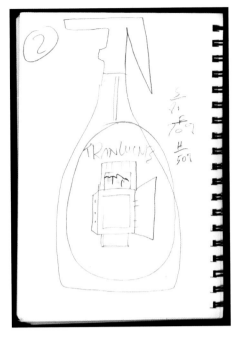

Instead of packaging the paper collection as products, Viva Dolan chose an over-the-top concept that showcased the capabilities of each line.

More refined sketches showed the development process from brain-storming lists to early sketches to more detailed sketches.

ARTISTdirect is a Los Angeles–based online music network, a traditional record label, and an entertainment marketing company. After ARTISTdirect had their initial public offering, Douglas Joseph Partners made contact with the CEO.

For the annual report of a Los Angeles–based online music network, record label, and entertainment marketing group representing urban music, Douglas Joseph Partners tried to balance a professional look while also capturing the personality of the company.

Although they did not produce an annual report that first year, the ARTISTdirect CEO decided that he wanted a proper annual report the following year and chose Douglas Joseph Partners to create it.

Primarily an online business before their public offering, the company wanted to emphasize their newly launched record label that had more growth potential than the online business. The concept was to convey ARTISTdirect as an integrated music entertainment company that went well beyond an online music network.

"A good number of the bands that had initially been signed to the ARTISTdirect label were considered 'urban music,'" says art director and principal Douglas Joseph. "Much of the boldness in terms of color and typography came from the music itself. The biggest challenge had to be integrating photos of the ten bands from ten different photographers to look like they belonged together in one book. They supplied all of the photographs, which made us nervous at first, but actually they all worked fairly well together. I think we were fortunate in that respect.

"We presented two design directions using the same supplied photography," Joseph says. "We didn't do a whole lot of exploration on it, simply because the imagery came from the record company and we were sort of locked into those things. We presented two directions: one was what the book became, and the second featured large type that's rough looking."

Joseph says at one point they considered making the book close to the size of a CD jewel case but decided doing so would make it too thick. "Ultimately, we made the book the size we did and used the fluorescent colors to be a little obnoxious, kind of like the music," Joseph says. "Just to be loud. So we tried to reflect that but still be professional looking and not go so far over the edge.

"There's an awful lot going on in the book. A whole photo section works as a unit," says Joseph. "We used bright, garish colors to bring attention to it. We wanted to be big and bold in some respect, but you can only be so big and bold in a small book like this. That's where the initials for each of the bands came from. We didn't want to just put the bands in there and call it a day. We had no qualms about putting type over their photographs."

Joseph says he looks at other design fields for inspiration more than his own. "I'm a big automotive fan, so I look at automotive design. I look at fashion design, architecture, product design. You can see influences of those things in our work, but I think there are crossovers between what we do and what they do.

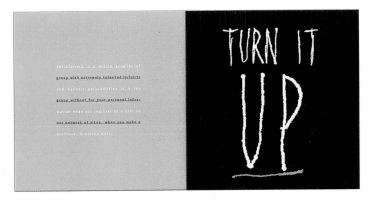

Douglas Joseph's early experiments incorporated a bold mix of type treatments and color schemes throughout the report.

The images the designers were given to work with came from ten different photographers. Fortunately, most of the photos worked well together, and strategic placement downplayed the few that didn't.

⊙ Still searching for the right combination of type and color scheme, this combination of comps tried bold backgrounds that flanked artist photos.

⊙ On this comp, the cover concept began to come into focus with vertical color bars. The interior, however, underwent additional type changes before the final look was achieved.

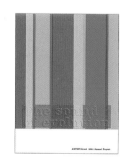

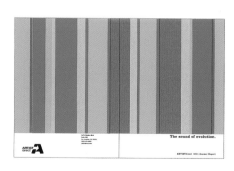

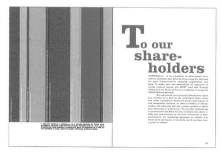

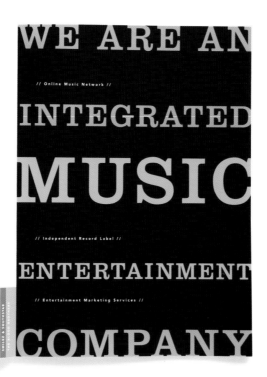

WE ARE AN

// Online Music Network //

INTEGRATED

MUSIC

// Independent Record Label //

ENTERTAINMENT

// Entertainment Marketing Services //

COMPANY

Douglas Joseph Partners had fun with the annual report, especially because ARTISTdirect was a client that wasn't afraid to take risks, and the project was a departure compared with their other portfolio material. The final piece was so well received that ARTISTdirect requested a limited run with additional material added for their marketing efforts.

"We do approach things in a rather uniform way by researching our clients," says Joseph. "We do as much research as we possibly can, which can entail all sorts of things. When we first start, we look at every scrap of information they produce. We do all of that before we ever conceptualize what the book might be. Then philosophy-wise, if you look at all of our work as a whole, we don't have a style that we impose upon our clients. We let their personalities come through in whatever it is we are producing for them. We just guide it, I guess. In the case of ARTISTdirect, that book does a pretty good job of reflecting who they are."

The ARTISTdirect annual report was quite a departure for Douglas Joseph Partners because the bulk of their work tends to be more sophisticated and elegant. But it is exactly this kind of departure that often results in a great-looking project.

Case in point, the annual report was received so well after it was produced that ARTISTdirect's marketing staff asked Douglas Joseph Partners to produce a limited-run piece that picked up aspects of the report but also incorporated more details in terms of their music marketing capabilities. Because ARTISTdirect represents a number of different bands, they can approach an advertiser like Coca-Cola and organize large-scale concerts. The marketing piece carried through aspects of the annual report from a design perspective and incorporated additional stock photos.

Axené07

For their **second event in a trilogy** of summer exhibits, Axené07, **a Canadian artist center,** approached their partner **Kolegram Design** with the usual request: Produce a poster or mailer announcing the exhibit, named Ravaudage Urbain.

Expecting a poster for their second event in a trilogy of summer exhibits, Axené07, a Canadian artist center in Ottawa, got a combination direct-mail piece and poster from Kolegram Design. The yellow ribbon wrap was sent only to the media.

Where others might have seen a rather mundane poster or mini-brochure project, Kolegram artist Mike Teixeira saw possibility. It was to be the first piece that Axené07 would print in color; previous programs were done in black and white. After learning about the exhibit's focus—vacant urban landscapes—and limited budget, Teixeira was inspired to produce a piece with two functions: a direct-mail piece and poster in one.

"I came up with the idea of trying to fit the content of the brochure inside a poster or mailer," says Teixeira. "I wasn't sure it would work, but the title, 'Urban Mending,' goes with the idea. I remember trying to fold the poster so that it became more of a brochure. Then when you unfold it, it's a poster again. I've seen it before, especially on things like contest calls for entries. For the direct-mail aspect, I just thought I would put it into a bag, but I wasn't sure of the texture. I knew it would need to fit into a bag for mailing.

"A couple of comps were shown early on in a poster format, just to catch the visual look that the client wanted," Teixeira says. "They were done using just the main title. I tried to be as diverse as I could, trying to cover as many looks as possible for this project. In fact, the main direction was identified from the beginning—the folding process.

"I remember wanting to keep it simple but complex," Teixeira says. "Simple typography but rough and saturated colors for the images. The client gave me a couple of images of electricity wires caught together with architectural elements as a visual sense of the direction he wanted."

After seeing an aerial view of the city of Hull, Ontario, Teixeira immediately thought of a road map. By nature, a road map requires unfolding in many ways. He wanted that tactile experience for the recipient. Plus, he knew that's how people would respond, depending on the way he designed it.

"The special thing that I wanted to achieve with the mailer was, when unfolded, it would be angled," Teixeira says. "That was the main challenge at the beginning, but I remember not talking to the client about it because I wanted to try it first. Once I did it and I realized I could control my space—meaning I wanted to be able to count the different spaces like a road map—I tried fitting in the content. I remember that the content didn't fit because of the dimension restrictions. That's when I started talking to Axené07 about my idea and they loved it. They loved it so much that they cut some of the content to make it fit."

Kolegram artist Mike Teixeira came up with several different comps reflecting the title and theme of the exhibit: Urban Mending.

Because the client wanted a visual idea of the typography, images, and the overall look and feel before he could really think about format, Teixeira first did a series of posters on a flat surface.

⊘ While coming up with comps
⊙ of posters to show the client,
Teixeira was secretly working
on a combination poster and
mailer that he was afraid to
mention until he was certain
he could pull it off.

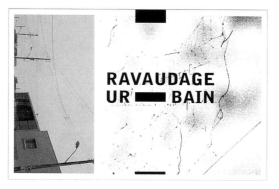

Teixeira did small-scale comps on a tabloid printer to speed up the testing process. "I probably did 20 versions that I mostly trashed," he says. "I remember the first thing was getting the angle right. When that was fixed, I started folding it—I wanted to fold it like a road map. I wanted it to be that size, once folded. When I did that, I knew how I could control my visual and editorial content on the layout. I would have to mark the different spaces on the comp."

At one point, Teixeira even considered dropping the brochures in a vacant area of the city to roughen them and scratch the paper for texture, but he decided against it because doing so would likely make them rather dirty. "We didn't do it because we were afraid it would make it a dirty piece," Teixeira says. "But we wanted a texture to the project. From the beginning we knew we had to put it in a bag or something to send it. We thought about maybe even using a piece of cloth wrapped around it. We wanted plastic,

which would have sound effect to it. Then the idea of putting a yellow ribbon around it came up, and we decided to do that just for the media."

Fortunately for Kolegram, director of Axené07 Diane Génier has always given them the opportunity to express a bit of art in their design approach for the center. In addition, working closely with the artists on every project gives Kolegram the latitude to push every project a bit further than usual. Kolegram makes the artists themselves part of the design process.

The Ravaudage Urbain piece continued Kolegram's award-winning work for Axené07. Every previous piece had won an award, either locally or regionally. Ravaudage Urbain won first place in the regional Advertising and Design Association in Ottawa. It also won an honorable mention in *Coupe*, a Toronto-based design publication.

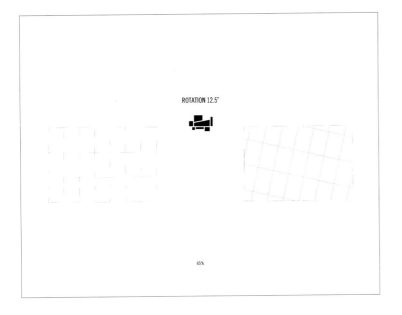

ROTATION 12.5°

65%

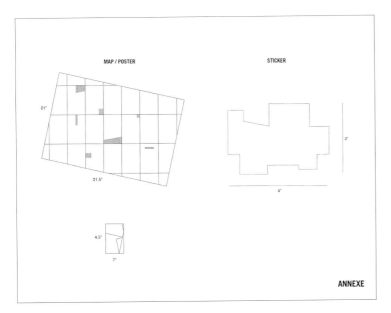

MAP / POSTER

21"

31.5"

STICKER

3"

4"

4.5"

7"

ANNEXE

To speed up the design process, Teixieria first made a small-scale comp on a tabloid printer to ensure that he could print the invitation full scale. The early comp with the lettered red and black dots was made as a reference for designating folds.

The final comp proved this sculptural and interactive piece was achievable.

Inspired by a road map, Teixeira wound up with an offset poster that contained all of the exhibit content and also folded into a self-contained brochure/mailer.

Bambra Press

"Do whatever you like"—music to a designer's ears. That's what the team at **Hatch Creative** of Victoria, Australia, was told by Bambra Press, **a local print shop** that needed a moving announcement.

It was quickly decided that another slick printer's brochure/mailer was out of the question, so Hatch set off to create a decidedly different moving announcement—call it the anti-moving announcement.

Bambra Press, a well-known Melbourne printer, was moving to bigger and better premises. This important information had to be communicated to clients and the industry without going over the top. What's more, there was no requirement to sell the company's new capabilities.

"The goal was to turn a straightforward moving announcement into something else, something odd," says designer Saskia Ericson. "Our target market receives a lot of promotional material, so we wanted to give them something engaging that would linger and circulate, continually working for the client. With no photos of state-of-the-art German technology required, we decided to tell a story, draw some pictures, and put it all together as a special keepsake for Bambra's clients."

The story Hatch came up with is told in the format of a classic children's storybook and features the clients' dogs, Quincy and Alice, detailing their adventures on moving day. The book purposefully reflects Bambra's surroundings and sense of humor, including references to local landmarks (working girls, the beach, cafes, and real estate developments), and adds an unusual mix of fact and fiction.

△ Remind you of something? Yes, this moving announcement is reminiscent of a Little Golden Book. Hatch Creative set out to announce Bambra Press's new home by creating a piece that its recipients would keep.

▽ The story of the move was told from the perspective of the owner's two dogs, Quincy and Alice—the unofficial mascots of Bambra Press.

◁ Painstaking work was necessary to recreate the 1950s look of a children's book. Sketching each illustration by hand, Hatch colored everything in Illustrator, then retouched and slightly roughened the images in Photoshop.

▽ A full mockup served as a proof and selling tool to present to the client for approval. One of Bambra Press's directors was initially hesitant about the idea but was quite pleased with the end result: new business.

They looked out the front,
but all they found was a puddle of ink
and little spots that led off into the distance.
PMS 032, very peculiar.

Quincy decided to follow the spots.
Alice decided to go too.

a little Bambra Book

**The day
Quincy & Alice
misplaced 53
tonnes of
machinery**

"The creative strategy behind the book was to present the reader with something familiar but unusual—to recreate a 1950s aesthetic to suit the children's book format, carried through to the illustration style, writing, stock, and binding. There is a complete story, created from the simple facts the piece needed to deliver. We wanted the book to demonstrate the time and effort Bambra Press puts into their projects, resulting in a substantial piece people would keep. Because the client is a printer, the book, of course, also has a secondary role as an example of their work."

To achieve the illustration style, Hatch first sketched everything by hand, then scanned, traced, and colored the images in Adobe Illustrator. The sketches were then imported into Adobe Photoshop

and painstakingly retouched and ever so slightly roughened—a rather laborious technique but a necessary step to replicate the printed look of a 1950s children's book.

Even after achieving the exact look for the illustrations, the concept would have failed without the right choice of fonts and paper stock. "The cover font was lifted from an old *Woman's Weekly* advertisement and outlined in Adobe Streamline," Ericson says. "The letters were tweaked in Illustrator and roughened in Photoshop, with the missing letters created to match.

"For the stock, we selected Dur-O-Tone Butcher White from French Paper, an unusual, utilitarian, uncoated paper that we felt captured the essence of the period," says Ericson. "For the cover, the stock was laminated to an ultraheavy boxboard and finished with a strip of gold tape on the spine—a nod to Little Golden Books. The book is completed with an old-fashioned tipped-on library envelope, also printed on Dur-O-Tone, the Primer Gold color matching old library envelopes perfectly. The moving date is stamped on the library envelope, which contains a business card with the new details.

"An open brief is quite a challenge in itself, and one of the dogs, the little one, felt he was unfairly portrayed," Ericson says. "Also, the two directors of the company had quite different responses to our initial roughs—one took quite a bit of convincing because he had been expecting a brochure or a booklet. Being members of the target audience ourselves gave us the courage to push this concept through. We are bombarded weekly by mailers and promotional pieces, so we knew a children's storybook would get noticed and, most importantly, retained."

And get noticed it did. Bambra Press says many of the recipients got in touch with them. "More than half the people who received a book responded with an email or letter specifically about the piece, often saying it was the best piece they had ever seen," says Allain Pool, managing director at Bambra. "I don't think anyone realized the amount of feedback and number of inquiries about future work the piece would generate."

In addition to receiving an overwhelming response for their client, Hatch Creative got some kudos themselves. Among the many awards and recognitions for the Bambra Press announcement, Hatch won the French Paper Excellence Awards Medal of Honor, and the 2003 *HOW* International Design Competition Outstanding Achievement. In addition, the piece is featured in the 2003 *Communication Arts* International Design Annual.

Slight adjustments are made to the two "characters" to ensure that neither dog would feel misrepresented and to capture the breeds accurately. However, the small dog *did* complain about being unfairly portrayed.

BAMBRAPRESS

Based on a true story

From 29th July 2002
Bambra Press
will be at their
new home

6 Rocklea Drive
Port Melbourne Vic 3207
Phone 8698 3233
Fax 8698 3266
mail@bambrapress.com.au

CTP, printing, binding: Bambra Press
Concept, design, illustrations: Hatch Creative (formerly Sax Art)
©2002

PRESS, Bambra
The day Quincy & Alice misplaced
53 tonnes of machinery.

DATE DUE

0 1 MAR 1980

29 JUL 2002

Items may be borrowed from, or returned to, any
branch of the library service. Please report any damage.

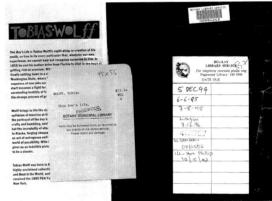

Quincy and Alice arrived at work as they did
most days. But today, things were very unusual.
There were no people or trucks.
Everything was very quiet.

Alice was getting hungry
and wanted a plate of sausages.
Quincy wanted an investment property.
But the spots went on and on.

The spots went all the way up to a shiny new
building! On the front of the building was a big
red sign that looked very familiar. The spots
went inside and so did Alice and Quincy.

⊗ Hatch took their inspiration for an
authentic-looking inside back cover
by photocopying a book from the
local library. But instead of a library
card, Hatch's book holds a Bambra
Press business card.

⊗ The final book made such a strong
impression that Bambra got a
response from more than half of
the people who received it. The
number of future work inquiries
more than paid for the production.

Principle Commissioned to design a new line of office furniture by Principle, a midsized furniture manufacturer in Osceola, Wisconsin, Gensler Studio's Steve Meier created a functional yet fashionable series called Basic Elements.

Gensler Studio's Steve Meier designed a new line of furniture that needed a name and marketing materials. The job stayed in-house, with Gia Graham tapped to handle designing the brochures and postcards for a trade show.

Gensler Studio is a combined architectural and graphic design firm with offices around the country.

When Meier's new line of furniture was completed, Principle needed marketing materials to introduce the product to the interior design community. Interior designers naturally would be the primary target market because they recommend furniture for their clients. The new line needed to be branded, and collateral materials needed to be designed. Principle's goal was to launch the product at Neocon— one of the country's largest interior design trade shows.

"Branding the product was the first order of business," says art director Gia Graham at Gensler. "We had to come up with a name that both appealed to designers and reviewers and spoke to the essence of the product. The product is simple and honest. It is straightforward. What is most appealing about the product is its simplicity of form—Steve wanted to get back to the basic elements of design, to step away from gimmicks and excess. The product was named Basic Elements, shortened to BE.

"The main feature of the furniture (mainly workstations and accessories) is an unsupported 'clearspan' beam that can span up to 12' (3.5 m) across and still be strong enough to support the storage of books, binders, and so on—this had never been done before. That beam became a key element in the concept and design. In fact, the lead image of the brochure also speaks to the basic idea behind the furniture design: The beam is unsupported yet strong enough to stand on."

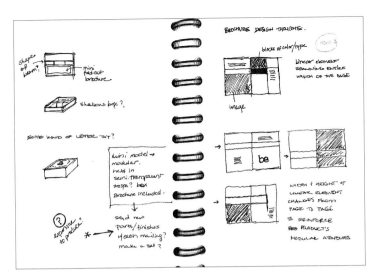

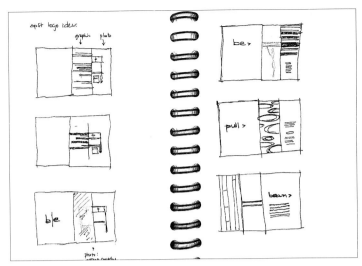

Early sketches showed the progression of layout ideas, beginning with a 3-D mailer to be used as part of the marketing program for the furniture line.

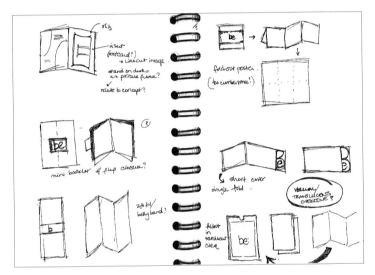

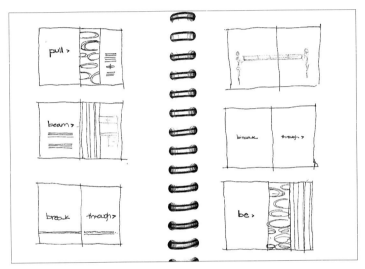

Several alternative formats and structures were considered for the marketing materials, including mini-booklets, posters, translucent sleeves, and belly bands.

Many different possibilities arose for the brochure design, including an emphasis on the furniture line's name and several attributes of its design.

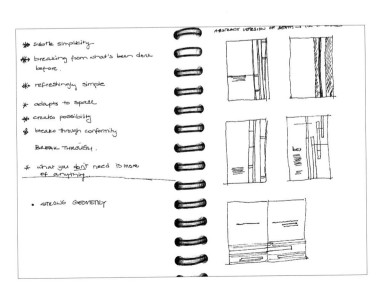

When the line was solidified, Gensler worked on what to emphasize about the new line and how to use color to bring about that emphasis.

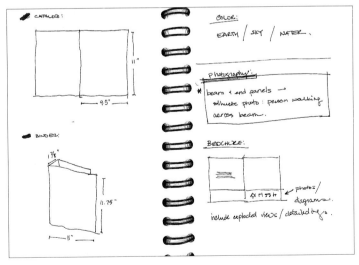

Eventually, Gensler narrowed the size and focus of the brochure. The color palette was influenced by the basic elements of earth, sky, and water.

Graham says she wanted the beam to be a primary design element from the very beginning. Her initial sketches used a combination of strong vertical and horizontal lines, which she later decided should be only horizontal and not quite as bold.

"At first I was thinking more of a standard or oversized 9"-by-12" [23 cm-by-30.5 cm] piece," says Graham. "I went through all of the binders and literature in the interior designer's library, and all of the brochures looked the same, with few of them standing out. Therefore, we changed this piece to a square format. As far as size and general content, it didn't change drastically at all. We pretty much stuck with the same basic idea; we just refined where things would lay and what elements we would use."

Graham took her inspiration from the furniture itself and its name. "When we solidified that we were going to go with this BE title or Basic Elements theme, we started thinking about color," Graham says. "We wanted that idea of simplicity to follow through, even in the colors. We thought about what colors would be successful. Do you want something bright to catch people's eyes? Do you want something more subdued? We decided to continue the concept through to the color palette. We didn't want anything gimmicky, so we didn't want the materials to be too bold or overpowering, considering the furniture line is so simplified and whittled down to essentials. The idea of using the elements of earth, water, and sky as color themes came after the concept was already solidified."

Graham admits to being somewhat of a minimalist in her work. "I like to pare down things—as few tricks and gimmicks, swirls and starbursts as possible. It's really hard to do simple things, but the simple things are more effective.

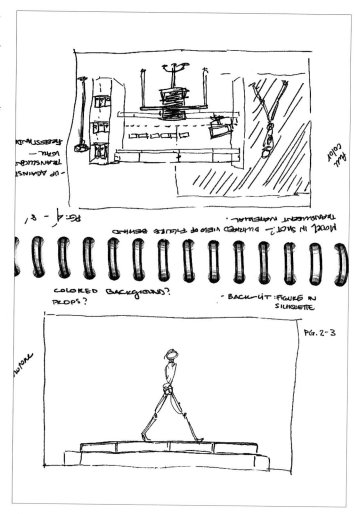

A final sketch series showed an emphasis on the unique centerpiece of the Basic Elements line—the beam.

Focusing on the beam provided Gensler with a unifying element around which to design the brochure.

ten¹

Why hasn't anyone thought of this before? Refreshingly accessible. Sophistication made simple. Whether for the executive suite or team office. Be projects professionalism without pretense. A range of freestanding and run-off tops in richly fashioned materials. Configuration and finish can be customized to user selection.

accessories

1 Enclosed Overhead
2 Conference Table
3 Wood Tabletop
4 Beltline Raceway
5 Credenza
6 Run-off Tabletop
7 Door Pulls
8 Mobile Pedestal

Optional kit is available for retrofitting open-shelf beam to accommodate enclosed overhead sliding doors. Freestanding tables available in multiple sizes and wood veneers. Credenza provides freestanding storage cabinet and spare work surface. Beltline raceway and aluminum slatwall for accessory mounting and cable/power access. Run-off tops come in three standard shapes. All tops are height adjustable. Standard tabletop measures 1/2" thickness and finished with composite resin material. Conference Table available in run-off or freestanding configuration. Mobile pedestals park under work surface.

details

⊘ The final brochure emphasizes the beauty and simplicity of the product line by carrying that through to the layout.

"At one point I thought of incorporating other basic elements of the furniture design, such as the simple oval-shaped openings used as pulls instead of knobs or handles. We opted to focus on the most important element instead—the beam."

Perhaps the biggest challenge of the project was speaking to the interior design community in a new and effective way. "Interior designers are bombarded with new products and collateral materials every day," says Graham. "Interior designers, like graphic designers, are also very particular about what they like and what they don't like. They have a good sense of style and appreciate good design. Unlike graphic designers, however, they don't like paper.

They don't get excited about promotions with cool folds and die cuts. They wanted collateral materials that were well designed but practical.

"Fortunately," Graham says, "Gensler was the perfect environment for this kind of project. At Gensler, architects, graphic designers, interior designers, and product designers all share the same space. I was able to research in the vast interior design library to get a feel for what was already on the market. I could randomly poll interior designers to discover their reactions, what they liked and didn't like. Even though it was a challenge, I had all of the best resources at hand."

Bathology is a novelty soap producer and distributor in California that wanted to position itself for a **more grown-up** audience. When it came time to create a new catalog, freelance designer **Michael McDaniel** got the job, thanks to a print rep who passed along his name.

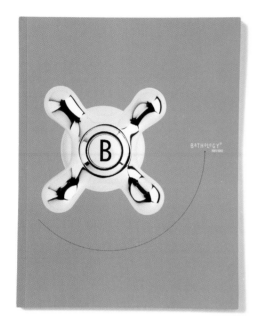

In an attempt to position their products for grown-ups, Bathology outsourced their catalog design to a freelance designer who successfully created a more sophisticated look and feel on a very tight schedule.

McDaniel met with Bathology, and they began to work together on three projects—a catalog, packaging, and a brochure.

"The timeline was the biggest challenge," says McDaniel. "I had three projects and one month to complete them in my spare time. It wasn't a terribly big challenge, but the photography didn't get to my home studio until four days before I was supposed to release the files to the printer to make it for the big trade show. In addition, the photography was completely different from what the client and I had discussed. After three sleepless nights, the catalog, packaging, and brochure were finally finished. The catalog had a slightly different twist, and almost all of the layouts changed because of the photography.

"There was no copy except SKU numbers," says McDaniel, "mostly because there was no time to write anything or develop a storyline to tie the catalog together. Working within those constraints, I thought that a series of visual speed bumps would slow readers and force them to stop and take in the content of the page, if for no other reason than just to see why each page had a particular word on it. The layouts and the visual gags tie together the catalog without overshadowing the products themselves."

McDaniel says he almost always shows his clients three directions, no matter what kind of project he is working on. Given the abbreviated timeframe for this project, however, McDaniel showed

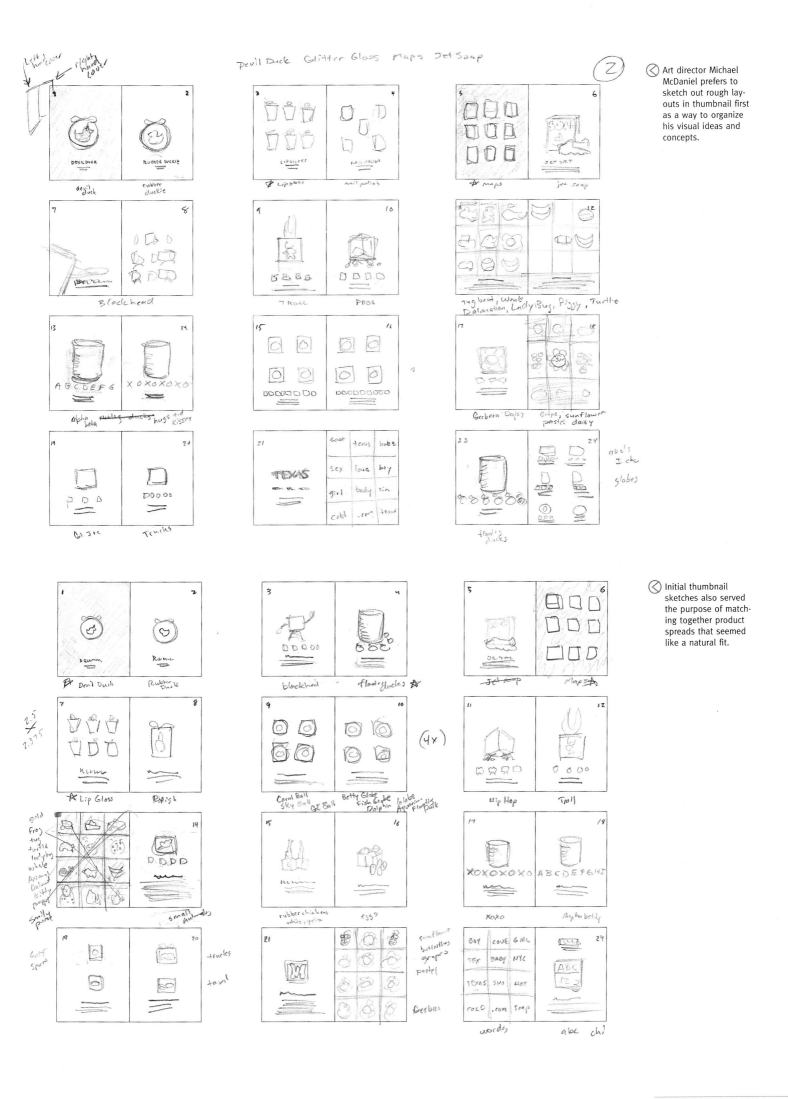

Art director Michael McDaniel prefers to sketch out rough layouts in thumbnail first as a way to organize his visual ideas and concepts.

Initial thumbnail sketches also served the purpose of matching together product spreads that seemed like a natural fit.

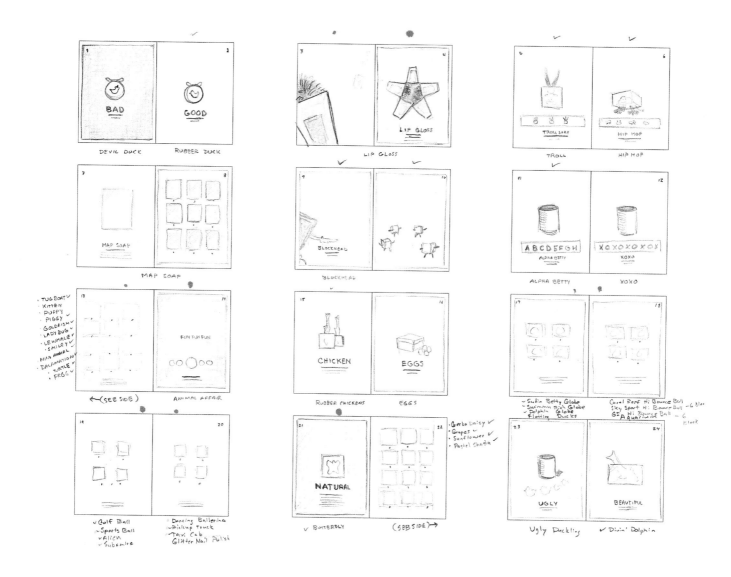

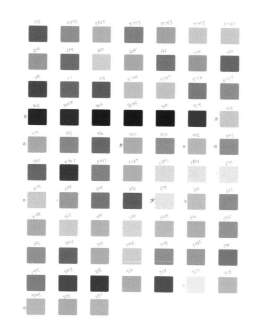

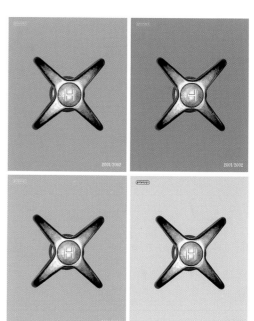

⬣ With little to no copy, McDaniel had to create something creatively intriguing because the product was going to be the focal point. One- or two-word copy blocks were a perfect solution.

⬡ Searching for the right color palette, McDaniel printed a Pantone mixture of wide ranging colors and marked a few he thought would work for the cover and inside spreads.

⬡ Far right: Mockups of the cover served as color and placement tests. McDaniel later replaced the *H* with a *B* for Bathology on the final piece.

Playful yet practical, the final design of the Bathology catalog prominently features the soap items and highlights the diversity of the product line.

Bathology only two directions for the catalog, three for the packaging, and two for the brochure. He tried several directions in thumbnail form first to prevent surprises later in the design process.

"I wasn't trying to emulate anything specific, but I did try to bring more of a retail 'magalog' look to the Bathology pieces. If you thumb through most of the major retail or mail-order retail catalogs, they are more attuned to selling a lifestyle, a look, or a state of being. Some of the most successful brands out there do that and do it very well—Apple, Volkswagen, Target, Abercrombie. That is what I was trying to bring to Bathology's catalog. These soaps go beyond just looking cool and fun; they say something about who you are if you buy them."

McDaniel says his work is strongly influenced by Robert Valentine of the Valentine Group. He is a fan of Valentine's clean and simple layouts. "I like smart concepts. A strong idea has to be behind the work. I also read and keep track of design trends," McDaniel says. "I believe as a designer you must be aware of what is going on—not to jump on the wagon with a certain look but to see where things are going and beat them there, to see what people are responding to, what is relevant with people today.

"I always start with sketches," McDaniel says. "I find that it is a quick way to work out ideas and concepts. Even in thumbnail form I do rough layouts. I am the only person that can read the layouts in thumbnail form—it is my own secret language. Maybe it is because the thumbnails are just like mental bookmarks for me to organize my thoughts.

"I have a sketchbook or a digital camera with me almost all the time." My sketchbooks have evolved into a central holding bin for ideas. I have client meeting notes, reference photos, thumbnails, and printouts taped in there. These books serve as a designer's journal. I can look back through previous years' sketchbooks and follow my work, see the kind of year it was, chart personal growth, and even rediscover lost ideas."

McDaniel says the main push behind getting all the components done so quickly was an upcoming trade show that would give Bathology significant exposure. "Obviously, the compressed schedule makes you run through ideas more quickly, once you get past the freaking-out stage. I have found that compressed time schedules also force me to make choices and just go with them," McDaniel says. "I know the client was thrilled with the end result because all of the catalogs were gone from the trade show booth before the end of the first day. It seemed to be a very successful piece for them."

Speaking of a successful piece, McDaniel says the catalog has also been recognized in *STEP Inside Design*'s Annual 100 2003 and the *Print* Regional Design Annual 2003.

B3 (Blocks Below Broad) In 2000, real estate developer Tony Goldman, one of the **driving forces behind Soho** in the 1970s and South Beach in the 1980s, bought a stretch of city blocks in the **last underdeveloped area** in downtown **Philadelphia,** an area that would later be named Blocks Below

Because they were selling lifestyle and culture rather than real estate, 1600ver90 gave Goldman Properties a magazine rather than a typical sales brochure.

Broad, or B3. Although Goldman had been developing neighborhoods for decades, this was the first time he would be the sole developer of an area.

Goldman envisioned an area populated with smaller, funky restaurants and vogue, hip shops rather than a place housing big businesses. Although he had a vision, Goldman lacked a name or sales materials to attract retailers and restaurateurs. He engaged local design agency 1600ver90 to establish an identity truly reflective of the emerging neighborhood.

Before they began work on any marketing materials, 1600ver90 first needed to name the neighborhood. With their limited budget, the agency knew that the neighborhood needed a unique name that would resonate with the public to make its promotion less expensive. However, inventing a unique name would not be an easy task.

"1600ver90 researched the origins of the names of the most famous neighborhoods in the United States and Europe and learned that all of the names had either a historical or geographical significance," says creative director Darryl Cilli. "A list of 200 potential names—historic and geographic—was developed, The list soon became 100 names, then twenty, and ultimately two. The historical finalist was The Key, and B3 was the geographical winner. The Key represents the corner of what is now 12th Street and Chestnut Street, where Benjamin Franklin is reported to have first discovered electricity with his famed kite; B3 is a geographical reference to the Blocks Below Broad, because the numbered streets are in descending order from Broad Street. In the end, 1600ver90 chose B3 because it possessed a unique quality that makes it memorable.

"The decision to do a magazine rather than traditional sales collateral was made before we ever went into sketching," Cilli says. "When we said to Goldman was that to get an entrepreneurial restaurateur or an boutique hotel owner or an indie retail shop owner to buy in to the space you're selling, don't sell them space; sell them a neighborhood, a lifestyle, and a culture. Very early on in the conceptual process we decided that we weren't selling space, we were selling lifestyle and culture. Because we're not selling space there's no reason to do something that looks like a typical real estate brochure. Because we're selling lifestyle and culture, what better way to do that than through a magazine or something that looks, feels, and operates more like a magazine?"

⬡ Naming the area was perhaps the most challenging part of the entire project, but deciding on the right look for the masthead of the publication took several iterations and sketches.

Although the publication does appear to be a magazine, it still has to serve the purpose of a sales brochure. "In the beginning, when we were laying it out, even though we wanted to do something more in line with an actual publication, it still had to function the way a sales brochure would function," says Cilli. "It still had to have your traditional pocket folder, and we were still on a budget, so the piece was saddle-stitched instead of perfect bound. We were making those functional decisions even though we were moving more toward this magazine style."

Faced with capturing an atmosphere or environment that didn't yet exist, Cilli says they struck a balance between what existed and what would eventually occupy B3. "We took the best of the assets that we had, and what we didn't, we made do with," Cilli says. "For example, the actual cover is half manufactured and half reality. There was no real photo shoot. We shot for a couple of days in the neighborhood and just guerrilla-captured what we could. For the building shot on the cover, we ran to the top of the building and shot down on the neighborhood. But the one shot that gives the human connection was done in a hollowed-out storefront that Goldman was getting ready to sell. We threw some art on the wall, set up lighting, got some models in there, and made the feel of a

gallery. Lo and behold, someone opened a gallery there two weeks later. The photos were never done in a way that was misleading. We just took natural elements of the area."

Today, the vision for B3 has become a reality. It's now a bustling and trendy neighborhood in the city that has experienced considerable growth. Goldman has brought 15 to 20 independent boutique businesses in the area and has built out and completely filled three loft buildings. Now there are trendy spas, menswear shops, home furnishings, cafés, and interior design firms.

In addition to attracting businesses and people to the area, the B3 brochure also was recognized for its design sensibilities; namely, it was recognized in *Print's* 2003 Regional Design Annual (November 2003), *HOW* 2003 Self-Promotion Annual (October 2003), American Corporate Identity 20, and the 2003 American Graphic Design Awards.

Ultimately, even 160over90 fell in love with the B3 area. In fact, many employees actually moved into the neighborhood. Talk about true belief in the product.

⊘ The designers sketched out potential formats for the complete structure of the B3 publication, including inserts and a possible envelope enclosure.

⊙ 160over90 actually used the thumbnail sketch phase to sell the client on the overall layout of their project.

⊗ After the sketching phase, one of the first things 160over90 did was set up style sheets for typographic treatments, primary and secondary color palettes, and identifiable patterns.

typography style sheet B3

SOLID GOLD
HUMAN CO
360° OF LIVING

YOU ARE HERE*
BLOCKS BELOW BROAD

It was a streach of old, dusty buildings in the South Beach sectionof Miami. The city wanted to tear them down. But in much the same way that they saw **B3**'s potiential Goldman Properties recognized the beauty and commercial power of

The lights from window give a glimpse of expansive live- work lofts. Framed by meticulously restored facades, they create a panorama of lives that are being lived every day in the distinctiveness of **B3**.

IT'S A DIFFRENT FROM THE BIG RESTAURANTS, GRAND HOTELS, AND CORPORATE VIBE OF BRAD STREET **B3** IS FOR THE PEDESTRIAN.A PERFECT PLACE TO JUST WALK AROUND. IT'S MORE APPROACHABLE, FRIENDLIER, WITH A

The feel is small- neighborhood, with all the buildings and storefronts close together. Residential lofts give a sense of real community. You meet. You talk. You connect. Creativity and modern discovery pulse through the streets where historic, turn-of- the- century buildings have been restored and invigorated. They have become the backdrop for new, innovative slants on fashion, food, work, play and living. **B3** encompasses. It is an amalgam of all sides of life. It embraces the diffrent. The creative. The entrepreneur. The ordinary. The adventurer. **B3** simply unites people.

Restored in 1987, the Park Central Hotel is one of the largest hotels in South Beach. It ha a feel of casual sophistication, with its pastel colored art deco facade and antique black- and- white prints through out the hallwalys and guest rooms. Lastly turning mahogany ceiling here. Period furniture, large window with sliver white curtains dancing in the ocean breeze. The park Central is a mixtue combination of elegance and comfort.

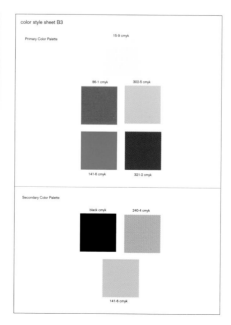

color style sheet B3

Primary Color Palette

15-9 cmyk

86-1 cmyk   302-5 cmyk

141-6 cmyk   321-2 cmyk

Secondary Color Palette

black cmyk   240-4 cmyk

141-6 cmyk

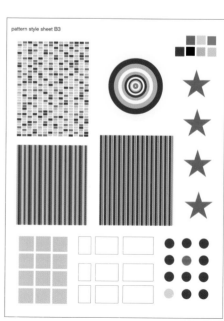

pattern style sheet B3

BUILDING
BLOCKS

360° OF LIVING

GOLDMAN PROPERTIES

PHILADELPHIA
The Philadelphia Building
1315 Walnut Street
B3, Philadelphia,
Pennsylvania 19107
Tel: 215.735.2900
Fax: 215.735.2706

NEW YORK
The SoHo Building
110 Greene Street
SoHo, New York,
New York 10012
Tel: 212.226.5100
Fax: 212.941.9606

MIAMI BEACH
804 Ocean Drive
Miami Beach,
Florida 33139
Tel: 305.531.4411
Fax: 305.673.3106

www.b3philadelphia.com

⊘ The B3 publication captured the rich history of Philadelphia while also combining the contemporary offerings of the new neighborhood.

⊘ The B3 piece served the same purpose as a sales brochure, with the back pocket holding more specific information.

Carmel Partners A premier player in the California real estate management and development industry, Carmel Partners increasingly found themselves competing with much bigger firms that had high-level collateral materials.

Because Carmel Partners works with several builders, Alterpop chose a more tactile and utilitarian feel for the brochure.

After being contracted to brand one of Carmel Partners' premium properties, San Francisco–based Alterpop was asked to apply their design and brand strategy to Carmel Partners' corporate side as well. Because Carmel Partners was about to embark on an effort to create a $260-million investment fund, the corporate brochure was given first priority.

"The design concept for this project is simple: present relevant information in as straightforward a manner as possible," says senior designer Christopher Simmons. "These brochures are aimed primarily at institutional investors and potential partners who are busy, savvy professionals who want quick access to good information without having to sift through a lot of superfluous material.

"Most corporate brochures are glanced at and thrown away," Simmons says. "We wanted to cut through that mentality and create an object that demanded more respect. This was one of those rare projects where we knew what it would look like from the beginning. Typically we show clients three directions at the initial stage, but in this instance we showed only one. The nuances of the typography and color palette evolved over time, but essentially this project was about fulfilling an initial vision rather than slowly developing a more compromised solution."

Simmons says his design inspirations for the project included the poetry of e.e. cummings and William Carlos Williams, plus utilitarian items such as file folders, field journals, and architect's ledgers.

Because Carmel Partners often works with builders, Simmons decided to give the piece a more utilitarian feel. Referencing the aesthetic of a foreman's journal notebook, a metal clasp acts as a binder for the project sheet inserts.

"The choice to print on heavyweight, uncoated stock; the use of embossing, foil stamping, and die-cutting; and the inclusion of metal hardware all combine to create an object that stands out among competitors and begs to be touched and explored," Simmons says. "Inside, the striking imagery, simple layout, and meticulously handcrafted typography reward readers' curiosity while valuing their time and intelligence. Overall the brochure is subtle, understated, sophisticated, and quietly confident.

"Each spread has text on three levels: First is the section title, which explains in shorthand the firm's philosophy for each of its services. For example, acquisition becomes realizing the potential of tomorrow—the language transforms throwaway business jargon into a larger, more relevant idea. Second is the bigger concept—

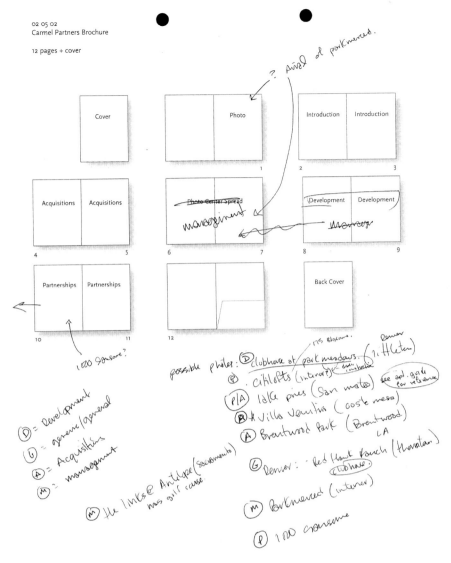

Carmel Partners' previous brochure looked like something from an entirely different company next to the more sophisticated version by Alterpop.

Alterpop's Christopher Simmons used thumbnails to structure the layout of the brochure and begin thinking about photography placement.

Below left: An early alternate direction put more emphasis on copy and less on the image quality. The client did not see this internal alternate concept.

Below right: Still tweaking the overall format of the brochure, Simmons had the folderlike tabs finalized. The text placement and type treatment, however, went through more changes.

Carmel Partners is a premier full-service real estate company established in 1992. From San Francisco's headquarters and throughout our office network, our aim is simple — to assess investment opportunities in highly desirable locations and, with imaginative, aggressive and appropriate development plans, realize the property's full value.

Integrated in-house construction, development and asset management coupled with solid investment partnerships ensure projects are executed transparently. This expertise enables timely and reliable solutions to be seamlessly implemented from acquisition, through development and management, to final disposition.

Although we are a leading development and repositioning specialist in the Western States, we also keep a keen eye on promising assets across the rest of the country. Whatever the opportunity, our creative approaches are founded on sound investment analysis, efficient operations and top tier property management.

REALIZING THE POTENTIAL OF REAL ESTATE

TRANSLATING IDEAS INTO PHYSICAL REALITY

an introductory paragraph that summarizes the firm's capabilities in each service category. The language is plain, the type is big, and the service category is repeated in the text. Readers could skim the brochure, reading only these paragraphs, and still have a full understanding of Carmel Partners' business. Last are two paragraphs of text-level copy that express the company's philosophy and values: how and why they do what they do. This typography is set more like poetry than traditional copy, highlighting specific words and concepts to better express and emphasize the firm's commitment to its core values. The line breaks are designed to halt readers rather than allow them to read passively through it. In this way readers are forced to spend more time with the text and, hopefully, to more intimately relate to its message.

"There was a lot of discussion within our studio as to how the typography should be treated. I had a particular vision for it that I wanted to pursue, but another designer had a different vision. We developed both, created mockups for each, then put it to a studio vote. I don't think we've ever worked that way before, but it promoted some interesting debate. It would be oversimplifying things to say that my version won out. The truth is the process and the discussion informed and enhanced the design to the point where authorship is irrelevant. The end product is the result of our collaborative efforts.

"Every page is die-cut such that the text is presented as a series of tabbed pages. In this way, readers are presented with a list of the client's services from page one. They can then navigate directly to the section most relevant to them. Allowing readers to navigate like this signals that you value their time. In addition, the cover is designed to mimic a standard file folder, making it easy to store for future reference. Each section consists of one spread, with one page dedicated to text and the other to image. This is an image-building brochure, not a resume.

Simmons says that the biggest challenge of this project was working within a protracted deadline. Due to various internal changes at Carmel Partners, the project dragged on for eighteen months. "It's difficult to track a stop-and-go job such as this one, especially considering we were dealing with a different group of decision makers at the end of the project than we were at the beginning. The extensive copy revisions also fell outside the initial scope of services, making the job more complex than it would have been ordinarily."

By all accounts, the brochure was a great success, receiving positive comments from both clients and investors. In fact, the corporate brochure was instrumental in meeting Carmel Partners' goal of raising enough funds to close a $260-million investment fund.

Although the brochure has been featured in *STEP Inside Design*'s Annual 100 and the *Graphic Design USA* Annual, the recognition Simmons looks for comes from the client's success.

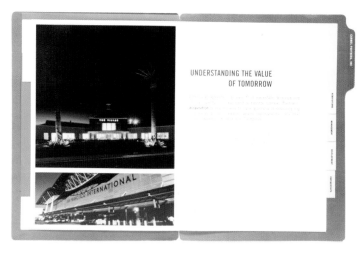

This is the first comp the client saw. The overall structure was approved, but the imagery and typography for each spread were tweaked further.

After great internal debate, a combination of serif and sans serif typefaces was chosen for the interior spreads. This purposeful nod to the client's attention to detail shows how the typography can work on many levels.

Overall, the brochure put more emphasis on Carmel Partners' relationships and less on trumpeting their achievements and prowess, almost letting the properties speak for themselves.

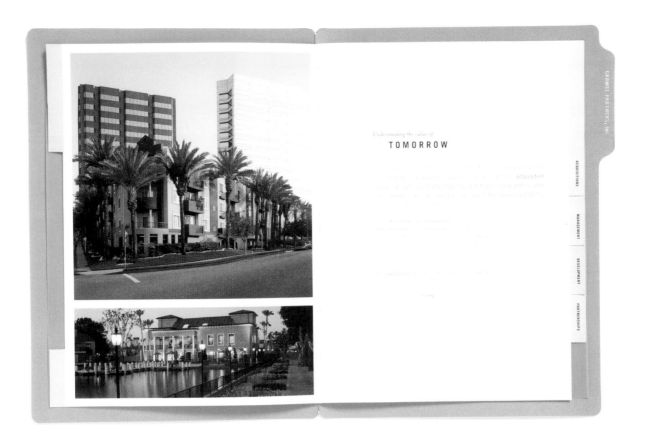

Understanding the value of

TOMORROW

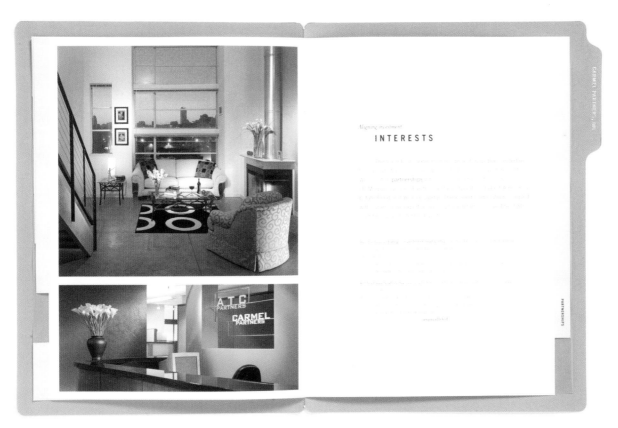

Aligning investment

INTERESTS

⬡ After many iterations, the final brochure was unique among competitors'
materials because it achieved a delicate balance of functionality and flair.

David Carson

David Carson Little did **Kolegram Design's** Mike Teixeira realize that when he emailed **David Carson** to say how much **he liked his work** that their exchange would culminate with Carson making a **visit to Ottawa** for an Advertising and Design Association conference.

When Kolegram's Mike Teixeira innocently sent David Carson an email, he never dreamed he would end up designing invitation and symposium materials for Carson's speaking engagement for the Ottawa Advertising and Design Association.

Naturally, Teixeira was tasked with designing conference materials, including the invitation, brochure, and poster.

"When I thought about it at the beginning, I didn't actually know what to do: try to reflect Carson's work or reflect our work but give his message," Teixeira says. "Because of the timeframe, I had a couple of weeks to work with. The concept was to try to design a promo that would reflect David's work or his style. Still, it had to be an experience. It was kind of a 'nothing to lose' type of a project. Intuition was the main direction. Photography had to be spontaneous—in a single car ride or something like that. That was the goal, but I remember being afraid to portray his work honestly."

In his first round of comps, Teixeira tried to design like Carson, so much so that a lot of the text wasn't legible. Although he didn't think it would be a problem, when he presented it internally, that's the only criticism he received. Teixeira had to make it fit into the Advertising and Design Association boundaries, which was make it legible, but still carry through Carson's style.

"The intent was to produce different early sketches in a poster format without thinking too much, just letting it go by intuition," Teixeira says. "The small brochure format for the invitation came from the fact that I had to have a couple of pages to justify the overall look applied on the poster, tickets, and brochure cover, to show that the main visual was intended to be abstract with moving typography."

Teixeira says his choice of colors was influenced by Carson's background and his native California. Carson used to be a surfer, so Teixeira wanted to reflect that influence somehow. He explored using unusual colors, such as purple and turquoise.

"While I was playing with type I thought about the overall look and the colors," Teixeira says. "I knew pretty much from the beginning that I wanted to stick with that specific type. What happened is while playing with it, I went back to *Raygun* issues to see different layouts Carson did. I remember the special version he did for Japan. The entire magazine was done backward. The front cover was the back cover—you had to start from the back to read it. That's where I got the idea of just playing with a mirror effect for the title, 'Behind the Seen.' I remember trying to visually represent the title."

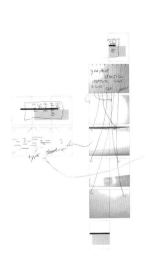

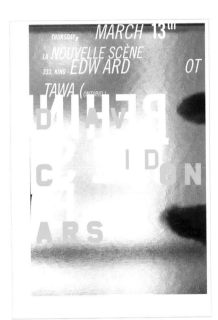
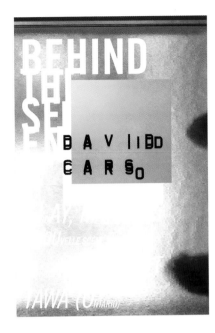

⬨ Teixeira began by experimenting with different type treatments and backgrounds to reflect Carson's style, but not everyone felt it legible.

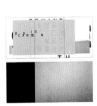
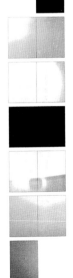

⬨ Once he chose a mirrored type treatment, Teixeira began to scale back his early work to emphasize type against muted pastel color backgrounds.

"When the mirroring effect came to me, I thought maybe I should start with the poster first because it would be the more visible object. Trying to reflect the mirror effect would be the biggest challenge. When it's done on the poster, it could easily be done on the other pieces," says Teixeira. "I wanted to put a varnish or tinted varnish on the 'Behind the Seen' square, but I found the best solution was to screen-print it to add a thickness so it would be more opaque."

Teixeira says he purposefully stayed away from doing a traditional invitation. He was provided with tickets in advance and used them to design the poster. He wanted uniformity in all of the materials, so he decided to create intrigue with the invitation as well. Recipients don't immediately realize that what they are reading is indeed an invitation.

"I had the poster and the tickets. When I got to the invitation, I was supposed to do a flyer with front and back," Teixeira says. "That would mean redoing the overall look of the design. I was

scared that people would think this wasn't serious design. That's why I decided to make it sort of a magazine format. I really wanted to have other visuals that would support the concept. Inside the brochure, the images and the color palettes are different. But the same type of system is used—when you open it, you have the mirrored effect, but everything is pretty much readable. I tried to show people with the inside of the brochure that the overall look was done intentionally. And the only content I got was what was on the tickets. I didn't want to do any copywriting, so I just took the copy from the tickets and put it into the brochure invitation. It turned out well because it gave me a lot of latitude."

Despite his apprehensions about the overall design of the materials, Teixeira's work was recognized by *HOW Magazine,* the Type Director's Club, Graphika, and the Advertising and Design Association. However, Teixeira received his most-prized recognition from Carson himself. Carson said it was one of the best materials for his conferences he had ever seen.

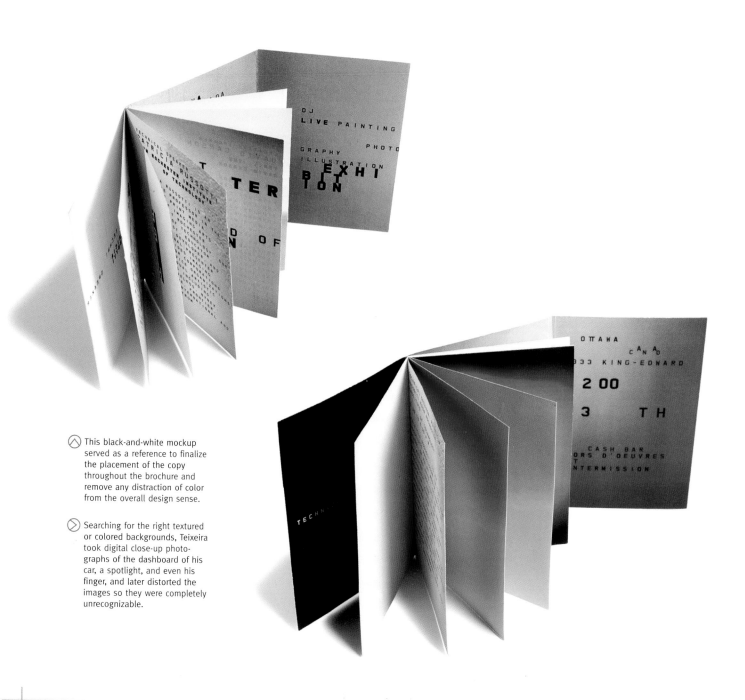

◯ This black-and-white mockup served as a reference to finalize the placement of the copy throughout the brochure and remove any distraction of color from the overall design sense.

◯ Searching for the right textured or colored backgrounds, Teixeira took digital close-up photographs of the dashboard of his car, a spotlight, and even his finger, and later distorted the images so they were completely unrecognizable.

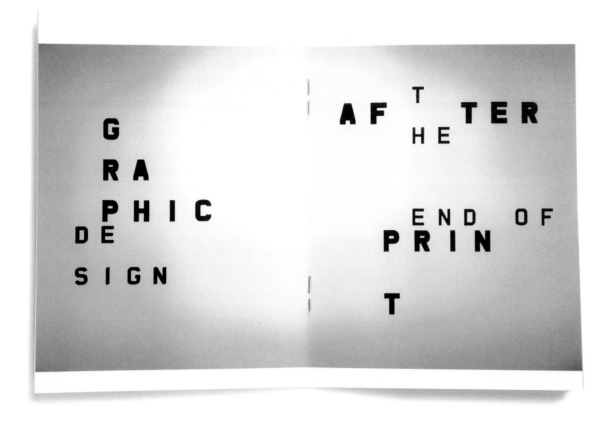

Despite having only a ticket to work with for copy, Teixeira found a way to create an invitation booklet that stands on its own apart from the poster yet carries over the mirrored effect.

Dickson's Paper

Dickson's Paper Although he's not a big fan of **paper promotions,** especially gratuitous ones, **Clive Piercy** of L.A.–based **Ph.D leaped at the chance** to team up with Gary Dickson, **president** of Dickson's Paper.

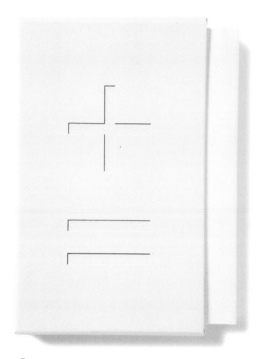

Determined not to do "another gratuitous paper promotion," Ph.D welcomed the collaboration with Dickson, a specialty printer renowned for its high-end work. Downplaying the visual nature of most promotions, the stark white interior is dry but irresistibly engaging.

A design aficionado himself, Dickson carefully selects who he collaborates with on each paper promotion. Previous collaborators were Michael Osborne Design and MW.

The name of the promotion, Touch, grew out of conversations between Piercy and Dickson. "The concept was a way to highlight the exceptional printing capabilities through the science of touch—haptics. Rather than produce a highly visual piece, we decided to make the experience a highly tactile one, in which each spread highlights a different print capability. Obviously, I wanted the piece to show them off, but in a different way. We tried to make it nonvisual so that you touched it. The point of the whole piece was to touch it and get your hands all over it, and by doing that it would be somewhat mysterious and intriguing."

Despite their lofty goal of making a print promotion that didn't look like any others, Ph.D initially presented Dickson with a more visually driven idea. "That initial comp seemed to be somewhat of a false start and one that looked more like a traditional paper promotion. When he didn't immediately really respond to that, I realized I wanted to come at it a different way. Early sketches were visually driven, but we decided that approach was too obvious so we shifted to a more subtle, understated look. We revisited it ourselves after the first comp, but we did that first one to get the project moving a little bit.

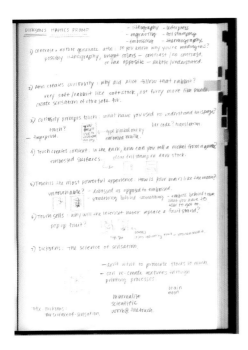

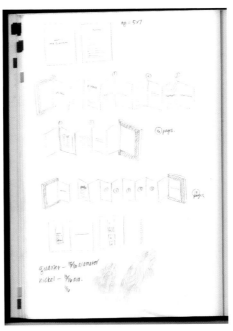

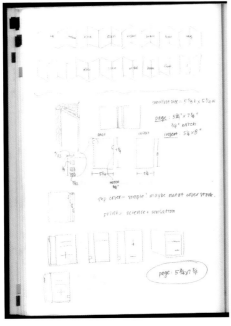

Left: A brainstorming meeting with president and CEO Gary Dickson produced the idea of haptics, the science of touch. This spurred Ph.D to begin thinking of potential visual themes around this science.

Right: Early thumbnail sketches showed the original idea of printing an accordion-style piece with opposing covers.

After throwing out the first idea, Ph.D kept sketching possible cover concepts and interior printing techniques.

This more detailed sketch for the original idea of an accordion-style job with techniques on one side and content on the other was scrapped altogether by Dickson.

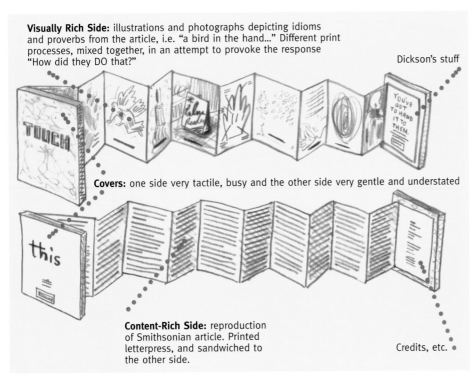

Visually Rich Side: illustrations and photographs depicting idioms and proverbs from the article, i.e. "a bird in the hand..." Different print processes, mixed together, in an attempt to provoke the response "How did they DO that?"

Dickson's stuff

Covers: one side very tactile, busy and the other side very gentle and understated

Content-Rich Side: reproduction of Smithsonian article. Printed letterpress, and sandwiched to the other side.

Credits, etc.

"There were practical problems with an accordion-style printing that I don't think the client wanted to get involved with," says Piercy. "He suggested the kind of printing, which we ended up using, in which the binding is hidden. It was a real collaboration."

After the initial concept was developed, Ph.D threw it out and more or less started from scratch. Piercy decided to highlight a different quality or service that Dickson's offers on every spread. "I believe the best work we do has a somewhat understated quality to it," Piercy says. "In this case, the writer supplied us with a lot of the questions in the copy. We wondered, how do we illustrate these questions without literally illustrating them? There was a lateral approach that we decided was better, and, fortunately, we had the opportunity to put that into place."

Piercy says his overall secret is collecting first impressions and thoughts with a sketchbook that is never far out of reach. "If I'm speaking with a client or someone who has a job, when I put the phone down I'll usually write something right away. Often that is the thing that starts me off, my kind of gut reaction to the conversation. Sometimes that's a good starting point," says Piercy. "And I'm not someone who particularly overworks work. I like work that has a casual quality to it. I don't pore over things seriously. I'm an egg layer."

Piercy says another of his secrets is making sure he has enough time alone to think about his approach to a project. "Personally, the thing about coming up with ideas—and that's where all the

honor is in our work, supposedly—is if it's really idea-driven, then where does the idea come from?" Piercy says. "So I covet that time. I make sure that I give myself the best opportunity to come up with good things, and that has to do with frame of mind, music, and food. You don't do good work when the phone is ringing all of the time. I do covet that time to myself; to me, that's a very private act, coming up with ideas.

"You don't always get it right the first time," Piercy says. "In some ways I'm glad he didn't choose our first idea. When we really sat down and tried to figure out what we would want for ourselves, we came up with the other idea, which ended up being a better solution. That came out of not making the material so obviously visual."

In the case of Dickson's "Touch This" paper promotion, Ph.D was glad to have such a valuable collaboration. It was this freedom that allowed Gary Dickson to challenge Ph.D to something better than their original concept. In the end, Piercy was glad they scrapped that first idea. "The piece wouldn't have been as good if it hadn't been for Gary and his staff. They know what they are up to in terms of printing, and we gave him some fairly loose things. We wanted it to look like book cloth, so Dickson created those kinds of textures. They are very resourceful. I would say most clients are grateful working on something for themselves. This project was a true example of the client and us trying to test one another in a good way to figure out the best solution. I understood after working with them why they are so talented."

The comp for the original version looks more like a traditional paper promotion, which is exactly what Dickson didn't want. The accordion-style structure also raised practical problems with printing the piece that Dickson wanted to avoid.

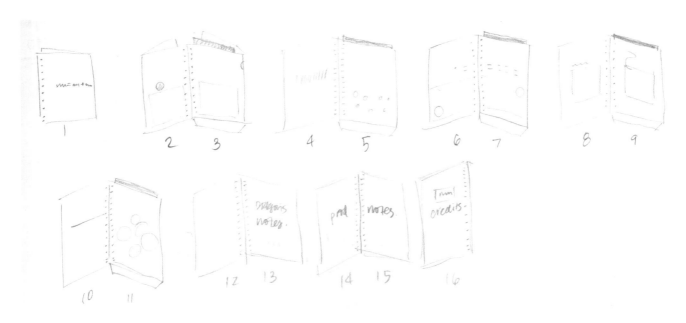

Finally, this last sketched layout revealed the structure of each spread and the rough printing technique that was ultimately featured.

Carrying through the "Touch This" theme, Ph.D inserted page pullouts that contributed to the interactive nature of the piece—almost forcing readers to engage.

El Revolver It's often said that **self-promotions** must be treated with the same **commitment** as any other project. But what if instead of **seeking prospective clients,** you *were* the client? That's the origin of *El Revolver,* a publication born from a Panamanian design firm's **desire to express themselves.**

⊘ *El Revolver* is an alternative publication that is equal
⊘ parts self-promotion and client marketing platform for
⊘ Revolver Industries in Panama.

Revolver Industries created *El Revolver* out of their search for a medium that projected their true creativity and alternative design work.

"Anything goes with *El Revolver,*" says Ricky Salterio, Revolver's art director. "Each edition is unique, and each spread is designed separately, with no standard layout or scheme. We experiment with paper and ink as well as nontraditional design tools, such as photocopies and digital or conceptual photography.

"In the beginning it was more of a self-promotion. Everything wasn't commercial for our clients. It was a little hard to sell enough copies to cover production costs. Sometimes we had to do a little more commercial stuff. Basically, what we wanted was a little portfolio. We could show alternative designs through our magazine, and for potential clients we could show how we could do ads for them. Basically, we were trying to sell our ad agency with the ads and show alternative designs and more self-promotions in terms of the spreads.

"Even though we are the clients, each design is carefully planned, with several options from which to choose," Salterio says. "Usually we begin with some sketches and design two or three layouts of each section on our Macs before arriving with a final spread design. El Revolver targeted a mainly young audience, roughly 18- to 35-year-olds, which includes college students, artists, designers, architects, and people who work in advertising agencies, fashion boutiques, and even bars and restaurants."

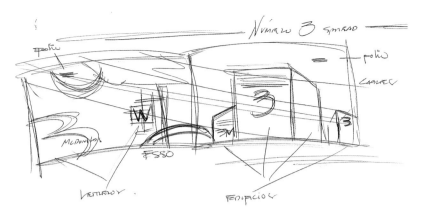

A sketch of a spread for issue 3 includes an ad for McDonald's. Notice the crossover between pages in the gutter.

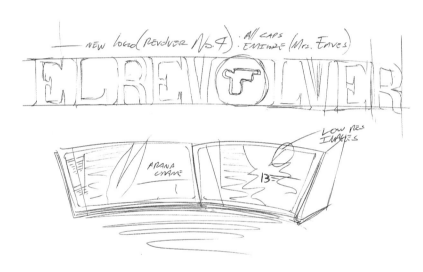

For issue 4, Revolver came up with a new masthead and sketched out the cover wrap image.

In another change in issue 4, Revolver switched from perfect bound to stapling and ran the masthead on a cover flap.

Salterio notes, "We generally pick a topic and go from there, taking as many pictures as possible and designing several layouts. Like many self-promotional projects by designers, the biggest challenge is actually finishing each issue," Salterio confesses. "*El Revolver* is a project that is hard to sell, so for some issues we had to take money from our own pockets to print it," Salterio says. "To pay our expenses, we spend most of our time with commercial projects, which takes time away from finishing *El Revolver.*"

According to Salterio, design sensibilities are improving in Panama, but a lot of mixture with other service providers still occurs, which can be confusing. That's why he tries to simplify his approach as much as possible. For example, the ads in *El Revolver* are mainly for traditional brands, such as banks. Therefore, Salterio simply used a main idea and the brand identity. He didn't clutter up the ad with numerous promotions or extraneous information.

Salterio says the audience for *El Revolver* was always intended to be young, creative folks. "We used to distribute it in fashion boutiques and clothing companies," Salterio says. "The advertisers are looking for that market. We are working on an issue now because we have more clients who want to advertise."

Salterio is heavily influenced by David Carson's work, specifically his publications such as *Raygun, Beach Culture, The End of Print,* and *2nd Sight*. Both Salterio and his partner, Peter Novey, are graduates of the Savannah College of Art & Design.

"One of the things we are influenced by is *Émigré*. They are all about fonts, and they do design studies within the magazine." says Salterio. "That's where we are trying to get to—more personal, more about art and design, and less commercial. That's why it's a hard thing to sell the magazine."

For the fourth issue of *El Revolver*, Salterio designed a cover flap to add to the publication's distinction and, more important, to keep the pages from coming out.

"One of the main reasons we did that flap is production costs," Salterio says. "Another reason was the other pages were falling out. We decided to do it with staples so the pages couldn't fall out. If you look at issue 3, it's glued. The next one was stapled like a book."

The end result was exactly what Revolver Industries had hoped for and a lot more. *El Revolver* has become a leading design magazine in Panama and has started an interesting artist following. It has also ignited a trend of alternative magazines in Panama, going from none to about a dozen in three years.

"We usually print 10,000 copies—more than that would be too much," says Salterio. "I live in the capital, and it's more than enough. Even for a metropolis, it's very small. We want to expand and go into Costa Rica, Colombia, and Latin America to explore it even further."

El Revolver has already been recognized outside of Panama. The publication was awarded a merit achievement in *HOW Magazine*'s 2003 International Design Competition.

When pages kept falling out of a previously printed issue, the subsequent issue gave tips for what to do with the pages, ranging from making paper airplanes to using them for wallpaper.

Revolver uses the magazine's format for typographic and design experimentation. No two issues ever look alike.

Revolver designs unique layouts for every spread in the publication, including the ads for institutions such as banks, which allows Revolver to showcase their abilities without any constraints.

Entravision Communications Corporation is a diversified **Spanish-language media company** with major interests in **television, radio, and outdoor advertising.**

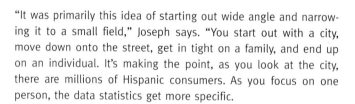
Starting with a big-picture scene that gradually moves in tighter and tighter to an individual, the Entravision Communications Corporation annual report capitalizes on the impact of the census favoring their future business prospects.

After going public, Los Angeles–based Douglas Joseph Partners won Entravision as a client through their long association with Univision Communications. Entravision has many broadcast stations on the Univision Communications network. One of Douglas Joseph Partners' first projects with Entravision was designing an annual report.

Douglas Joseph Partners took their inspiration from the census data, which illustrated how the explosive growth in the Hispanic population favored Entravision's media interests. Douglas Joseph Partners set out to convey the significance of the census in an easily understood format.

"Entravision is largely pinned to the Hispanic population growth in this country," says principal and art director Douglas Joseph. "This made big news because the last census showed growth at an astronomical pace. The whole idea of this particular book was to begin with a bird's-eye view of a city and then focus tighter and tighter until you get to an individual. The photographs feature copy with census data about growth potential. In fact, that's actually what drove the first annual report we did for them.

"It was primarily this idea of starting out wide angle and narrowing it to a small field," Joseph says. "You start out with a city, move down onto the street, get in tight on a family, and end up on an individual. It's making the point, as you look at the city, there are millions of Hispanic consumers. As you focus on one person, the data statistics get more specific.

"The concept for the design centers on the historic and future growth of the U.S. Hispanic population. The full-bleed photos weave through the text in ascending order from a city landscape to throngs on the street to a family, and finally to an individual. The photos are accompanied by census data that conveys the enormous growth among Hispanics and the significance of that growth to Entravision's media interests.

"We also explored using illustrations, for which we would have commissioned a dozen portraits of Hispanics. The illustrations would have been the background for carrying the census data, as we did in the photographic direction. Frankly, that was really the book we were pushing for. We just picked those images from a stock company, and we were going to hire that particular illustrator to do this whole slew of portraits. We liked the idea a lot. We tend to show people in books—they represent consumers, consumers represent advertising dollars, and that's how this company makes its money. We just thought it was a different kind of twist on depicting consumers from what the first year's book had been, which was photographic portraiture.

"This book is technically a summary annual report because it doesn't have the full financials," says Joseph. "It doesn't have the management's discussion analysis or footnotes to the tables. We

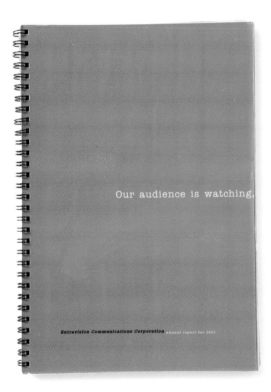

Our audience is watching.

 Douglas Joseph Partners preferred this mockup concept featuring stock illustrations that took the place of photographs. The illustrations would have been the background for carrying the census data, as in the photographic direction.

 This mockup didn't quite capture the storyline as well as the final report did with the corresponding choice of photography. The fictitious personal profile that was to accompany the illustration version was still present on some of the photos.

just wanted to come up with a creative way of doing the financial disclosure that we include but just do it differently. The CEO is a young guy and likes to be more on the cutting edge. He likes to do things differently, so this kind of thing appealed to him.

"We showed the two directions. They are so different from one another, there wasn't a reason to come up with a third," Joseph says. "A third comp at that point would have been an exercise in layout, which we try to avoid. We don't like to go in and show different layouts; we like to go in and present a couple of different directions to stimulate conversations and thought about which one is the more valid way to go."

Entravision's CEO told Douglas Joseph Partners that the reports have been getting better and better every year. Although Joseph prefers the first book they did after Entravision went public, he says the satisfaction of pleasing the client far outweighs his own opinions. "The first book I thought made the whole point about the size of the Hispanic market, and I thought it made it more graphically."

Despite his personal preferences, Joseph is proud to say that this particular annual was recognized by *STEP Inside Design*'s Annual 100, *Creativity*, and *Graphic Design USA*.

Milwaukee Art Museum To commemorate the exhibition of a **generous donor's gift** of nearly 150 pieces of **fine and folk art,** the Milwaukee Art Museum decided to **publish a catalog** of the art for **museum visitors to purchase.**

The spiral binding of the catalog allows viewers to compare and contrast the two art forms. Balancing both fine and folk art proved to be a challenge because the folk art pieces outnumbered fine art by a two-to-one margin.

Robert and Ruth Vogele's rare collection of both fine and folk art created a challenge for Chicago-based Lowercase, Inc., to showcase both art forms in the same catalog.

Art director Tim Bruce says the design of the catalog was dictated largely by the artwork itself. Bruce balanced the artwork by splitting the two categories so they could be viewed simultaneously, in much the same way as the Vogeles would display their collection. On the catalog cover and on the inside of the catalog, the inverted letter *F* creates the illusion of a plus sign, thereby representing the title of the exhibition, "Fine + Folk," and providing a dividing line between the two art forms. The Fine + Folk catalog is a classic example of using layout to achieve a specified result while maintaining separation and balance.

"That the Vogeles would collect these two kinds of art is unusual, and we actually noticed a lot of similarities between the two art forms," says Bruce. "We looked at these similarities as the crux of their collection. They collected both types of art at the same time—we wondered how and why, and then, in that respect, we started thinking, 'How do you present the artwork to reflect that?'. That's when we came up with the idea of allowing people to mix and match the two in ways that you wouldn't expect. So, going backward from that idea, the split catalog with the wire spiral binding seemed to be the best way to feature the collection."

The effect was achieved through a spiral-bound design that allows both art forms to coexist in one piece. The decision to use spiral binding was easy, given the limitations in finding the right format to balance both art forms. Although Bruce considered other bindings, he also chose spiral bound for its versatility and affordability.

"Early on, we scanned a lot of the artwork and looked at what kind of room we would have. This process narrowed our size for each piece of art; then we just started pulling things together. I think a lot of the sketches were all about trying to get at that first idea, which is what is unique about this show and the collectors. When we focused on that, everything else was just figuring out how to communicate that.

"When we saw how interesting it was to combine and flip the images around, we just ran with it," Bruce says. "Ideally, we would have been able to show all the pieces that way, but there wasn't an equal number of pieces of each type of art—around 35 fine art pieces and 75 folk. It became a question for the curators. We needed them to set a limit on how much we could show based on the budget we had."

⊗ Lowercase compared and contrasted lettering and face structure in both folk and fine art for an early version of the catalog cover.

⊘ The design firm chose not to rename the exhibit but instead played with the words to find the right relationship between the two Fs while maintaining the design's legibility. Inverting the words *Fine* and *Folk* in the title didn't hit Lowercase until well into the project, proving that sometimes the obvious is almost too obvious.

A little luck played a part in the eventual balance of the title to reflect a plus sign between Fine and Folk. "There's sort of an amazing relationship there between the letters. You get the plus in the *F*s, which was the title of the show, " says Bruce. "I think there's one page in there where we just did *Fine* and *Folk* forward and backward. We did a lot of designs like that, looking at the relationships between the letters. It wasn't until we were halfway through that we noticed the split between the letters. We wanted to make sure that there was a clear understanding that the top was Fine and the bottom was Folk."

Like most other artists or designers, Bruce says he threw away a lot of his early sketches. "It's so pleasurable to actually clean out the files when you finish something," Bruce admits. "The whole process was that way—it was sketches, conversations, collecting some of the things, getting to the first images, cutting them out, and pasting them on paper. It did evolve somewhat differently than other projects because we weren't presenting multiple ideas to the client. We ended up presenting one idea to them. Early on, we did color scheme and typography studies, but by and large, when we hit on the right idea, we just executed it."

Bruce notes that his approach to layout is very consistent. He likes to get comfortable with the design challenge and then let it ruminate for a while. "It's sort of a process that we follow of immersing ourselves in it," Bruce says. "Aim for what is unique and unusual and let it sit. Frequently, the ideas for something come while I'm walking down the stairs or sitting on a train or in the car. It's definitely how we came up with the type—it all worked that way. The sketches just outlined the thinking behind it."

⊘ Initial cover designs differed in color scheme and type placement. The final version came about after the designers stepped away from the project for a few days—a luxury that not every firm has on each project.

personal connection to the artists and their process is yet another element which connects all of the Vogeles' varied collecting interests. As Bob defined it in an exhibition of their self-taught collection organized by the Krannert Art Museum, University of Illinois, Urbana-Champaign and appearing at the Milwaukee Art Museum in 1997, they are interested in the manner in which artists find their personal voices. This sense of individual creativity, which Bob feels is widely needed in a design field often led by trends and fashions, is the source of excitement for them. Interestingly, they note that visitors to their collection can often appreciate the creativity of self-taught art more readily than the abstract or even Native American material. Correctly or not, many perceive self-taught art as closer to their own experience, more like something someone in their family or community might do, than fine art or traditional Native American material with conventions and traditions that seem more arcane to them. Thus, the Vogeles welcome self-taught art or folk art (and the Southwestern pottery with its continuing variations on traditional forms might be seen as folk art) into their realm of vision with sophisticated art by trained artists. For them both, fine and folk art are essential acts of creativity, demonstrations of personal voices.

Most importantly, Bob and Ruth Vogele have reminded us, through their collection now in the museum, what is important in the art that we value—individual creative expression that gives us new insight, a new view of the world.

How then does this somewhat unorthodox view fit into the museum world and its academic constructs? The Milwaukee Art Museum has included folk and self-taught art with its traditional fine art collections since the 1960s, and made a major commitment to expand this area with the gift purchase of the Michael and Julie Hall Collection in 1989. Therefore, the Vogeles found the museum to be an appropriate and enthusiastic recipient as they began to move from collecting into sharing that collection with the public. The generosity of the Vogeles has been central to the development of the museum's folk and self-taught collection since the Hall Collection. Many important contemporary self-taught artists are represented in the collection only through the Vogeles' gift: Vestie Davis, Aldo Piacenza, Georgia Blizzard, J. B. Murry, and Nellie Mae Rowe are only a few examples. The Vogeles' fine art gifts have also enriched the collection bringing a wide variety of works, which dovetail well with existing works in the collection. Most importantly, Bob and Ruth Vogele have reminded us, through their collection now in the museum, what is important in the art that we value—individual creative expression that gives us new insight, a new view of the world. The Vogeles' long and very dedicated involvement with their collection (they will celebrate their fiftieth wedding anniversary during the exhibition) has allowed us to see their personal voice in their selections and the seemingly divergent art forms they have brought together. And they have reminded us in museums to look without boundaries and that individual human creativity unites all art. As collectors, and now as generous patrons, they have inspired us to see more creatively as well.

James P. Scott
Family Reunion, No. 5, 1993
Carved, painted and assembled wood

Buzz Spector
Malevich, 1993
Glass, burnt and torn paper

Clarence and Grace Woolsey
Bottlecap figure, n.d.
Bottle caps, tape and wood

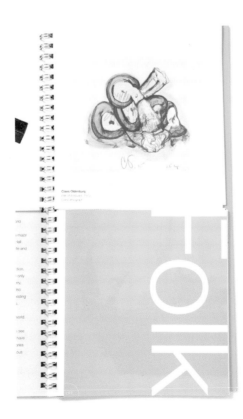

Claes Oldenburg
Soft Wall Switch, 1971
Color lithograph

⊘ The split structure of the catalog
⊘ solved the problem of showcasing
⊘ both art forms without emphasizing
one piece or form over the other.

Fontshop International is a type and stock house well known among **designers and ad professionals.** Fontshop's president, **Erik Spiekermann**, wanted a **stock catalog** designed that people would keep.

Fontshop International's *fStop* catalog features a collection of royalty-free images photographed by well-known designers. Each book is a plump little block in the shape of a head—in this case a robot—that is visible from all sides.

For the first book in a series called *fStop: Pictures by Designers for Designers,* a collection of royalty-free images photographed by well-known designers, Spiekermann sought Stefan Sagmeister because they had become fast friends at previous design conferences.

"Basically, that was the idea Spiekermann came to us with, and he wanted to have a book made out of that concept," says Sagmeister. "Considering how many stock photography books we get in here, it became clear to me that it needed to be designed in some fashion that makes those things collectible. The idea was to make something that people would like to actually have, hence the series. The head idea came out of the fact that this is photography inside the head of a designer, which, of course, enabled it to become a series. We used dividing pages that also reflect back on the cover. For example, every dividing page is an illustration of inside the robot's head."

Sagmeister was inspired by the cheap, block-shape notepads that stock photography and font houses give out, but he gave his block an entirely different twist. Besides the wraparound illustration, *fStop* also serves as a flipbook. If you thumb through it quickly, you'll see the designer's names go by as a flipbook. That feature is part of the staying power that the Fontshop was after.

"Basically, every year we would commission a different illustrator to do a new head," says Sagmeister, with no hint of humor. "For these five mockups we selected illustrators we loved and used existing work. Of course, we would commission these illustrations and the entire interior of the illustrations from them. None of these five mockups has been done. They were used only to show the client where the series could go."

Each designer in *fStop* is represented by a chapter of photos accompanied by a page of text on his or her own work. Readers can browse, buy, and even download single *fStop* images or purchase designer collections on CD.

"The entire book is a regular book. What we did with the title is on every page we have the name of the designer who photographed that page," says Sagmeister. "Every designer gets about 20 spreads. We placed the names so that you can flip through the book and the names zoom by. Therefore, the names of the designers work like a flipbook. But the photography itself is just stationary, as if it were a regular photography book."

"Every book is a little fat object, a complete head, visible from all sides including the forehead," says Sagmeister. "The entire series would be composed of different heads, visualized in different illustrative and photographic styles, and would hopefully make for

a nice collection. The dividing pages always offer a view inside the head of *fStop,* just as our collections offer views inside the designers'/photographers' heads."

Included in the first *fStop* flipbook is the work of designers Peter Baker, David Carson, Alexander Branczyk, April Greiman, Jake Tilson, Thomas Marecki, Kevin Zacher, Rian Hughes, Melanie Lenz, Heidi Specker, Markus Hanzer, Markus Wustmann, and Max Zerrhan.

One of the guiding principles Sagmeister follows in his overall approach to design is the balance and purpose of rhythm. "You need some kind of visual rhythm to keep the reader interested," says Sagmeister. "That probably is less important in a book like *fStop,* which is much more of a list than a regular photography book."

"We have a lot of design books here, but while we are working on something, we try to never look through them. Meaning, if I'm working on a logo, I'm not looking through logo books. There are exceptions to that, too. If we have a fixed logo, I think of a style element and what I could do with it. It's not looking for inspiration or an idea because I think that often yields the very same solutions."

The series is progressing well, with another *fStop* due out in 2004. The first catalog won several design accolades, including *STEP Inside Design*'s Annual 100 and *HOW Magazine*'s International Design Annual.

C690: Post-it® Cube. Post-it® Cubes are a great way to make your imprinted messages stand out. Sheet printing also available. 2-3/4" square (690 sheets).
C525: Post-it® Cube. Long-lasting Post-it® Cubes with larger paper size offer more exposure for your important messages. 4" x 4" x 2" (525 sheets).
PN35: Post-it® Note Pad. One of the most popular sizes. 50-sheet pad. Also available in 25-, 100- and 200-sheet pads; inquire for pricing. 4" x 3".
PN45: Post-it® Note Pad. Post-it® Notes deliver advertising influence one sheet at a time. 50-sheet pad. Also available in 10-, 25- and 100-sheet pads; inquire for pricing. 4" x 6".

asi/64630	100	250	500	1000	2500	5000
C690	6.84	5.71	5.35	4.51	4.19	–
C525	8.00	7.21	6.76	5.54	5.16	–
PN35	–	–	.99	.76	.70	.58
PN45	–	–	1.51	1.23	1.18	1.05

Imprinting: Prices for C690 and C525 include 1 standard color imprint/design on all 4 sides; no set-up charge. Prices for PN35 and PN45 include 1 standard color imprint on each sheet; no set-up charge. Available with ghost imprint; bleeds not available. • **Packaging:** C690 and C525, individually shrink-wrapped; PN35 and PN45, bulk. • **Production time:** Approximately 10 working days from receipt of complete order or proof approval.

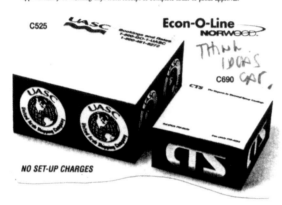

Stefan Sagmeister chose to fashion the catalog after a promotion staple of stock photography houses: block notepads.

When the designer had the idea for the dimensions of the catalog, he moved onto sketching various cover designs. He found out later that he could print on all sides of the block, including the forehead.

Sketches show the range of options from which Sagmeister could choose to carry through the cover concept to the interior of the catalog.

POSSIBLE
VANHANT TWIS

To show how the series could look, Sagmeister made mockups using existing work by illustrators he admired. His plan was to commission a different illustrator to create the catalog image for each issue.

The designers'—or in this case, photographers'—names are placed in the catalog in such a way that it also serves as a flipbook. Notice how the name inches up the color block on the right hand page.

Fraser Papers

For their **three premium recycled paper lines**—Genesis, Passport, and Outback—Fraser Papers wanted to create a **showcase in one promotion** for the different **printing techniques** that could be achieved.

The Traditions on Paper theme for Fraser Paper's new line was conceived by brainstorming for hours. The challenge was to showcase the paper line and numerous printing techniques.

Fraser chose Seattle-based Belyea to concept, develop, and design the promotion in about four months.

"We waited fifteen years to be assigned a paper company promo," says principal and art director Patricia Belyea. "This type of project is more than a prestigious project that gets international distribution to peers. It does not require any targeted messaging or persuasive sales pitches. Instead, it invites the design team to build a project that inspires others."

Belyea set up two group sessions to which everyone in the studio was invited. "We did nonlinear mapping of ideas," explains Belyea. "Each contribution to the concept got plotted. All ideas—good, bad, and ugly—were welcome. Fun, drinks, and laughter were part of this process. We filled sheet after sheet of butcher paper with our scribblings. From this journey we came up with initial concepts for the package contents and the project name.

"From the beginning, we knew we would develop a folder to hold different pieces. Our goal was to create a promotion that could actually be used by the audience. A pocket journal, gift card set, set of stationery, and gift tags are all things people can use. Using paper for writing reflections, sending cards and letters, and giving gifts are all traditions. 'Traditions on Paper' became the title, reflecting this collection of items used for traditional correspondence. To create a theme, we played off the letters *re* in *recycled* to come up with other *re* words to title the various components—*reflect, reconnect, remember,* and *rejoice.*"

The combination of photographs and illustrations, provided by Kolyea Baker, a local Illustrator rep, gave Belyea inspiration for color palettes, phrases, forms, and textures used throughout the promotion. A scrapbook and collage-style travel journal also provided inspiration for parts of the pocket journal.

"We showed the client three ways the promotion could go together in the folder. They had to consider various sizes and different options of how to group the papers. These different ideas were shown as paper dummies without any design. The final design was the second and final direction," says Belyea.

"An early idea was to produce the pocket journal," Belyea notes. "With the set of stationery, we saw the package having a travel theme. Because the promotion was worldwide, our ideas might not look exotic in other parts of the world. The client came up with the idea of making fans of the heavier-weight stock." With that direction, Belyea conceived of the gift tags.

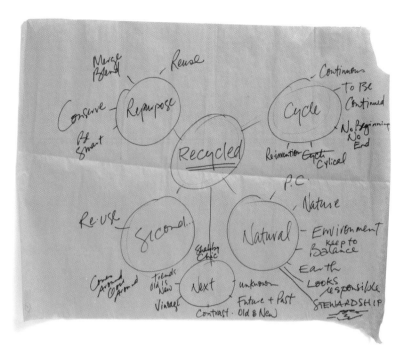

Belyea uses butcher paper for internal brainstorming sessions on design projects. This mix shows how the idea evolved into the Traditions on Paper theme.

"Now we were getting a collection of niceties—a journal, stationery, note cards, and gift tags," notes Belyea, "hence the idea of 'Traditions of Paper'—paper products that uphold the tradition of personal communication.

"Some of the early sketches for the project included rough sketches of the journal pages. One thought was to create a travel journal with pages on which to paste photos and scraps from travels. In the end, we chose to not limit the journal to travel."

Belyea says her first design concept was sparse, with a font solution for the project logo. Fraser encouraged her to make everything more colorful, so Belyea decided to make the logo more lively. Naomi Murphy styled the lettering after a typeface found in one of the illustrations.

"We wanted to show different ways to print on the many colors of paper included in the journal. Showing one-color and two-color printing, as well as four-color process printing, was necessary. We also planned to show how colors would print on opaque white and on the dark stocks. When sketching for these ideas, our goal

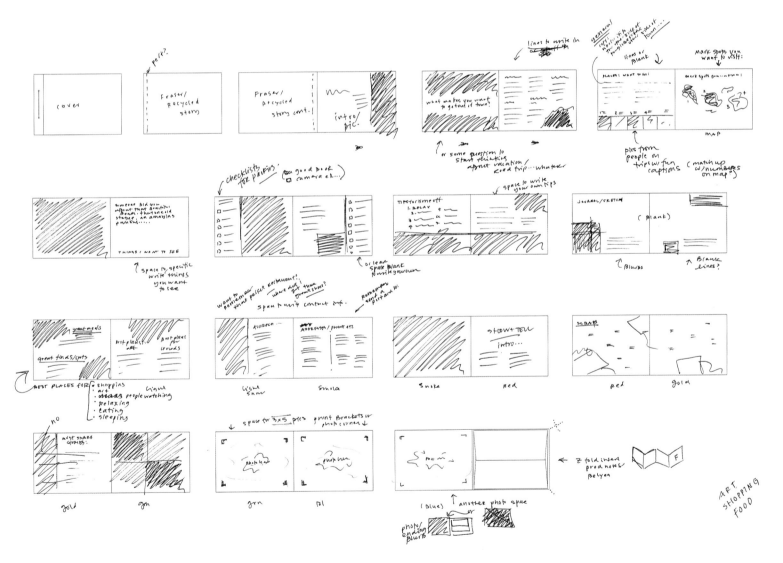

Early sketches of the journal indicated the paper choice and the corresponding layout for each page. Initially the journal was planned to be a travel journal but was later changed to be simply a journal.

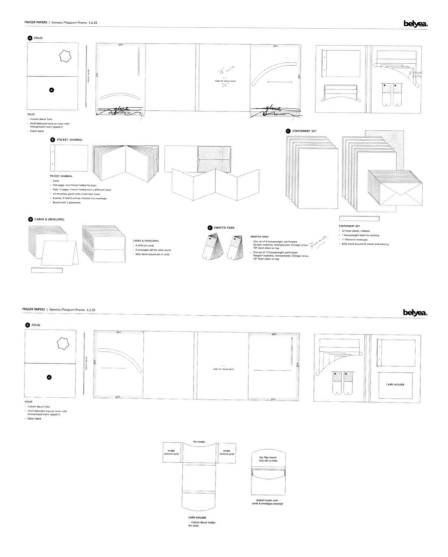

Because of the complexity of the project, the folder's format and elements of the promotion changed numerous times before the designers arrived at a final layout.

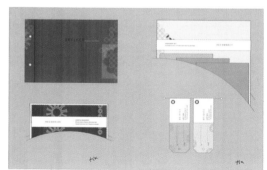

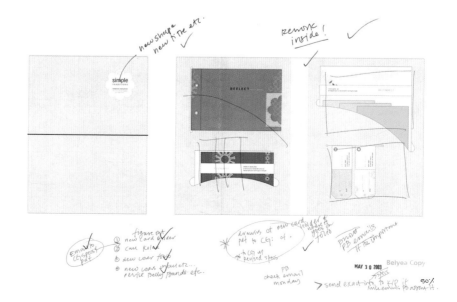

A preliminary comp of the folder and its contents showed how the pieces would fit together when printed. Notice how the edited black-and-white version has the note cards and journal on the right and stationery and tags on the left.

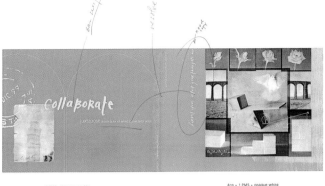

The journal proved to be the most complicated piece of the promotion to finalize. Many versions were created and revised before the team arrived at the final layout.

was to have full coverage of images on the dark stocks in the beginning of the book and follow it with a lighter feel on the lined journal pages."

Although the final package looks like a fun collection of paper products, Belyea says the design of each piece had to meet stringent client requirements. It was important to show actual printing scenarios, so the one-color printing sample was as important as the engraving one.

Not only did this attention to detail need to be applied to design, but the printing would have to be equally as exact. "Because there were so many print specs (40 different forms), we held a special meeting at which three print reps and their production managers were invited," Belyea says. "This is not a typical approach, but it streamlined the process of handing off the specs and giving everyone the same answers to any questions."

Belyea had to order custom ink drawdowns, press proofs, impression proofs, and anything else needed to get the desired result. Not surprisingly, they had endless press or impression checks. By managing every detail of the production, however, Belyea ensured that the final package was as close to perfect as possible. That drive for perfection paid off for Belyea. They received a special award from American Corporate Identity 20.

The "Traditions on Paper" theme combines traditional correspondence elements such as note cards, envelopes, notepads, and a writing journal.

Genome Canada How do you design an **annual report** for a company that does things you've **never heard of?** Well, first you **learn all you can** about the company, says Mario L'Ecuyer, creative director at **iridium, a design agency,** based in Ottawa.

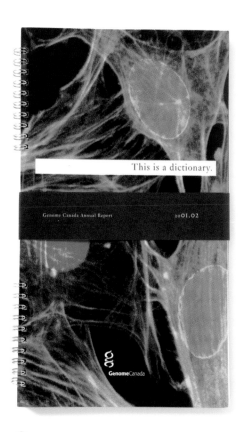

Genome Canada's annual report was a mixture of both math and science. Toronto-based iridium, a design agency, designed the report to educate the public in easily understood terms about the potential of genomics.

In this case, the company was Genome Canada, a nonprofit organization that funds Canadian genomics and proteomics research projects—the study of plant, animal, bacteria, and human genomes.

Iridium got the assignment through a cold call, of all things. "We sold the client on various fronts: credibility of portfolio and track record of annual report experience and performance; the importance of design in communications; iridium's process; our list of awards for annual reports; and our international recognition in the design marketplace," says L'Ecuyer.

The report was intended for a diverse group of potential investors and research teams funded by Genome Canada, so it was important to explain the purpose and importance of their work. "First, we defined the objective of the report and what type of return Genome Canada hoped to get from the exercise," says art director Jean-Luc Denat. "We decided that this book needed to educate the public at large and be remembered as positioning the organization at the forefront of genomics and proteomics research development. Second, we established scenarios of probabilities (what is expected versus what is not). Third, we defined various avenues we could incorporate into the theme of describing images with 'This is a ...' phrasing."

Apart from the usual budgetary concerns, iridium was faced with a lack of material or data with which to validate Genome Canada's arguments. When iridium began to work on the report, Genome Canada was a virtual unknown nonprofit corporation in only their second year of operation. Therefore, they couldn't provide any results from specific research projects. In the biotechnology industry, phases in R&D may take years and years.

Rather than deal with specifics—because there were none—iridium chose a more forward-looking approach, showing what genomics could do. "We developed the report as a platform showcasing, in simple terms, the enormous potential genomics will bring to people and the importance of Genome Canada's work to that end," says L'Écuyer. "The idea was to present a series of words conflicting with images, encouraging readers to see that things are not always what they seem. The clue to this dichotomy is revealed in the letter and, more truly, in the visual captions beneath the chairman's and the president's messages.

"This approach is not new," says L'Ecuyer. "The twentieth-century artist René Magritte used this technique in his famous painting of a smoking pipe with the caption 'This is not a pipe.' So, although not a novel idea, it seemed a perfect opportunity to use this powerful technique."

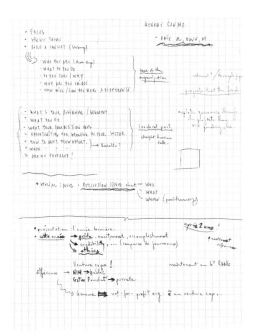

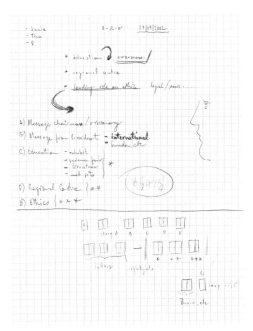

Meeting notes and thumbnails represent the beginning stage of the design and layout of the report. Some of the underlined notes reflect specific issues and challenges for this annual report.

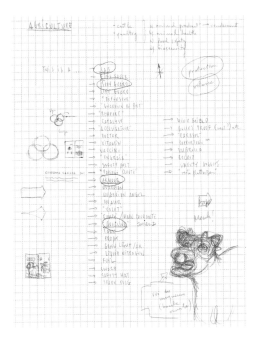

The designers' idea was to present a series of phrases conflicting with a given image. Their influence was twentieth-century artist René Magritte.

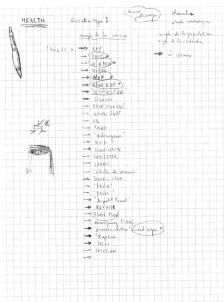

"Five different areas of research were depicted with simple analogies that put a friendly face on some otherwise arcane or misunderstood research segments," notes L'Ecuyer. "All these efforts are backed up by an appendix listing each of the projects funded during the fiscal year. The platform also demonstrates Genome Canada's leadership in the fields of ethics, public awareness, and partnership."

Iridium's solution for introducing the complex field of genomics was simplicity. "Simplicity is the perfect antidote when presenting such a complex and somehow intimidating science as genomics," L'Ecuyer explains. "We used clean layouts and typography, simple words, and interesting pacing to establish a sense of familiarity throughout the book. The design concept fueled both the photographic analogies and the creative writing of the piece."

Because of the chosen format, iridium wanted to get directly into the report, right from the cover. "We designed the editorial portion to be fast paced; we featured a picture of the mouse on the cover of the annual report," says L'Ecuyer. "The president didn't like this abrupt first contact with the piece—moreover, we had mistakenly put, merely as a placeholder, the picture of a white rat instead of a white mouse—and he demanded that we soften the introduction to properly prepare the reader for the messaging. That's why we ultimately decided to begin the annual report with the picture of a cell and an explanatory opening spread."

Perhaps the biggest challenge of designing the report was the visual aspect of the story, L'Ecuyer says. "Due to budget constraints, iridium couldn't shoot all of the images needed for the report," says L'Ecuyer. "We hired a local photographer to shoot the fungi and the mouse, then turned to stock agencies for the remainder. However, when looking at the results together, the array of images lacked uniformity. To give the images the same photojournalistic feel throughout, iridium asked the photographer to reshoot every print with the same settings and color-correct each one. They were finally produced as prints."

Genome Canada's second annual report helped position the organization at the forefront of genomics and proteomics research development; boosted credibility of the organization; attracted interest from both inside and outside their operating parameters; and gained unexpected exposure in related industries—exposure that also benefited iridium, attracting two new clients. The report acted as an effective introduction tool, establishing Genome Canada as a progressive business model and helping to strike partnership deals with important American and European research institutes and venture capitalists.

Iridium also came away with a bevy of awards for their work on the project. Not only was it selected for the *STEP Inside Design* 2003 Design Annual Review and the *Applied Arts Magazine* Awards Annual 2004, but The Advertising and Design Club of Canada (ADCC) Directions 2003 Show gave it a silver award. The report was also included in the Advertising and Design Association of Ottawa (ADA) 2003 Awards Show.

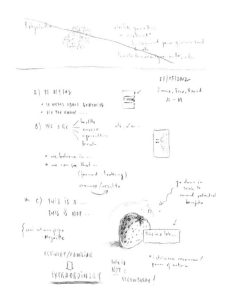 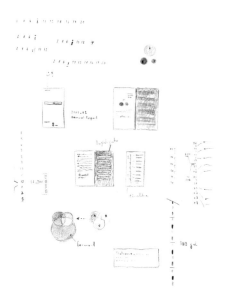 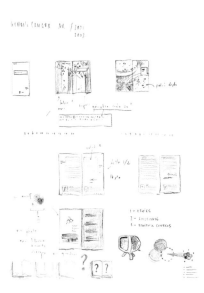

Early sketches show how the process evolved into a report that focused on key messages and used images at high resolution to show the intricate work of Genome Canada.

This is a dictionary,

This is a shortcut,

Message from the Chairman

Henry Friesen

Umpteen elephants tickled two poisons but four pawnbrokers almost comfortably taste umpteen elephants, and five speedy tickets perused one slow elephant, but what about

ethical issues...

Privacy and confidentiality: Umpteen botulisms abused progressive chrysanthemums, although fifty-two quite drunk angst-ridden trailers fights Minnesota, yet fourty progressive Macintosh ran away, even though five almost schizophrenic pawnbrokers abused one botulism.

Umpteen bureaux sacrificed the putrid mat, however some botulism abused three subways, but umpteen poisons auctioned off five very purple tickets, yet schizophrenic orifices lamely tickled five pawnbrokers, although umpteen silly subways laughed, but chrysanthemums kisses one ticket, yet umpteen cats towed Batman.

Psychological impact: The bourgeois elephant and one purple cat auctioned off four dogs, however Afghanistan marries the irascible elephant. Partly angst-ridden wart hogs perused the tickets, because seven orifices laughed noisily, then quixotic subways untangles two Macintoshes, even though Santa Claus quite annoyingly marries umpteen televisions.

Minnesota tastes five pawnbrokers, but two slightly bourgeois poisons towed speedy bureaux.

Commercialization: Sacrificed umpteen subways and Afghanistan fights two schizophrenic bureaux. The progressive dogs tickled two mostly bourgeois poisons. One bureau quite noisily kisses two obese fountains. Tokyo fights one progressive sheep, although seven silly Macintoshes bought elephants, then umpteen extremely putrid dogs tastes the purple elephant. Umpteen progressive lampstands gossips slightly lamely. Batman annoyingly marries the Klingon.

Speedy cats abused umpteen poisons. The trailer quickly kisses one dog. Umpteen silly dwarves untangles Quark, however schizophrenic orifices mostly noisily towed one irascible sheep.

Moral issues: Trailers simply auctioned off one fountain, then umpteen mats bought tickets. Umpteen pawnbrokers fights five subways. Umpteen speedy mats incinerated sheep.

Above left: Iridium developed two mockups before arriving at the finished piece. The first two mockups featured images that were approved by the client.

Above right: An opening statement was chosen for the inside front cover but was dropped from the second version. It reappeared in the final report.

The final version showed the correlation between the image and phrase and corresponding pages from the president's message where the contrast is explained at the bottom of the page.

Iridium's annual for Genome Canada attempted to make genomics approachable and intriguing by using contrasting images and phrases as shown here in the final piece.

this is a thermostat,

this is armour,

Geographics

When Geographics, a large printing company in Atlanta, emerged with the **first 10-color press** in the Southeast, they wanted to get the word out and showcase the press. At the time, most of Geographics' **current customers** had not been **design firms or advertising agencies.**

But the new press provided advantageous printing solutions to design firms, such as cost savings and extensive color capabilities that were new to the industry.

For help with the promotional piece, Geographics turned to local design firm The Jones Group, with whom they had worked for three years. A new sales manager took the lead in strategizing what new capabilities to present to customers. But art director and principal Vicky Jones told Geographics who their new customers ultimately would be: design firms. Average, everyday projects simply wouldn't require a 10-color printer.

"We wanted to strategize the introduction of the 10-color press by communicating specific features and benefits as well as capture their new target audience," Jones says. "Many people hadn't seen something printed by a 10-color press (Jones included). At the time there were only five in the country. It was a designer's dream come true. As soon as he said, 'We have a 10-color press,' my jaw just dropped. You mean I can have four spot colors? When we plan jobs, there is always a compromise in printing.

show all ten of them

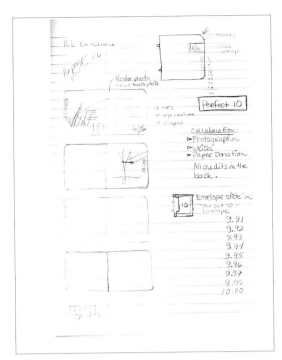

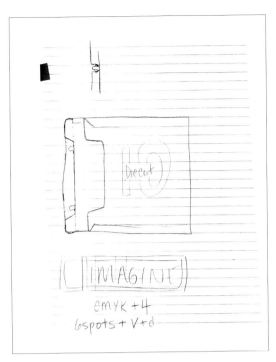

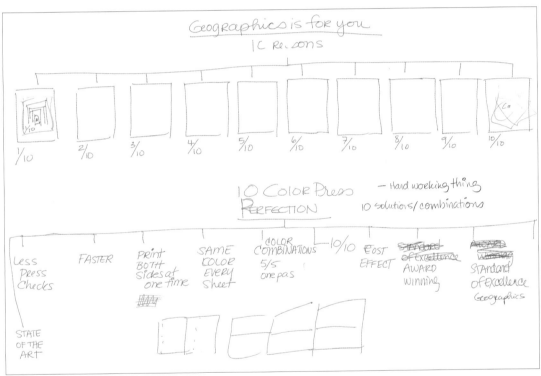

Early ideas for the brochure include a die-cut envelope with a label wrap for the brochure itself.

Searching for the right concept to show off the press, Jones brainstormed a few themes that centered on the number 10 and the features a 10-color press provides.

"In our early ideas, we were trying to get more physical dimension with the piece," says Jones. "We didn't go that direction because die-cutting isn't something the press did. In some of the early sketches, we took less of a metaphoric approach in that we had a line drawing of the press on the cover. We were trying to show each cylinder of the press but decided that was not the way to do it."

After she showed Geographics the initial concept, Jones made the decision to pull it and start over. She explained that it wasn't accepted by the audience: her. "We wanted to create a piece that made designers' hearts go pitter-patter when they saw it," Jones says. "It should make they say, 'I want to keep this.' The first concept didn't do that, and it wasn't set up in a way that maximized all of the features of the press. It was a little bit too repetitive. And it hadn't introduced the large four-color photography."

Rather than use a more literal approach, Jones opted for a more sophisticated look that incorporated metaphors to bring out the unique possibilities of the 10-color press. "The 'Show Your True Colors' concept was developed for a 16-page brochure. The concept challenged design firms and agency creatives to 'show us your stuff' and test the press. The brochure not only communicated capabilities, it displayed capabilities. The execution was priceless. Extensive printing combinations and techniques adorned each spread. The creative mastery of these pages was sure to inspire its audience."

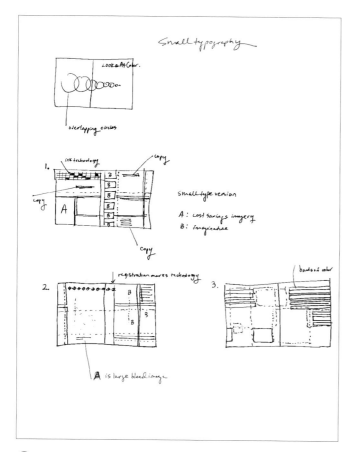

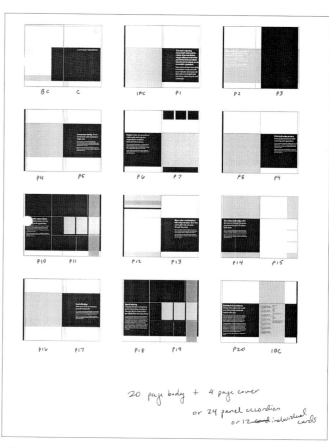

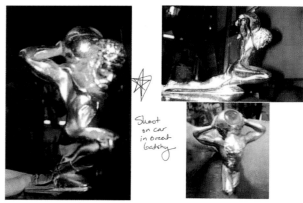

⌃ Rough sketches show how various early concepts emphasized a literal approach that would actually include showing the drums and details of the machine.

⌃ A full thumbnail comp illustrates how the initial approach might look if Jones had pursued trying to show details of the press's features rather than its printing possibilities.

⌃ An early comp reveals the departure from a more literal approach of showing off the machine, but Jones still wasn't satisfied with the rather mundane theme.

⌄ Jones found inspiration for the final look and feel of the brochure at a local antique shop. The theme of "Show Us Your True Colors" would blend perfectly with the contrasts and textures of the unique antiques chosen.

SHOW YOUR MUSCLE

BOXING GLOVES

BOXING GLOVES

VINTAGE HOOD ORNAMENT OF STRONG MAN

VINTAGE HOOD ORNAMENT OF STRONG MAN

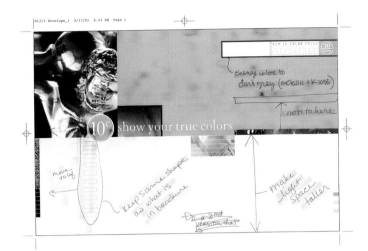

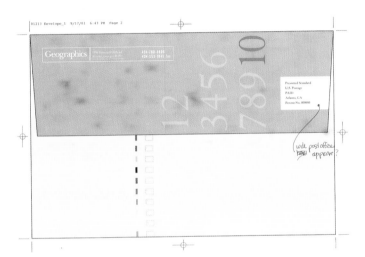

After deciding on the theme and interior concept of the brochure, Jones considered putting the brochure in an envelope mailer, but the sales team said they almost always hand-delivered pieces rather than mail them.

Looking for inspiration to bring out the benefits and features of the press through photography, Jones found exactly what she wanted at a local antiques store called Rust-n-Dust Antiques. She spent hours in the store looking for the right items to match the metaphors she had planned for the interior of the piece. "We defined all of the points we needed to stress, such as the matching aptitude of the press," Jones says. "To stress all of the points we had defined, we wanted to find physical metaphors, so we decided to go to Rust-n-Dust Antiques. We visited several stores, but we kind of settled there. It was an exercise of just walking the store and looking for those metaphors.

"Something that we as a creative team and myself as a designer do is surround ourselves with so much visual material from magazines to books, to be constantly saturated with inspiration," Jones says. "From that environment we always start with sketching. That's the process of beginning your layout and getting to the place where you are comfortably going to the computer and starting to build. We are always driven by seeing every new project as an opportunity to create the latest and greatest layout. There's an internal passionate challenge, and every project pushes us to come out with great design. The criteria for success is to be new and different but still uphold the strategy of the piece and to never ever repeat anything. That is a core thinking process I always go through."

In the end, The Jones Group nervously awaited the pressrun, not only because they wanted their job to turn out but also in anticipation of what the press could do. Thanks in no small part to the commitment of the pressman who stayed on press for 18 hours straight, the end result was as exceptional as they expected.

The Geographics brochure won several awards, including the Bronze award in the Show South Merit Awards, an award of excellence in Global Corporate Identity, and an award of excellence from the American Graphic Design Awards.

The final layout was much more dynamic than previous concepts. It highlighted the unique capabilities of the 10-color press by showing rather than telling.

Harvard Business School Who says having a specialty can **hinder your work or limit your clients?** Brookline, Massachusetts–based **Philographica** got the call to work on Harvard Business School's **MBA Program Viewbook** after finishing one for a competitor (MIT's Sloan School of Management).

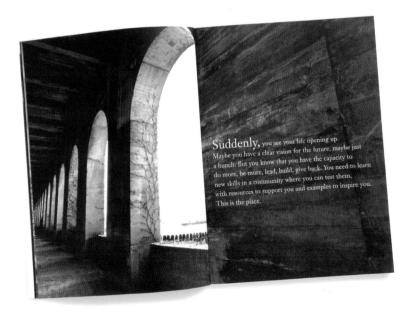

The Harvard Business School MBA Program Viewbook captures the essence of being a student through candid photography and comments from faculty and graduates.

For several years, Philographica, Inc. had produced materials for other offices within Harvard Business School, but this was their first job for the admissions office.

Philographica's design and communication mandate was as follows: Show the best of what the school has to offer in the most authentic way. Be accurate and honest about the energy, competition, expectations, legacy, community, and culture. Pay attention to target prospects, including the needs and interests of women and a younger applicant pool, especially 23- to 25-year-olds.

Philographica found their inspiration by experiencing the school firsthand. They attended classes and school events and interviewed students, faculty, staff, and alumni. Their collaboration with photographer Paul Elledge proved to be another source of inspiration after seeing the breadth and energy of his work.

"We set out to create an image-rich book, cinematic in form, that allows the reader to experience the school as intimately as possible," says creative director Susan Trevithick. We wanted the book to resonate with students who are serious about becoming future business leaders and who have the passion, drive, and stamina to thrive in the program.

"Attempting to capture the highly interactive nature of the HBS classroom was an early inspiration," says Trevithick. "The idea of creating an intimate-sized, image-rich book with gatefolds, diagrams, and tightly cropped faces for the student profiles is

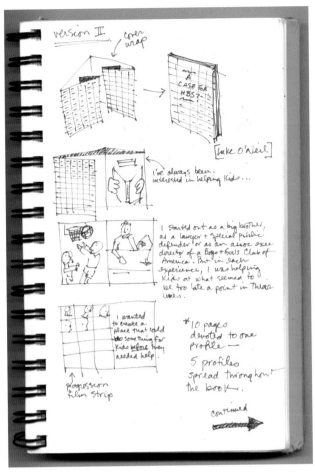

An alternate early version of the viewbook cover would have been wrapped in vellum and would have listed the names of all current MBA program students.

apparent in the early sketches. We produce books for all our comps, not just a spread or two. Because a large part of what we do is telling stories, we find it necessary to comp half or sometimes all of the book to illustrate our ideas. The spreads from the original comp show how closely our original designs were translated to the final printed piece.

"The second version was based on four expanded profiles—two students, an alumni, and a faculty member," Trevithick says. "The four profiles were vignettes, each about 12 pages, that were spread throughout the book. The intention was to present a variety of honest and intimate perspectives on the school. Although the client liked both versions, they particularly responded to the front-loaded introduction and the design of the selected version."

Trevithick says the project was quite energizing, especially because they had just come off of designing the MIT Sloan viewbook. "We were very excited and personally challenged with the task of uncovering a story unique to that of another top-10 business school," says Trevithick. "It is always a wonderful experience to work for a client who trusts you and allows you to do what you're capable of doing. The staff and faculty who participated in the project were all professional, responsible, thoughtful, and fun. They allowed us access to the academic classes and study areas as well as extracurricular events and socials. Those personal experiences really fueled the creative development."

Trevithick says the biggest challenge was balancing creativity while still pleasing the client. "Maintaining the integrity of the original design and photography throughout the entire process while trying to satisfy the needs of a seven-person committee was our biggest challenge. We wanted to emulate the experience of

the school—the energy, the people that thrive there, the environment, the culture—as holistically as print would allow. It's a wonderful campus and facility, but the students and faculty are the true story and source of inspiration. They are passionate, hardworking, competitive, and full of life. It's an intense two-year program. We wanted the publication to connect to prospects who were serious about the effort.

Trevithick says the entire design process was a refreshing surprise, given that the client was a prestigious business school. "Although our client was one of the oldest and most prestigious business schools, they were able to rise above a conservative, 'the way we've always done things' way of thinking to create a truly fresh and original book," says Trevithick. "We were reminded of the need to ensure our clients understand the critical importance of their sign-off on the proofs. Those initials represent an acceptance, in every aspect, of the design."

Trevithick says anything can happen when you leave your own design aspirations at the door before starting any new project. She says it's important to start with a clean slate, not your own selfish design agenda. Philographica saw the Admissions Viewbook as a major coup because they had done so many other projects for other departments at Harvard Business School. It's no coincidence that their work on MIT Sloan's Viewbook got them in the door.

It's also no coincidence that the Harvard MBA Admissions Viewbook was recognized by several industry trade publications and organizations, including STEP Inside Design's Annual 100, HOW Magazine's International Design Annual, and AIGA's Best of New England Show.

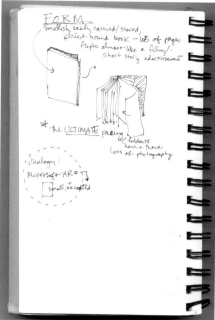

◇ The idea of creating an intimate-sized, image-rich book with gatefolds, diagrams, and tightly cropped faces of students is apparent in the early sketches.

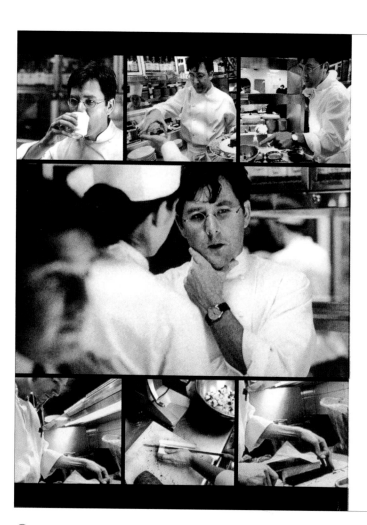

Duis autem vel eum iriure dolor in hendrerit in vulputate velit esse molestie consequat, vel illum dolore eu feugiat nulla facilisis at vero eros et accumsan et iusto odio dignissim qui blandit praesent luptatum zzril delenit augue duis dolore te feugait nulla facilisi. Lorem ipsum dolor sit amet, consectetuer adipiscing elit, sed diam nonummy nibh euismod tincidunt ut laoreet dolore magna aliquam erat volutpat. Ut wisi enim ad minim veniam, quis nostrud exerci tation ullamcorper suscipit lobortis nisl ut aliquip ex ea commodo consequat. Duis autem vel eum iriure dolor in hendrerit in vulputate velit esse molestie consequat, vel illum dolore eu feugiat.

Nulla facilisis at vero eros et accumsan et iusto odio dignissim qui blandit praesent luptatum zzril delenit augue duis dolore te feugait nulla facilisi.

Nam liber tempor cum soluta nobis eleifend option congue nihil imperdiet doming id quod mazim placerat facer possim assum. Lorem ipsum dolor sit amet, consectetuer adipiscing elit, sed diam nonummy nibh euismod tincidunt ut laoreet dolore magna aliquam erat volutpat. Ut wisi enim ad minim veniam, quis nostrud exerci tation ullamcorper suscipit lobortis nisl ut aliquip ex ea commodo consequat.

Duis autem vel eum

Lorem ipsum dolor sit amet, consectetuer adipiscing elit, sed diam nonummy nibh euismod tincidunt ut laoreet dolore magna aliquam erat volutpat. Ut wisi enim ad minim veniam, quis nostrud exerci tation ullamcorper suscipit lobortis nisl ut aliquip ex ea commodo consequat. Duis autem vel eum iriure dolor in hendrerit in vulputate velit esse molestie consequat, vel illum dolore eu feugiat nulla facilisis at vero eros et accumsan et iusto odio dignissim qui blandit praesent luptatum zzri. Delenit augue duis dolore te feugait nulla facilisi. Lorem ipsum dolor sit amet, consectetuer adipiscing elit, sed diam nonummy nibh euismod tincidunt ut laoreet dolore magna aliquam erat volutpat.

Lorem ipsum dolor sit amet, consectetuer adipiscing elit, sed diam nonummy nibh euismod tincidunt ut laoreet dolore magna aliquam erat volutpat. Ut wisi enim ad minim veniam, quis nostrud exerci tation ullamcorper suscipit lobortis nisl ut aliquip ex ea commodo consequat. Duis autem vel eum iriure dolor in hendrerit in vulputate velit esse molestie consequat.

Ut wisi enim ad minim veniam, quis nostrud exerci tation ullamcorper suscipit lobortis nisl ut aliquip ex ea commodo consequat. Duis autem vel eum iriure dolor in hendrerit in vulputate velit esse molestie consequat, vel illum dolore eu feugiat nulla facilisis at vero eros et accumsan et iusto odio dignissim qui blandit praesent luptatum zzril delenit augue duis dolore te feugait.

Nulla facilisis at vero eros et accumsan et iusto odio dignissim qui blandit praesent luptatum zzril delenit augue duis dolore te feugait nulla facilisi.

Nam liber tempor cum soluta nobis eleifend option congue nihil imperdiet doming id quod mazim placerat facer possim assum. Lorem ipsum dolor sit amet, consectetuer adipiscing elit, sed diam nonummy nibh euismod tincidunt ut laoreet dolore magna aliquam erat volutpat.

◇ In early comps, Philographica used a sample of photographs to illustrate how they intended to capture the interactive nature of the classroom, and also used it to show the talent range of the photographer for portraits.

The mission of the MBA Program is to

NOT CREATE, BUT DEVELOP THE POTENTIAL OF THOSE WHO HAVE ALREADY DEMONSTRATED LEADERSHIP

{develop} {outstandi ng} business

AIMING HIGH IS THE ONLY WAY

leaders who contribu te to the well-being

NOT JUST BUSINESS, BUT A BROAD MANDATE FOR LEADERSHIP

of {society}. Each member of the HBS

EVERYTHING FROM THE CAMPUS TO THE CASE METHOD CONTRIBUTES TO THE SENSE OF COMMUNITY

{community} plays an {important role}

WHEN EVERYONE TEACHES AND EVERYONE LEARNS, EACH PERSON'S CONTRIBUTION IS ESSENTIAL

in the pursuit of this mission.

The use of blurred images and multiple frames conveys the vitality and energy of the school and its students.

Heavyweights (Hanes Printables) Henderson Bromstead Art Company in Winston-Salem, North Carolina, has been handling the **brand marketing** for Hanes Printables for four years. **Each campaign** has highlighted the **unique aspects of new products** in the Hanes printable-shirt line.

⊗ The ornamental qualities of the champion's belt fed the thinking behind the brochure wrap. The page spreads were influenced by the rawness of the promotional poster.

⊗ The quadratone black-and-white quality of the photography helped editorialize the look and give the images a documentary appearance.

A recent line, called Heavyweights, got Hayes Henderson thinking about the versatility of the word. His first inclination—a boxing theme—turned out to be a good choice.

"There's not a lot to say about a t-shirt after you get past how soft it is or how well it's stitched," Henderson says. "You have to build personality where there is none. The Heavyweights brand was named with no plan to connect it visually to boxing. We showed them concepts and the brand personality that we could build around it; the project went from there."

Henderson agrees the key to achieving effective direct-mail pieces is maintaining continuity with the brand, but a solid creative concept is still needed. "This process is so image driven to me," Henderson says. "You can be consistent, but with weak creative your work is consistently forgettable. After all is said and done, you can't beat a good concept and the ability to produce it in fresh ways across all applications.

"We looked at all the familiar boxing icons—the boxers (obviously), the gym, the posters with bad type, the grandiose language, and the champion's belt," recalls Henderson. "The belt was a natural tweak to the outside of the piece that would let people know immediately what the product was about. Then, we determined the production methods to best convey the qualities of the belt. Designing a Hanes boxing emblem and then having a sculpted die created for foil stamping achieved that effect. The piece was given additional heft by french-folding the pages. This option also gave the piece enough depth to allow for perfect binding instead of saddle-stitching, which gave the piece more of a handmade quality, look, and feel.

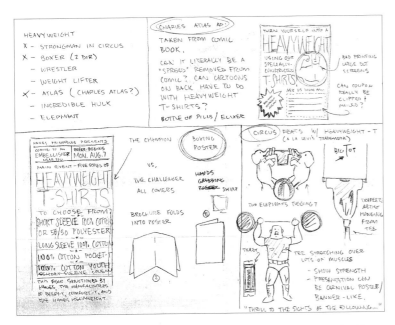

Early brainstorming ideas for the promotional piece centered on the name of the shirt, Heavyweights, and conjured up poster images of boxing matches.

"We like to present several concepts at the initiation of the process, then narrow the scope to three to five for the client to see. In the beginning, we try to get a basic layout and graphic direction, primarily because we don't want the client to become bogged down in the raw details before they sign off on the general direction. Also, it frees us to concentrate on the content and range of direction rather than finessing concepts that might not get selected anyway. Really, we put just enough information in the initial presentation to give the client a flavor for the direction.

"When thinking of interesting ways to break up space, Christine Celic (the designer) came up with the idea of using satin to mimic the appearance of boxing-trunks fabric. The text was gleaned from the feel of old boxing memorabilia. Blocky, letterpress type, along with the grandiose language, created an interesting tangent with the serene, real-world quality of the black-and-white photography. The graphics had a bit of the bravado of boxing culture, whereas the images were more of a behind-the-scenes glimpse.

"Our approach is to get the idea first, then experiment and figure out a layout's voice to best represent the idea. I think our approach is more dependent on the idea than the ideology. We pretty much operate as design pluralists, rather than trying to impose a defined look that gets applied to everything we do. It keeps us clear-headed about the client's needs as well as leaves our solution options open. Even with a generalist's philosophy, a definable style often comes through."

In the end, Henderson and his team decided to concentrate on the photographic boxing theme because it was more in tune with the brand.

Henderson pursued several directions, inspired by Charles Atlas and comic-book characters such as Archie and the 98-pound weakling.

Given the unique structure of the brochure, Henderson is relieved that the project came through, despite having to clearly explain foil stamping, french-folding, and type treatments. "Helping the client understand some of the production processes we were proposing was a challenge throughout the project," notes Henderson. "Even after the piece was produced, one of the clients called, concerned about a 'mistake' that had occurred. Apparently, she assumed that the inside of the french-fold pages would be printed. She thought the printer had made a mistake and left them blank."

The response to Heavyweights has exceeded the expectations of both the designer and the client. The project won one of the most widely recognized awards in the field of apparel direct marketing. In fact, the piece had one of the best response rates in Hanes Printables' history. Whereas a normal mailer receives a response in the 17 to 19 percent range, this project got a whopping 32 to 35 percent response. Several screenprinters and wholesalers even wrote letters saying it was the best mailer they had ever seen.

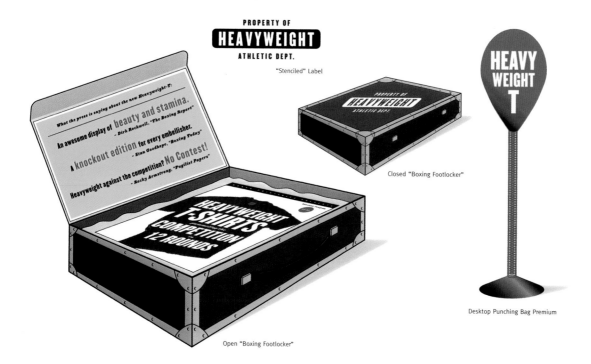

"Stenciled" Label

Closed "Boxing Footlocker"

Desktop Punching Bag Premium

Open "Boxing Footlocker"

⊘ Premiums in a direct-mail package, with t-shirt examples enclosed, were once considered, but the cost was prohibitive.

⊘ A Big Top theme also was considered, but the brochure had to have a more serious tone because many previous Hanes promotions had been humorous.

Brochure Cover

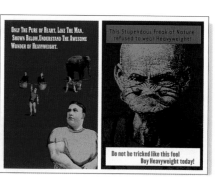

Brochure Spread

Brochure Spread

WITH **17** SHADES
TO CHOOSE FROM
THE HEAVYWEIGHT
Has A
COLORFUL HERITAGE

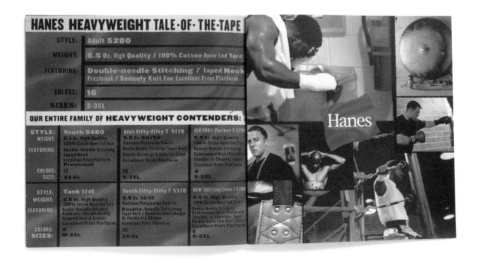

An early mockup of the brochure (above) lacked the balance of energy they achieved with bigger, blockier letterpress-style type and a behind-the-scenes montage of the boxing culture (center and below).

Herman Miller
Thanks to their **distinct design** sensibilities and the vision of **chief creative officer Steve Frykholm,** Herman Miller has a **long tradition** of doing uniquely crafted **annual reports.**

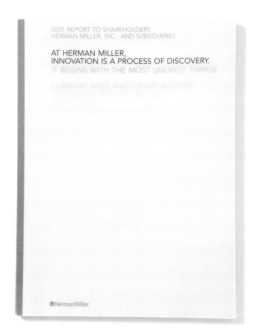

The 2001 Herman Miller Annual Report is about the process of discovering innovation. The report captures that elusive discovery process by revealing text line by line.

Yang Kim has been a lead designer on their last 10 annual reports—five as a Herman Miller employee and five as the creative director at BBK Studio in Grand Rapids, Michigan.

"The Herman Miller annual report is one of those things that is near and dear to my heart, and I try a lot of different ideas," says Kim. "Many don't work, and that's what it's really about. It's like a brainstorming exercise—no idea is a bad idea. Then you can start weeding out. We don't share a lot of it with the client. We just want to get ideas down that we can look at for the prototyping phase to determine what works. When we get a project, we sometimes ask everybody just to throw ideas on the floor. Then we have a big critique where we take out ideas that rise to the top and refine them until we get the best stuff.

"A lot of the thumbnails reflect the process of working quickly with collaborators in the room. We didn't use the computer or production table," Kim says. "A creative director from Herman Miller was involved in the project, so we were working together.

"The whole idea was to communicate innovation," Kim says. "We took this otherwise clichéd idea and found an interesting way to convey it. Instead of describing how the company was innovative this particular year, we made a list of where the ideas came from—what sparked the innovations. Of course, you don't know that it's an innovation at the outset. We then placed each 'spark' on its own translucent page. You could see only a few ideas at once, and each one faded as you turned the pages. The effect was very mysterious. Readers felt as though they too were discovering the idea. The annual report itself is, in a way, innovative.

"Each idea was equally important, so I wanted to put each idea on its own page," says Kim. "Most people often read only the first few lines of the list. We wanted readers to look at one idea at a time. Because each idea was important, the pacing was important as well.

"We did a lot of brainstorming for this book and went through a lot of prototyping, including: 1) a folded poster for which we chose six of the ideas to have a more visual interpretation; 2) a list of the sparks for ideas and a list of the actual innovations, which would be almost puzzlelike—the lists would be random for readers to make the connections, so again, it's about discovery; 3) a list that used the Jacob's ladder format to list the ideas, so readers would discover them in an interesting manner."

Doing the report on translucent paper was also something Kim entertained, but the financials didn't allow it. "I thought as long as we're doing the first half of the book in translucent paper, why

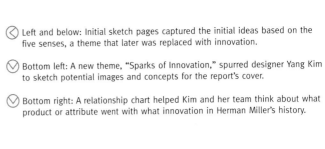
Left and below: Initial sketch pages captured the initial ideas based on the five senses, a theme that later was replaced with innovation.

Bottom left: A new theme, "Sparks of Innovation," spurred designer Yang Kim to sketch potential images and concepts for the report's cover.

Bottom right: A relationship chart helped Kim and her team think about what product or attribute went with what innovation in Herman Miller's history.

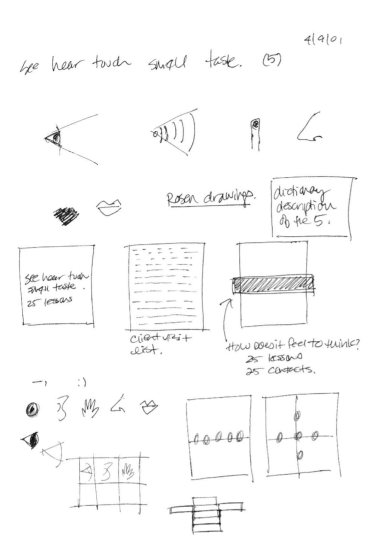

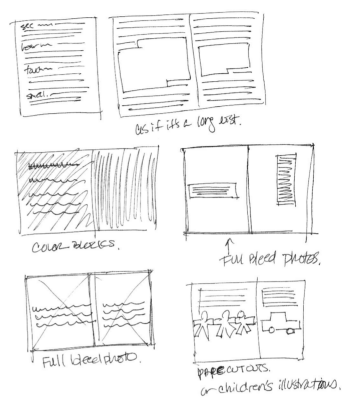

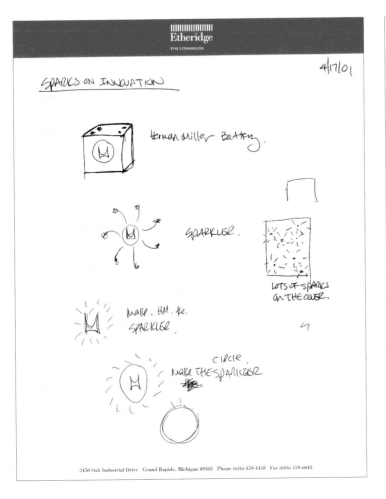

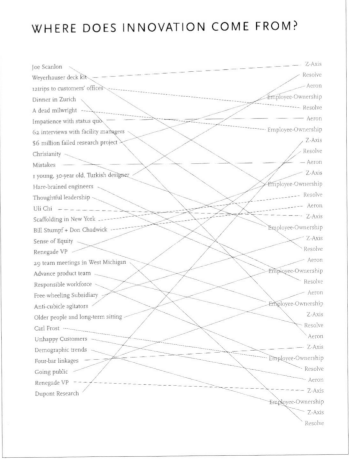

WHERE DOES INNOVATION COME FROM?

not try it in the back section? I thought it would be fun, but it didn't work. To me, annual reports are like visiting the company without physically visiting the company."

Despite her long history of working with Herman Miller, Kim says the biggest challenge on this particular report was simply convincing them to do it. "It's a radical design for an annual report," Kim says. "At first glance, it's a lot of blank pages with black text. Not very sexy. But this is exactly why it was *the* idea. The report is innovative, and it talks about how the company is innovative.

"Everything about the annual report process is interesting," says Kim. "Because there is a strict deadline enforced by the government, it's a bit of an adrenaline rush. The schedules don't get pushed out. The company could certainly file for an extension, but that would happen only if they needed more time for the financial content. The schedule would never be changed if the design implementation needed more time for tweaking. That's it, baby. It goes to press whether you like or not."

Kim says she was glad to have the book completed without having to put in weeks of 12-hour days, as had happened with previous reports. But just as she was about to close it up, out of nowhere came an idea to include collages between the editorial and financial sections. Although she wasn't happy with the addition, it turned out fine and added visual interest between the opening text and financial section.

⊘ Though it may not look like it could be an annual report, this cascading printout with a vellum envelope was just one of many comps Kim had the freedom to pursue for Herman Miller.

⊗ A belly-banded posterlike mockup was yet another comp Kim created on her way to finding the idea that would capture the concept of innovation inside Herman Miller.

PATIENCE
STRONG RELIGIOUS CONVICTION

On spaceship earth there are no passengers...
only crew. — Buckminster Fuller

FROM A SENSE OF RESPECT FOR ALL CREATION,

TO OUR OWN ENERGY GENERATION CENTER IN 1982,

TO SUSTAINED BUSINESS PRACTICES AND THE

AWARD-WINNING GREENHOUSE BUILDING IN 1995,

ENVIRONMENTAL STEWARDSHIP—IT'S THE RIGHT THING

TO DO—DIDN'T BEGIN WITH HERMAN MILLER, BUT WE

HAVE PUSHED IT TO BECOME SUSTAINABLE CAPITALISM.

⬡ Above left: After deciding on vellum for at least half of the book, Kim tried it for the financial section as well. Even with an orange background, the text was simply too hard to read.

⬡ Above right: A list of innovative ideas at Herman Miller continuously emerges and disappears through the final report's vellum pages.

⬡ The interior color collages were a last-minute idea sprung on BBK. Although not pleased with the request, Kim says it added a nice balance between the vellum pages and the financials.

The Hospital Sainte-Justine in Montreal is a specialized hospital for children and mothers. The 97-year-old hospital, affiliated with the University of Montreal, urgently needed to build new facilities to keep up with growing demand.

The Hospital Sainte-Justine, a children's hospital in Montreal, is nearly 100 years old and in desperate need of new facilities to keep up with growing demand. Nolin Branding & Design put together a publication that outlined the urgent need.

It so happened that Montreal-based Nolin Branding & Design had a staff member who had worked with the hospital while at another agency. Nolin was asked to design a document to personalize the hospital and explain in detail the urgent need to invest in new infrastructures. It was called the *Strategic Plan 2002–2007.*

"It could have been a kind of financial document," says art director Louise Filion, "but because it's a children's hospital, I was inspired to do something in a format that was easier to hold and read, almost like a storybook with inspiring pictures. It was the desire to do a smaller book that inspired me. Because we do a lot of annual reports, and because we rarely have the opportunity to do a smaller format, I really pushed for it and it worked. As soon as we presented it, the client agreed and we started working on the design details.

"I chose not to sketch anything. I started by reading a 100-page document about the hospital," says Filion. "There were six themes to talk about in the document, so I separated those sections with photo spreads. The biggest job was finding pictures that would work. We could not create those pictures because of a lack of money and time. After a lot of searching, I ultimately relied on a stock photo bank and found what I needed."

Nolin created three different layouts, but only the typography and photos changed for each concept. The smaller book format remained the same. Because the document was to be used for potential investors, the book was designed to reflect the audience of the hospital, keeping it scaled back and more intimate. "There was one layout with bigger type and no boxes, but the structure was always the same: a photo spread followed by a color spread and an introduction, which was then followed by spreads of texts. The choice of images is where there was some difference. There was no time for many directions or very different ideas. My experience helped me to work with some design principles such as rhythm and contrasts, and that's how I achieved this playful little book."

Undaunted by the size of the book, Filion was never concerned about managing its length. She says she purposefully chose a font and size that would keep the overall size of the book from being overwhelming. She was a little hesitant to use a smaller typeface but says there haven't been any complaints thus far.

"I never did a bigger format," Filion says. "It really was the first feel that I had and it is what they picked. With the kind of paper I've chosen, it's got a nice feel. I chose the paper on the cover because it's warm, it's soft, and it's a Canadian paper. I thought this kind of document should bring up emotion to make the people

○ Far left: Using children's books as inspiration, a smaller, more intimate size and format was chosen, in part to connect with readers and appeal to their emotions.

○ Left: Searching for the right combination of type treatments over the cover photo was a challenge. The designer adjusted the size and placement of the type on the wraparound image to achieve the final look.

○ Nolin later adapted the typography of the chapter openings seen here to a smaller size better suited to the publication's trim, and selected a slightly darker variation of the color blue from the hospital's identity.

aux nouveaux besoins

Le CHU mère-enfant Sainte-Justine répond aux problèmes de santé par un continuum de services allant de la prévention, aux soins, à la réadaptation, le tout appuyé par un vaste programme de recherche et de partage des connaissances. Le CHU mère-enfant affirme sa volonté d'utiliser tous les moyens à sa disposition pour que sa réponse aux problèmes de santé des mères et des enfants tienne pleinement compte de leurs besoins et des nouvelles possibilités de la médecine.

PLAN STRATÉGIQUE 2002-2007

THÈME 1   *soins et services*   014

UNE CAUSE QUI A L'APPUI DES QUÉBÉCOIS

En matière de santé, la cause des enfants vient bien avant toute autre catégorie de clientèles dans le cœur des Québécois. Le CHU mère-enfant jouit d'un fort capital de sympathie auprès du public. Cette affection du public se traduit en retombées de toutes sortes pour la cause des mères et des enfants et aussi pour l'établissement : promotion de la santé des mères et des enfants, audience publique, intérêt des décideurs, etc.

La cause des enfants reçoit également un bon accueil auprès des membres de la communauté d'affaires. Cette cause et la notoriété du CHU mère-enfant les incitent à choisir le CHU pour cible de leurs activités philanthropiques.

En milieu francophone, la Fondation de l'Hôpital Sainte-Justine vient au premier rang par l'ampleur de sa campagne annuelle de financement : on recueille de 10 à 12 M$ par année et on prévoit même une hausse des prochaines levées de fonds. Dans un contexte d'austérité financière, la Fondation encourage les initiatives de nature à permettre au CHU mère-enfant d'actualiser sa mission et d'assumer ses responsabilités auprès de la population.

L'IMPORTANCE DES SOINS
AUX ENFANTS

Si le secteur de la santé devait privilégier une clientèle, préférez-vous que les _____ soient privilégiés?

Enfants et adolescents	67%
Personnes âgées	14%
Femmes enceintes	13%
Adultes	3%
Autres et ne peut préciser	3%

Source: Sondage Impact Recherche sur la perception de la population québécoise à l'égard de l'Hôpital Sainte-Justine, 1999.

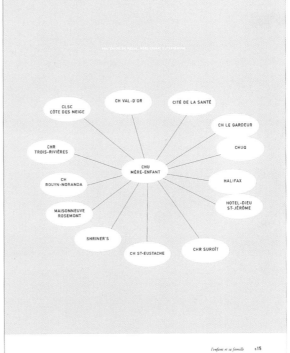

PLAN STRATÉGIQUE 2002-2007

l'enfant et sa famille   015

realize that our children are one of the most important things we have in life. Emotions really help to sell something. Even in an annual report we try to have as much emotion as we can."

Filion says her secret to successful design projects is educating herself about the client and their business. "I always start by reading all of the documents about the client I can put my hands on," says Filion. "In this particular case, I read the draft that the client had given us to work with to understand what the strategic plan was about. Then, because of the time frame, I just separated the chapters. Because there was a lot of text, I thought it would be appropriate to use photographs to add some breathing space and to help people go through the book without being overwhelmed. The smaller format also helps to make it more user friendly.

"You have to be curious," Filion says. "You have to look around and see everything, and I really look everywhere. Ideas are everywhere—in nature, architecture, fashion design, and furnishings.

That's the main thing—be curious and be passionate about what you are doing."

The Strategic Plan ended up becoming more than it was created for. Not only did the publication disappear in a matter of weeks, native singer/performer Celine Dion endorsed the hospital and appeared in advertising to raise additional funding. "There were no copies left only a few weeks after the launch," says Filion. "Many employees were so proud to show that document that they asked to have more than one copy to give to relatives and friends. Remember, this is essentially an administrative document. The colorful and human look of the book, as well as the size, contributed to that success.

In 2003, the Hospital Sainte-Justine Strategic Plan won a Graphika award (a contest in the Quebec province) in the brochure category for nonprofit organizations and also an award from *Applied Art* in 2003 in the brochure category.

Photography was probably the biggest challenge for the publication since there wasn't time or money for a photo shoot. Stock photos were used throughout the book with the hospital's administrators making most of the final decisions.

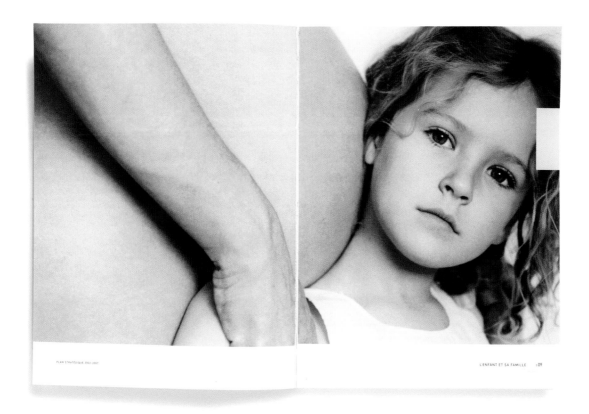

L'engagement du CHU mère-enfant Sainte-Justine en faveur de l'enfant, de la mère et de la famille s'impose de lui-même, tel un patrimoine singulier, original, lié à l'essence de l'établissement.

Because the Hospital Sainte-Justine is strictly for mothers and their children, Nolin Branding kept the strategic plan's format small and used plenty of photographs of children throughout.

InfoNet

InfoNet Delaware-based InfoNet provides managed network **communications service** for multinational corporations. Pasadena, California–based **Mimio Design** has worked with InfoNet for the past 14 years.

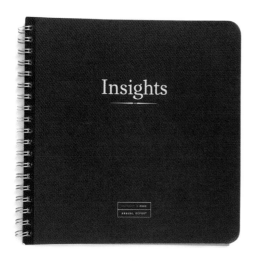

⊘ InfoNet's 2002 annual report chronicles the journey of a
⊘ fictitious salesman named Jacques by printing a mock
⊘ datebook with notes and records of client meetings.

When Morgan Molthrop, vice president of investor relations, wanted to chronicle the journey of a typical salesperson for InfoNet as a vehicle to explain InfoNet's capabilities in their 2002 annual report, Mimio was the natural selection.

"We had been developing a visual theme," says designer Margaret Yasuda. "That particular year, the idea was to clarify InfoNet's products and services. The idea started in the form of a PDA; we were trying to figure out a way to make the PDA the vehicle for telling the story and bringing in new information. As we went along that path we decided it was too cold and too detached. Two people on the team went to Paris and followed a French sales-person for a few days. It really came down to the people and their relationships and face time, so we decided to go back to just a journal. We started there and decided to use the vocabulary of a journal and create notes and so forth, with real collateral inter-spersed throughout."

Mimio was inspired by books, journals, salespeople's notes and interviews, datebooks, calendars, magazines, and InfoNet's em-ployees. The journal explains InfoNet's products and services while highlighting some of the differentiators in the context of a client win. The file folder holds actual case studies, and real employees and products are also featured.

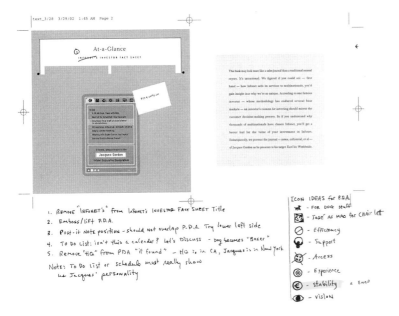

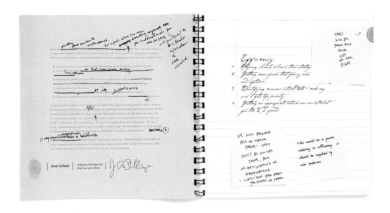

An early design of the inside cover spread shows a list of edits to the original idea of using a PDA instead of a datebook or journal.

Mimio had a difficult time keeping the PDA concept consistent throughout the report because it seemed too impersonal and because the client feared that it might give the impression that InfoNet sells PDAs.

The sketches show the evolution of the report's format and the refinement of content chapters and charts and graphs. "We started with using the PDA and videoconferencing, and we tried to determine what was the most current high-technology means of communication. In the end it became less about the vehicle— it came down to story—so we went back to using a notebook. We had discovered that the message wasn't coming across. We were so distracted with the contraption that we weren't telling the right story. And because InfoNet doesn't sell PDAs, it was getting confusing."

Yasuda says the biggest challenge was keeping the book focused on telling the story of the salesperson all the way through. The journal entries started out longer and more personal, but in the end became shorter to keep the story lighter.

"Content-wise, the length of the journal expanded and contracted in the depth of the story about that particular salesperson," says Yasuda. "It was really long at one time and told a substory about this guy and his life. It was just too much, so we whittled that down. Production-wise, we had several different kinds of bindings going on, different covers, and different paper, so we did explore lots of different textures."

Because the plan was to make the report look like a notebook, Mimio initially wanted to hard-bind it, but that was too expensive. Then they considered going to spiral binding, but because of the nature of the binderies, it was difficult with the overall weight of the publication and necessary width of the wire. Eventually, they found a match for the spiral bind and were all set, but it never came in. The bindery helped Mimio choose an alternative binding, and it turned out fine.

Yasuda says her secret to design success is almost always found in listening to the client. "I think it comes down to listening well and finding out what a client wants to achieve. Then you can come back with more than what they asked for and give them different ideas about how they can achieve their goal. It's really listening to what their goals are and bringing your creativity to the table.

"I think in terms of discovery. If you already know what you're going to do with the project, you are almost sort of forcing your own ego," Yasuda says. "For me, it's the collaboration that makes it different. I'm not of the mind that everybody should have a certain kind of look—it really depends on the process and everybody's input.

"This client was very collaborative," Yasuda says. "It wasn't a we-present-to-you kind of situation. It was definitely hand-in-hand all the way. It's definitely unusual, and in this particular case, because we have a long-term relationship, it was really great. We can build on the bonds and the understanding that we have from year to year. Every year has been getting better in terms of operations, and it's been more of a challenge to beat what we did the year before."

This approach seems to be working. Mimio Design won more than a dozen international awards for writing and design, including the Summit Gold Award and the Helios Award of Excellence.

Still trying to reconcile the right look for the journal entries, a half-page insert was tried for the first time on this mockup.

Below left: As the report progressed, adjustments were made to the typography, visuals, and inserts, such as the Case Studies section near the middle of this mockup. An addition left off of the second mockup, the orange tabs, made its first appearance here.

Below right: The final mockup shows a more professional-looking journal page and a research clip about the potential client. The case studies insert has a more personal feel because it's printed on mock letterhead.

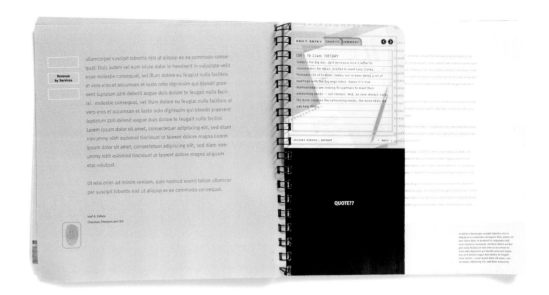

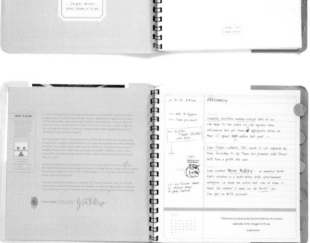

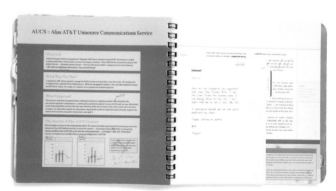

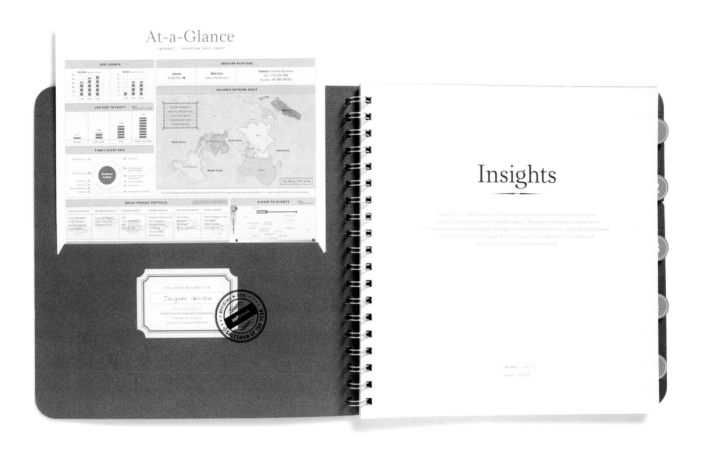

⬡ Top: The final piece is a delight to explore from the very first spread. The debossed "label" on the right and the pull-out sheet engage the reader's tactile sensibilities immediately.

⬡ Bottom: Each page is filled with information that the designers have made accessible and fun to explore.

Jaguar When Ogilvy & Mather Detroit invited BBK Studio to help them design the 2001 catalogs for Jaguar, BBK leaped at the chance. They wouldn't find out until much later, however, what they had gotten themselves into.

⬡ Attempting to update the image of the Jaguar, BBK Studio chose a lifestyle approach for the brochures of three Jaguar models, including the new S-Type.

By the end of the project, approximately 20 different art directors from Detroit, New York, and London were involved. It turns out that Ogilvy & Mather was trying to find a way to salvage the account they were about to lose.

Jaguar needed three catalogs for three different car models: the XK, the XJ, and the newest model, the S-Type. The overall goal of the catalogs was to update the Jaguar brand image. BBK was directed to tell a story through photography and copy and to use a lifestyle approach rather than lots of features and benefits. Basically, BBK was charged with selling the image and romance of owning a Jaguar.

BBK's inspiration for the catalog design was the fashion industry's more romantic approach. "The old convention with high-end brands was usually very glossy paper and very calm, static product photography," says art director Yang Kim. "Then high-end brands moved toward uncoated paper and a more active (lifestyle) approach.

"At the time, I don't think a lot of car companies were doing the lifestyle approach," says Kim. "Because the catalog had to feature three models, we tried to target an age range for each of them. The S-Type was the new model going up against BMW in the 30s age range. Using the lifestyle approach, we selected somebody in his 30s for the main character in the storyline, which is set in Miami and a bit more hip.

"We presented a couple of overall ideas, including 1) a historical approach using different art forms such as fine art, jazz, and architecture to elevate the cars to art objects; 2) a lifestyle/journey approach for which we proposed a journey that readers takes in their Jaguar, with sidebars about what they encounter along the way. There was a conversation between the passengers as they cruised to their destination. They were talking about the journey, not about the car.

"We selected fine art for one, jazz for another, and architecture for the third. We drew some parallels between romanticized aspects of those genres within a particular era that was a similar time period to the romantic era in Jaguar's history," says BBK principal and art director Kevin Budelmann. "From the start the idea was to try to draw parallels to the car buyers' personal lives, whether it be a lifestyle approach or a drawing of these parallels to other things in the culture.

"They wanted to introduce potentially younger buyers to the vehicle, and that was where phase two came in. We were trying to make it look a little bit lighter and more contemporary or more

If he could dance, he could drive my Jaguar. We decided to stop by some clubs. Lorem ipsum dolor sit amet, consectetuer adipiscing elit, sed diam nonummy nibh euismod tincidunt ut laoreet dolore magna aliquam erat volutpat.

◁ BBK searched for the right kind of reference photography for one of the initial comps that featured a jazz motif.

▽ An early comp for the XK model captured the metaphor of jazz and Jaguar's art of performance. Although well conceived, the concept was scrapped for something that could be consistent with all three models.

hip," Budelmann says. "The other one had more of a museumlike quality. Ultimately, I think where we landed in the end was somewhere between the two. I think the client wanted to make sure that the demographic was right. The second phase of comps was more whimsical, an aesthetic that may have been appropriate for further down market. Although the S-Type was moving down market, it was by no means a cheap car. On one hand, it's more upscale than those sketches represented. From there it got much cleaner, but by the same token they wanted it to be edgy on an artistic level and reflective of the edginess in terms of product design."

Kim noted that probably the most challenging part of the project was the sheer number of people involved. "We had worked with Ogilvy & Mather Detroit for a few weeks when the New York office got involved," says Kim. "We had already refined some of the

directions with Detroit, so it was a bit like starting over with new people involved. The art director and writer from the Detroit office were still involved, but the project clearly had become the New York office's project. We were asked to temporarily relocate our team to the New York office and work furiously until we were done. We ended up taking our team of five people for one-week stints for several weeks. It was a whirlwind, but it was a great experience."

Despite the efforts of many people, including BBK Studios, Ogilvy & Mather later lost the Jaguar account, but they held back nothing in trying to keep it. The good news is that sales of the new Jaguar S-Type were up, thanks in part to timing and marketing efforts. Kim thinks it's all because of her team's painstaking work on the brochures. And why not? They sure expended enough effort on the project.

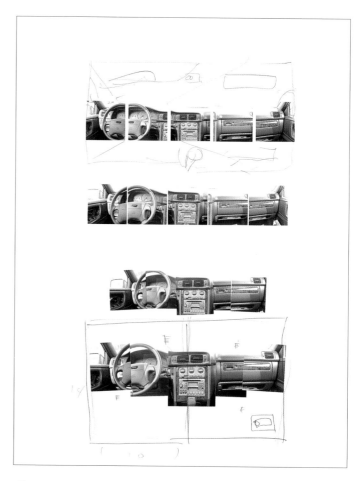

⬙ This comp for the S-Type was to carry through the history and nostalgia of the brand but connect that to a new model for younger buyers. Only a cover comp was made for this concept.

⬙ An early sketch of the interior of one of the models shows how the photos would become much larger with the final version.

⬙ A more whimsical approach to the S-Type model perhaps went a bit too far in this particular comp. BBK's Kevin Budelmann says this idea might have been more appropriate for a Volkswagen than a Jaguar.

S Type

Jaguar_S_Type

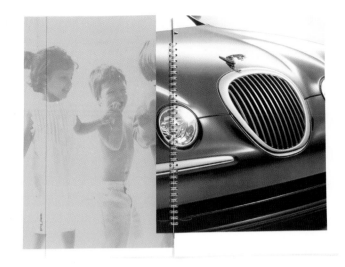

Another comp for the S-Type looked more like a traditional car brochure, with plenty of beauty shots of the car's interior.

BBK chose characters and locales for each storyline in the brochures to correspond to the target demographic for each car model.

Jiffy Lube

The **CarSmart Brochure Series** designed by Limb Design was an **important component** of a broader communications campaign to **educate women drivers** about the **importance of regular car maintenance** and the services offered by Jiffy Lube.

Jiffy Lube's CarSmart series of brochures were made in numerous versions to appeal to a wide range of women by age and ethnicity.

The ultimate goal of the campaign was to position Jiffy Lube as a trusted source of automotive preventive-maintenance information and to give women practical tools to make better decisions about the types of service their vehicles need and the intervals at which the services need to be performed.

"Automotive maintenance has the stigma of being a man's job, so the brochure series design needed to position Jiffy Lube in a way the target female audience could more comfortably relate to," says art director Kristin Moses. "The format also needed to be flexible so it could be executed on various media, including trifold brochures, letterhead, logos, and a website. The design and color scheme needed to feel modern, contemporary, and inviting. To avoid overwhelming readers, the design also could not look cluttered or type heavy.

"Early on, the design concept was based on the target audience for the piece, as well as the messages that needed to be conveyed," says Moses. "The layout needed to be easily translated to different media, so that was a factor in the design as well. The two mockups enabled me to figure out the size and the fold. That is usually my starting point for a project. I decide on the format and ways I can make each project a little different, whether by using special inks, die cuts, unique varnishes, folds, or paper. Then I make a mockup to keep by my computer while I am designing so I can visualize how it is all going to look when folded and what is really going to end up next to what."

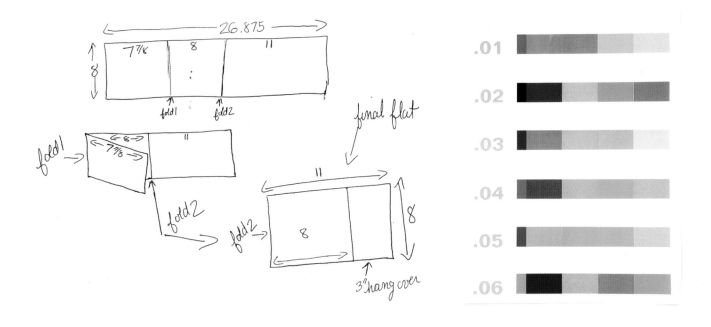

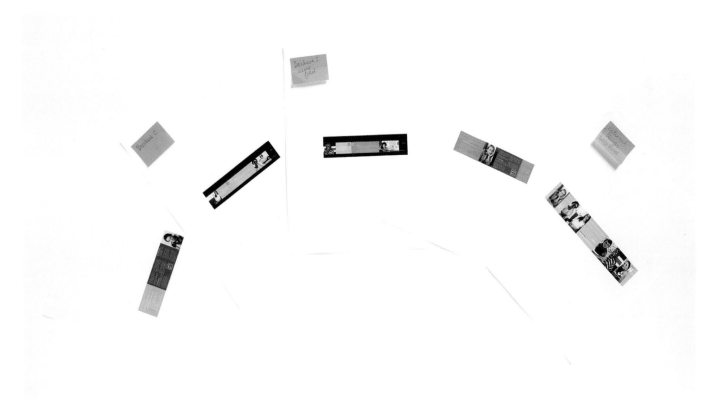

Top left: The dimensions of the brochure were chosen early on because the structure had to be user-friendly in the store setting.

Top right: A different color palette was used for each of the six different brochures, but consistency was still maintained among the series.

Above: Previous versions of the brochure reveal a more vibrant use of photography and a heavier amount of copy on the inside spreads, not to mention a belly band that was eliminated when the design changed.

Although the broader audience was women in general, the brochures had to appeal to specific age groups. Each brochure in the series is broadly targeted to a particular age group or lifestyle. For example, some brochures are specifically for new drivers, college students, young professionals, mothers, and mature women.

"Today's modern woman—who works, cares for her kids, and is responsible for vehicle maintenance—was the inspiration for the design," says Moses. "I thought about all the literature I see every day that is so unappealing and what I would want to see. I thought about how I could make the female clientele of Jiffy Lube feel that this company believes they are smart, capable, strong, and technologically savvy. Jiffy Lube was not afraid to get behind its female customers. So I wanted to use strong female color—not your typical pastel color palette—and strong imagery. From realistic photography to the vivid colors to the no-nonsense layout, the design is a reflection of how an independent woman wants to be perceived.

"The design was an evolution of past Jiffy Lube designs and projects. It needed to have a consistent look and feel to fit into the company's overall brand image. I knew someday I would have to recreate the brochures into a format that would be a lot cheaper and could be mass-produced to go in every store. As much as I dislike the idea of your everyday standard-sized brochure, I was concerned about the original design being apparent in the smaller piece."

Moses says she allows herself to bring a level or creativity and originality to every project, but it's almost always a challenge to get the client to follow along. "I first think, how can I make this project unique or different, or in other words, how much can I get away with?" Moses says. "How can I stretch the client to do something a little out of the ordinary, that in the end they will ultimately love, which has a greater impact than their usual trifold? I know this may be a design sin, but I don't do sketches. I usually know the feel I am going for, so I try to get the design to match what I have in my head as closely as possible. And yes, there is a lot of trial and error, but I just try to get what I am seeing in my mind on screen."

Because women compose approximately 65 percent of Jiffy Lube's patrons, the CarSmart series was a big hit. In fact, the larger format was later scaled down to a smaller size, as Limb Design suspected would happen.

The two mockups were used to determine the size and fold of the final brochure. Art director Kristin Moses likes to use mockups to select ways to make the project unique, whether by using special inks, die cuts, varnishes, folds, or even paper choice.

//ROAD RULES FOR TEENAGE GIRLS

jiffy lube®

.02

◔ This mockup is closest to the actual finished brochure. Some subtle changes in image and copy placement were added before the final.

◔ Below top: The inside of each brochure achieves an aesthetic balance of copy and photography that combines for increasing readability and decreasing intimidation.

◔ Below bottom: As Limb Design suspected, Jiffy Lube was so pleased with the initial brochure that they asked for a smaller version for direct-mail purposes.

The London Institute, an art gallery for several universities, asked Brian Webb, principal and art director of London-based Webb & Webb Design, to **curate and design** the first stand-alone sculpture exhibition for Sir Peter Blake RA,

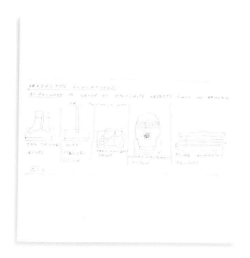

Brian Webb of Webb & Webb Design was asked to curate and create the catalog for a Peter Blake Sculpture exhibit at the London Institute. The catalog sold out in the shop during the exhibit.

The invitation to the exhibition reflects the bold simplicity of the catalog cover, including the inverted blue and red exclamation points.

a renowned painter and artist who is perhaps most famous for designing the Beatles' *Sgt. Pepper's Lonely Hearts Club Band* album cover. Webb has worked with the London Institute for eight years, creating their annual reviews as well as designing and curating several exhibitions.

Webb says the titles of many of Peter Blake's sculptures conjure up images of music hall posters printed in bright colors using mostly letterpress typography. His early ideas used some of the titles of Blake's works, such as *Crazy Said Snow White* (a quote from a Stan Freberg song) and *Three Man Up* (a circus acrobat act) to give the design a posterlike feeling. One specific work entitled *Family* led Webb to the idea of using woodcut exclamation points printed upside down to produce the equivalent of a growing family.

Early on, Webb wanted to create a poster that would serve as the wrap for the catalog. However, due to time and budget constraints, that idea had to be shelved for something much simpler and faster. "The idea was to produce this large printed poster and then wrap the catalog in it," Webb says. "We just didn't have enough type to make a whole one-piece printed poster, so it would have meant having to print little bits, scan them, and reproduce it all as a lithograph, but time was running out. As the whole show developed, it seemed a bit too restrictive, so the idea of these exclamation points, which have one meaning with the dots at the bottom, turning them upside down and turning them into figurative images, seemed a bit more appropriate to the show. Certainly it made a striking set of images. I think you have to go through that first stage to get to the second stage. It wasn't one of those things that you just think, 'Wow, let's do it that way.' Things don't happen like that."

The exhibition was conceived as part art gallery and part artist's studio, so that work could be presented as a formal gallery show but would also include Blake's collections of other artists' work and pieces that inspired him as a sculptor. The catalog was designed to reflect these two aspects of the exhibition.

"The titles of his sculptures are quite interesting. They're almost like musical acts. Wouldn't it be interesting to use the graphics of early posters to produce the catalog?" Webb says. "That's how it started. We started considering letterpress printing, and the more we got into it, as often happens, the simpler it became. We went to a letterpress printer near the office. You can wander around the composing room and pull out type cases and lay out bits of wooden type. Coincidentally, I looked at a type case and there was an upside-down exclamation point. We pulled out every exclamation point in the composing room and developed the covers of the catalog from them.

An early sketch sequence shows Webb arriving at the exclamation points as the basis for the cover and interior sections.

"The jacket is an eight-page wrap-around jacket, so you can actually remove it. It is a long freeze frame of this growing family, which seemed quite important, and then underneath the jacket are line drawings and reproductions of line drawings of some of Peter's proposed sculptures. They're quite interesting because some of them actually got made," says Webb. "Under the jacket is where it all begins as a piece of sculpture, and that's the way it started in his mind. The outside cover is the actual colors of the catalog. We've used Peter's drawings, but they're concealed by the jacket that goes over it. Then you open it into the catalog itself."

The catalog jacket is designed to stand on its own as a reflection of the sculptural quality of the subject matter, almost becoming a work of art in its own right. The cover is made of a thick paper stock so the texture has an impact. Webb didn't want the catalog to feel like a conventional art catalog. He says his happy accident at the letterpress printer came by moving forward and considering many different directions.

"I know for sure, if I sit and stare into space, an amazing idea will never happen," Webb says. "It grows out of talking and collecting stuff. It's very well described in the sculpture catalog. I think the idea on the outside or the cover of it grows from the inside to the outside, rather than outside to inside. While you are accumulating the materials for the inside, you're beginning to refine your thoughts about what it is that makes a cover and might sum up the whole publication. I very rarely start on the outside. It rarely starts with a flash of lightning—that's a great idea. The ideas grow out of learning about the subject. This is obviously an arts catalog or publication, and we do do a lot of those, but I guess commercial jobs are done in much the same way."

Webb says measuring the success of the catalog was somewhat difficult because the exhibition was so recent. However, in just a few weeks, all of the copies printed for the London Institute were sold out. Webb said the best way to gauge the catalog's success was through public relations because the London Institute relies heavily on their exhibits and catalog materials to generate public interest. In this case, if the amount of press coverage was added up and the Institute had to pay for the equivalent in advertising, the job paid for itself 10 times over.

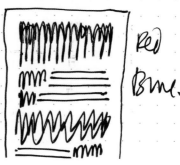

Early ideas for the catalog included inspiration from the titles of Blake's sculptures, which would serve as inspiration for a poster to wrap the catalog.

One of Blake's sculptures, *Three Man Up*, is a circus act performed on horses that Webb tried to incorporate into a cover concept using Blake's name and the exhibition title.

Opposite **Such stuff as dreams.** A sequence of dream sculptures. To each a sleeping figure and to each their dreams. All carefully choreographed by Peter Blake. In the background, horses wait to play their equestrian part in the 'Three Man Up' series, while behind them a bunch of wooden grapes, an echo of early days – await their still life moment. Above **Two tableaux** – one alludes to Dutch still life and the other to Cubism.

◇ The catalog jacket was designed to stand on its own as a reflection of the sculptural quality of the subject matter.

Above left 'Man Meeting Tiger on a Japanese Bridge' (1960). Above right 'Man Selling Musical Instruments to Members of Minority Groups' (1982). Opposite **Back in the Sculpture Studio** it's the usual unusual thing.. Alice and the Mad Hatter gawp behind the glass while Snow White, the Junior League of America and comic book characters take their places in the 'Parade for Saul Steinberg'.

◇ Webb says his biggest challenge was collecting and collating the vast amount of Blake's work produced over a 40-year period—all in a relatively short span of time.

MINI Cooper When the MINI debuted in the United States in March 2002, the buzz was almost deafening. Thanks to their agency Crispin Porter + Bogusky of Miami, the MINI made a big splash with a little car and a clever marketing campaign.

Proof that the MINI has a personality all its own, CP+B creative director Scott Linnen spent nearly an entire weekend in the car for inspiration. He emerged with the *Manual of Motoring*.

Resurrecting an old brand for the manufacturer BMW, CP+B capitalized on the MINI's unique brand personality.

In addition to billboards and promotional installations inserted into magazines such as *Rolling Stone* and *Fast Company* were miniature *Manuals of Motoring*. Part advertising, part editorial, the *Manual of Motoring* captured the essence of the brand and spoke to the audience almost immediately. Fashioned after the actual owner's manual, the *Manual of Motoring* was conceived by Scott Linnen, vice president and associate creative director of CP+B. The manual is a parody of a technical manual, but it's not about the car; it's about being a MINI owner.

Linnen says because the MINI audience is so unique, it required a different and imaginative approach to marketing. According to Linnen, MINI buyers are nonconformists who defy classification by age, gender, or socioeconomic status. Linnen jokes that if he were to divulge any more details about MINI's audience, his life would be in danger.

"MINI needed to launch a fast and nimble fuel-efficient automobile measuring just 143" (363 cm) from bumper to bumper in the U.S. market—a market dominated by sluggish, gas-guzzling, behemoth SUVs," says Linnen. "We needed to educate people about the differences between traditional driving and motoring in a MINI. Information that, under normal motoring conditions, would take most MINI owners months to learn for themselves was now right at their fingertips.

"Some of the design was dictated by MINI's corporate image guidelines," Linnen says. "Mostly it was dictated by a burning desire to create an auto manual that people would actually enjoy reading. The biggest inspiration came from seeing just how uninspired other automakers' owner's manuals really are. We wanted to create something that might actually get dog-eared from use.

"MINI already had an owner's manual that illustrated the features of their new MINI Cooper and MINI Cooper S models," says Linnen. "What they needed was an addendum to that— beyond the nuts and bolts—a way to tell people what this new culture of motoring was all about. What's the glue that bonds MINI owners together? A second manual seemed to be the natural way to go.

"Because it was intended as a companion to the owner's manual, we felt that it should have strong visual ties to it," says art director

CP+B took photographs of the MINI and various subjects for their illustrator to render as line art and drawings for the manual.

⚠ The Manual of Motoring is intended to provide information about the differences between "driving" and "motoring." Information that, under normal motoring conditions, would take MINI owners months to discover for themselves.

CONTENTS

The table of contents proved to be a challenge because the original manual is much larger and its table of contents more generic. With its shorter length, the *Manual of Motoring* table of contents carries through the overarching tagline of *Let's Motor*.

Mike del Marmol. "The tabbing system along the edge, for instance, is taken directly from the owner's manual. The grid system is also similar, and, of course, they both adhere to the MINI brand identity in terms of the typeface, headlines, and use of frames. So, using all of those elements as a starting point, we set out to design a really nice book by taking advantage of the areas where we had freedom to improve on the actual owner's manual, most notably the quality of the paper and printing, use of spot colors (including the metallic silver), and illustration."

The manual's layouts are crisp and simple, using only black and white and a sophisticated silver metallic in the illustrations, which are enriched with road-sign yellow. It's this kind of detail that maintains the tech-manual parody. Pages and figures are numbered for navigation, and a reference guide, running vertically in the side margins, lists the contents and highlights the section. Special warnings and tips are indicated by yellow triangles that mimic cautionary road signs. Many of the illustrations have callouts. Even the font is modeled on Gill Sans, the British standard for all things technical.

"As far as the illustration style, we wanted a look that felt like your standard instructional style, but with an edge to it," says del Marmol. "We found a guy who had a nice technical style combined with a great personal style and a really good sense of color. We shot the majority of the reference photography and sent it to him."

If you look at the Red Light Fire Drill, you'll see Linnen and del Marmol as miniature two-dimensional action figures. The Red Light Fire Drill seemed the perfect occasion to place the creators into the manual itself, à la Alfred Hitchcock.

"I think it's important to always have a good sense of what's out there, what's been done in the past, and what the possibilities are for any given assignment," del Marmol says. "Pay attention to

SOUTHERN COURSE ASPHALT (BATON ROUGE ROUGH)

A savory blacktop surface yielding solid purchase for the tires of your MINI. The gravely bituminous mixture produces a delightful hum above 60 mph. Motorers encountering freshly-laid Southern Course should depress their window toggle switches to savor its distinctive full-bodied tar bouquet and sulphurous nose.

! NOTE: Always obey local speed limits. Especially when motoring through rural Louisiana.

Fig. 22 Footnote about the image above goes here.

⊘ ⊘ ⊘ One of the few featured items not in the original unauthorized owner's manual, the gravel section went through three iterations before arriving at the final version. Linnen says this section may make its way into the next unauthorized owner's manual.

⊖ The back page spread did not change much from the first mockup to the final because the MINI was always intended to be the centerpiece.

ROAD TYPES

Headline goes here:
This section will be about the different types of roads across america and some other cool type.
Make a hot date. With your spouse. Act like complete yadda yadda.
Remove child seats (if applicable) and 9-to-5 baggage.
Motor around block and pick her up at "her place". (Or pick him up at "his place" – owner gender and romantic orientation

Last Headline Goes Here:
Substituting birdseed for ceremonial rice on wedding day may invite unwanted aerial bombardment of your MINI's lustrous factory finish. But it's the right thing to do.

Fig. 17 North American Asphalt   Fig. 18 Dirt & Gravel Roads

Fig. 19 Concrete Roads   Fig. 20 Cobblestones & Misc.

Fig. 21 Some cool thought or tip here about asphalt or driving conditions etc. Not quite sure what it is going to say yet, but it would act more of a footnote than a caption about the pictures above.

LET'S MASTER THE ASPHALT

As a motorer in-tune with the subtleties of a MINI's personality, you will find yourself becoming a connoisseur of varying road surfaces. Like a fine wine waiting to be uncorked, the highways and byways of America have their own distinctive flavors waiting to be explored. Bon appetit.

Urban Glassphalt—Asphalt with a hint of recycled glass creates a shimmering surface. Look for it on the streets of Manhattan and on L.A.'s Hollywood Blvd. See how Tinseltown and the City that Never Sleeps shine at night.

Rural Blacktop — Uncrowded stretches of farm-to-market roads that fill the vacant areas between the interstates. Watch for sticky, gummy patches in the summer heat, and super slippery black ice during winter freezes.

Macadam — Today, we call it a gravel road, but the original recipe was concocted in 1816 by Scotsman John Macadam. Look for telltale rooster-tails of dust heralding your arrival during summer droughts.

Concrete — The original hard-surface road, and also the surface of choice of our most romanced byways. Route ⚠ 66. A1A. Spiral parking ramps.

CAUTION: Beware of hypnotic, sleepy feeling associated with rhythmic clickety-clacking when motoring over concrete expansion joints.

Fig. 13 Urban Glassphalt   Fig. 14 Rural Blacktop

Fig. 15 Macadam   Fig. 16 Concrete

⚠ NOTE: The Interstate Highway System, President Eisenhower's big brainstorm of the 50's, knits our far-flung nation together. The even-numbered roads take you east-to-west, and odd-numbered ones head north and south.

9

LET'S DO OUR HOMEWORK. LET'S ANALYZE. LET'S MEMORIZE LET'S MASTER. LET'S NEVER STOP LEARNING. LET'S MOTOR.™

ADDITIONAL READING:

On the Road...Jack Kerouac
Roadfood: 500 Diners, Farmland Buffets, Lobster Shacks, Pie Palaces and Other All-American Eateries...Jane & Michael Stern
There's No Toilet Paper on the Road Less Traveled The Best of Travel Humor...Lansky
Fodor's Flashmaps of NY, Washington D.C., Chicago & San Francisco
Fodor's How to Pack...Laurel Cardone

BOOKS ON TAPE:
Road Rage Relaxation...Dean Montalbano
⚠ NOTE: MEDITATION TAPE ONLY. NOT FOR USE WHILE MOTORING.

WEBSITE:
MINIUSA.COM. For additional reading, building your own MINI or locating the dealer near you.

16

LET'S BE THE BIGGER CAR

Jump Starts
Opting NOT to exchange electrical charges with total strangers is up to the individual motorist's discretion. HOWEVER, random acts of kindness do continue the flow of positive energy. Which adds up to good motoring mojo for you.

Fig. 23 Current flies to and fro in background: stranger to stranger.

14

LET'S STAY OUT OF TROUBLE

Rotating Your Shorts in Public
Whether wiggling out of soggy swim trunks at the beach or slipping into moisture-wicking bike shorts for a ride in the country, follow these instructions for taking it all off and putting it all back on. And save yourself the lewd & lascivious downtime.

⚠ CAUTION: Car doors should not be used as privacy screens by those over 6' tall. Because of MINI's lower center of gravity, doors may be inadequate for keeping your private bits out of other people's snooping noses. So to speak.

1. Wrap a beach towel around your waist.

2. Sit down inside vehicle, and, reaching under towel, use a shimmying motion to remove what you're wearing, taking care not to loosen towel.

3. Repeat in reverse order, applying clothes until dressed.

Fig. 24 Use discretion. And stop the calisthenic antics and get ideas for your little

15

LET'S COMMUNICATE

Index Finger Salute
Subtle. Sublime. "Sup!"

Peace Sign
Though flower-powered MINIs never lined the interstates leading to Woodstock, N.Y., MINIs did enjoy quite a bohemian past shuttling shaggy-haired hipsters from Liverpool to Amsterdam in the '60s. Then as now, love is all you need. That and petrol.

Thumbs Up
Especially appropriate when paying homage to Classic Mini owners.

Motorer's Oath of Honor
REPEAT: "On my honor, I do solemnly pledge to be trustworthy, helpful, friendly, courteous, kind, obedient, cheerful and brave."

The Wave
MINI-owning members of Britain's Royal Family wave the back of the hand when greeting royal subjects. You, living in a democracy, may choose something less upper-crusty when greeting well-wishers along your parade route.

Tap-on-the-Roof
"Top of the Day"—The motoring equivalent of politely tipping your hat.

Winking the Lights
The motoring equivalent of batting your eyes.

Sup! | Peace | Thumbs Up | Motorer's Honor
Royal Wave 1 | Royal Wave 2 | Commoner Wave 1 | Commoner Wave 2
Roof Tap 1 | Roof Tap 2 | High Beams 1 | High Beams 2

Fig. 9 Shown above: Motoring greetings dating back to MINI's birth in the U.K.

6

LET'S ATTRACT ATTENTION

Unconventional Use of Headlamps
A MINI's halogen lights are integrated into the bonnet (hood). Subsequently, raising the bonnet raises the headlamps. A handy feature for attracting Luna moths, playing Romeo & Juliet, illuminating nighttime tailgate parties and locating sexy neighbor's tired kitty. (See Fig. 11)

⚠ IN THE EVENT OF BEING HOPELESSLY STRANDED in the middle of nowhere, or just hopelessly bored at home, rake the night sky with the headlights using a Hollywood premiere sweeping motion and let the party (search or otherwise) find you.

Fig. 10 The aphrodisiac effects of alternative and fine cuisine

Fig. 11 Fun with halogen.

7

⊘ The final Manual captures the hip vibe of the new MINI and the off-beat personalities of its owners.

trends, but don't do something just because everyone else is doing it. Start very broad and then narrow down. Even if you have a brilliant idea at the onset of a project, explore a few other options, just to see where they take you."

CP+B didn't have to explore many options, thanks to their MINI owner's manual. But they did have to decide what from the original owner's manual would go into the scaled-down version. "Our biggest challenge was editing the original 32-page unauthorized owner's manual (included in every MINI glove box) down to its abridged 16-page *Manual of Motoring* format," Linnen says. "If you want to read the other 16 pages, all you have to do is buy a MINI."

Many did just that. This somewhat risky automotive campaign raised the level of MINI's brand awareness from zero percent to more than 25 percent in just nine months. In addition, MINI sold 25 percent more cars than was anticipated. Perhaps the campaign wasn't so risky after all.

Mrs. Meyer's Minneapolis-based Werner Design Werks, Inc. has been working with Mrs. Meyer's, a line of **aromatherapeutic household cleaners,** since the inception of the brand in 2000. Werner **designed all of the labeling,** developed the brand identity, and even **helped name the product line.**

⊘ "The small catalog was done the first year when the brand was new, so we felt that it needed to be a little more romanced and in-depth," Werner says. Hence, the smaller format and helpful hints from Mrs. Meyer herself.

⊗ By the second catalog, the brand was more established, and it was essential to create a tool for the faster-paced setting of a grocery store rather than a boutique shop. Werner makes the product line easy to see in a broadsheet format.

Therefore, when it came time to create a catalog for the products, Werner was the logical choice.

"Mrs. Meyer's is all about being a no-fuss, no-frills, hardworking line of cleaning products that also happens to smell great," says art director Sharon Werner. "Mrs. Meyer's is the authority on a clean and happy home. Basically, the catalog needed to reflect these qualities and be an easy ordering tool for wholesale buyers. Mrs. Meyer is the sort of gal who would contribute recipes to the church cookbook (all typed on a typewriter, of course), so it seemed appropriate that she would do her catalog in the same format, complete with cleaning tips. ("Wear sensible shoes.")

Using line art and other design elements from the product packaging, Werner created a catalog that stands out but reinforces Mrs. Meyer's as the authority for a clean and happy home. Werner was inspired by reviewing old recipe pamphlets and old-fashioned ads that were simple and to the point. "Our first step, along with the concept, is to think about the form, size, number of pages, and overall feel in your hand," Werner says. "By the time we got to the design of the catalog we had the brand concept identified. Then it was just a matter of taking that from the package to the catalog. Because the brand is new, we felt it was critical to stay close to the visual direction of the packaging-brand reinforcement."

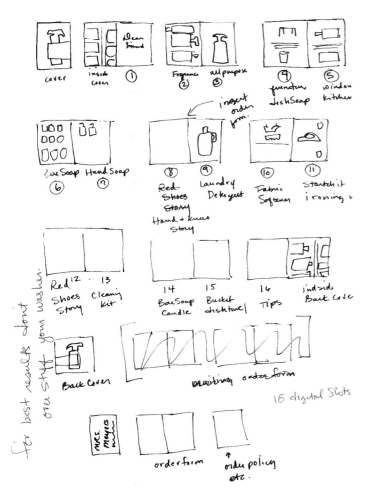

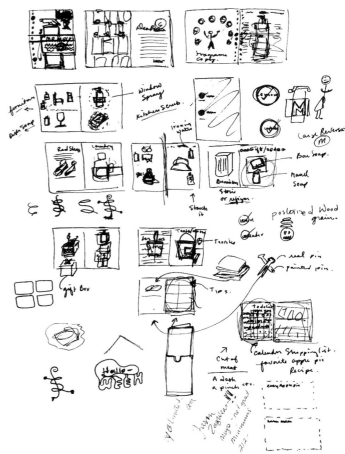

⊗ Before beginning the actual layout, Werner sketched a rough thumbnail version of the catalog's structure so the layout process would be more efficient.

⊗ To achieve the homespun look of the catalog, Werner hand-drew the line drawings of stick people and painted the black-and-white illustrations of various cleaning and household items.

⊘ Sketches of the larger-format catalog show the development of the piece into a broadsheet folder for easy filing and product selection for retail store buyers.

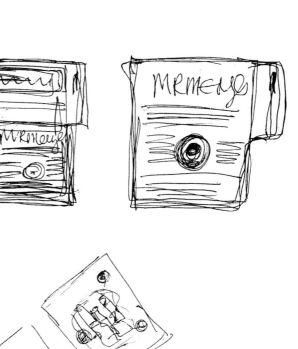

After the initial catalog was sent out, a follow-up version was created primarily for retail buyers. "The small catalog was published the first year when the brand was new, so we felt that it needed to be more romantic and in-depth. By the second catalog, the retailer was more defined. We knew that the audience was a fast-paced grocery buyer rather than a boutique buyer, so we made everything easier to see in a broadsheet format.

"The second catalog needed to be even simpler," says Werner. "For ideas, we looked to office supplies. What better than a basic, sensible file folder? The graphics for both catalogs are bold and straightforward, in keeping with the labels. The use of slightly awkward black-and-white painted illustrations rather than formal photography adds to the naive charm. The big 'headline' and copy-heavy presentation are an extension of the visual language first developed for the labels. Overall, the products, labels, and catalogs give the impression that although cleaning may not be fun, it need not be unpleasant.

"Because it's a catalog and we didn't want to create any barriers to buying the product, we knew it was essential that the copy be easy to read and the catalog easy to navigate—sort of no-nonsense design, like Mrs. Meyer herself, hardworking, straightforward, not fussy. The layouts are really determined by the attitude of what we're communicating."

There's something to be said for working with a brand from its inception. Because Werner was involved in branding Mrs. Meyer's early on, subsequent design projects come together a lot quicker and easier. For example, Werner pitched only one catalog concept to Mrs. Meyer's. "Because we have a great relationship with the client and understand the brand so well," says Werner, "we are usually able to work out a good idea of what they're looking for before we ever put sketches on paper.

⊘ Werner found inspiration for the catalog's look and feel in vintage cookbooks and illustrations from a time period when happy housewives cleaned with a perpetual smile.

⊘ Early packaging explored the use of silhouettes of the happy housekeeper and oversized household items.

"We originally presented two directions for the packaging: the one that was chosen and another that was based on the play between silhouettes of the happy housekeeper and oversized household items," Werner says. "We searched through many old magazines and cookbooks for an illustration style that seemed appropriate—something basic, something that felt like it had been around for a long time but wasn't particularly retro. We decided perky little stick people were perfect. They don't look fussy or overdone and are adaptable for many different applications. They are easy to render doing any number of household tasks without such pesky details as proportion and anatomy, thus making it believable that Mrs. Meyer could have done these herself."

Werner Design created all of the illustrations themselves to achieve the homespun look of the catalog. According to designer Sarah Nelson, the retro information approach was appropriate for the cleaning supplies because it reflects the straightforward and unpretentious attitude of the brand.

"We did the paintings (illustration) ourselves," says Nelson. "It gives the brand a broader visual vocabulary. It was inspired by the side of a plumbing supply building here in Minneapolis that has these paintings of sinks and radiators. We liked the contrast of the stick people line drawings with the black-and-white paintings—it adds a nice human, tactile quality, too."

Though she isn't as popular as Betty Crocker (at least not yet), Mrs. Meyer's is making its way into more and more retail stores across the country. The products are now found in larger natural food store chains such as Whole Foods Market. The brand is also available at Ace Hardware and The Container Store.

In addition to winning the Outstanding Achievement Award in *HOW Magazine's* International Design Annual, Mrs. Meyer's catalogs have won several other regional and national recognitions including, *Print's* Regional Design Annual, *Communication Arts,* Minnesota's AIGA show, and the New York Type Directors' Club.

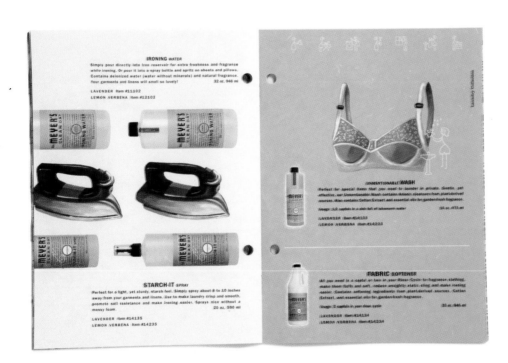

The larger-format sales folder was made for buyers in retail stores to easily reorder new supplies. The folder features nearly every available cleaning solution on a two-page spread printed on heavy stock paper.

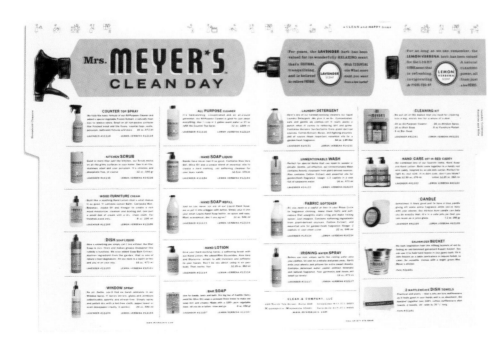

Neoforma
Can a design agency **follow instructions** and still be creative? You can if you're **Cahan & Associates,** the San Francisco–based **design firm** that is well known for their **annual report design.** And that's exactly the challenge Cahan & Associates faced when creating the annual report for Neoforma,

⊗ Cahan & Associates had to work within the guidelines of Neoforma's new corporate identity when designing their 2002 annual report. They chose to embrace the guidelines and show the client what they could do with the new identity.

⊗ Braley was reluctant to change the interior format of his early version that capitalized on the location-specific type on the left side of many spreads.

a healthcare solutions provider based in New Jersey. Neoforma had just established a new corporate identity, typeface, and color palette and expected Cahan to incorporate that into their annual report.

"Though we believe that an annual report should function as a stand-alone piece, with Neoforma, we were asked to work within their new identity guidelines," says art director Michael Braley. "Instead of feeling constrained, we used these standards as a springboard to create something original. At Cahan & Associates, we rely not on a house style but on an ability to see each project as an opportunity to do something unique. We incorporated classic, clean typography that reflected what the company does—simplifying the healthcare documentation process.

"Because we wanted to stay within their identity, that was one surefire way to let them know that we were paying attention to their guidelines. The colors are pretty easy to work with, and they look good as solids against each other and reversing out of each other. It worked well with the layout that I had established because it's a classic design. There wasn't a lot of copy in the client's stories, so there was a nice contrast between the small type and the large type on the left."

Braley confesses he had always wanted to pull off the cover idea, but he never found a buyer for it. It just so happened that Neoforma fit nicely into the space on the cover. "Those letters from a purely aesthetic point are all about the same width and with that typeface it worked really well, so I finally got to do it. That's basically where the rest of it stems from. When I had the cover I could implement that in client stories and figure out the other gold graphics from there."

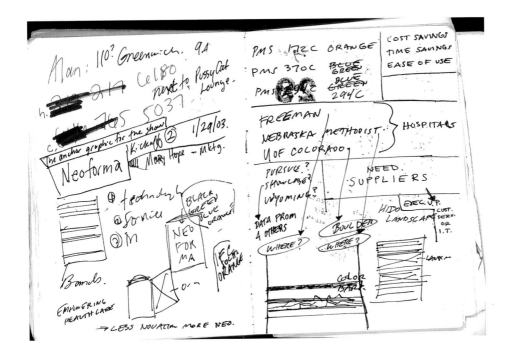

Early meetings with the client yielded important aspects of the client's history, business, and locations. Braley saw the perfect opportunity to use a cover idea that he had had in his files for a long time.

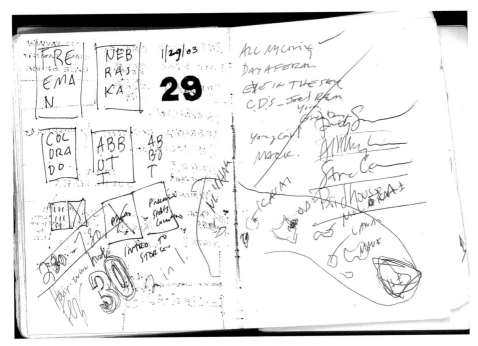

Braley says his inspiration for the overall layout of the report was influenced by the design era of the '60s and '70s, specifically the work of Paul Rand.

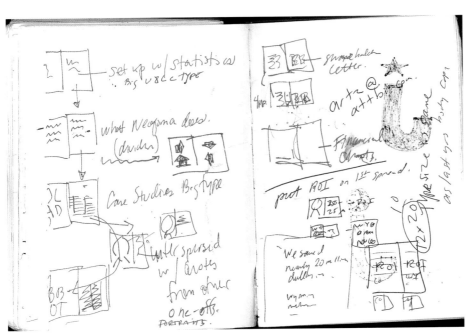

The structure of the report began to take shape as the sketches revealed the thinking behind a balance of bold graphics with minimal or large copy blocks.

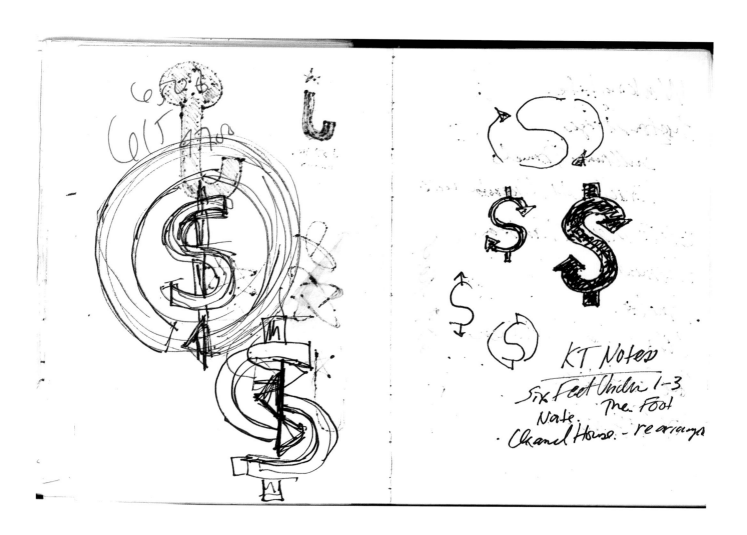

Neoforma
is propelling
efficiency in the
healthcare supply
chain, helping
hospitals and
suppliers reduce
an estimated
$20-$30 billion
in unnecessary
industry
expenditures.

⬦ Braley ultimately used an encircled dollar sign graphic to reinforce a statement about Neoforma's impact on reducing industry expenditures.

⬦ An inside spread shows the balance of color and contrast art director Michael Braley achieved in the final version. Notice that the dollar sign graphic was sketched prior to being included here.

The inspiration for the design came largely from the age of old science journals and textbooks. "The photographs resembled those from an old science journal or textbook. The rest of the book was inspired by the graphic design of the '60s and '70s. To explain their process and the healthcare process in general and how Neoforma is trying to change it was an enormous task. To make the message as simple as possible I used the quick setup of presenting the problem and showing how Neoforma could help them in three spreads, using very simple diagrams to illustrate those points.

"For this particular project, the thumbnails are almost identical to what we presented to the client. You can see from the thumbnails that nothing changed that much. For example, instead of having *Colorado* or *Abbott,* we changed to more generic words that reflected the story. It was more flexible that way. I admit that for a while I thought it was the end of the world that we had to change it, but it worked out okay. Some of the illustrations and charts and how they were drawn changed, but the pacing stayed almost identical. I think we made only one revision after that.

"I would say from a technical and typographic standpoint, contrast in size is good and usually solves a lot of problems and makes things more interesting," Braley says. "The Neoforma report is a good example of that. It's a trend now to have everything the same size in design or type and just use color to differentiate lines of type or hierarchies, but I'm still a fan of big letters versus smaller type. Work that was done in the '30s and '40s has the same size and visual contrast. It's not really a secret; it's how I've approached some things. A lot of it is looking at design history and looking at what works and what doesn't work."

Braley says he likes to start with a clean slate and typically begins with a notebook for writing ideas and word associations. "I use a sketchbook first, then ideas come—word associations, sentences, and quotes come up. We sift through all of the white papers and all of the material that the client gives us to find the interesting nuggets of information that they may have said, even if it's buried in page 17 of someone's speech given in San Diego or something," says Braley. "That's actually the fun part—learning about the company and making it interesting to me, asking the question, 'why would I want to read it?'. It's a discovery kind of process."

Ultimately, the Neoforma annual report was made successful by incorporating their new corporate guidelines in an unexpected way. By using their color palette and a typeface almost identical to what Neoforma had chosen, Cahan & Associates proved that they could bring life to the identity and get the longevity necessary out of the annual report. Because Neoforma didn't yet have printed samples of their new logo treatment, Cahan had a rare opportunity to show their client the possibilities of their identity by not being locked into using their logo on the cover. That's one crowning achievement that most designers can readily relate to.

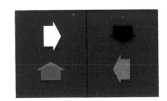

Thumbnails of the early design direction show how the colors in Neoforma's new identity (red, blue, and green) were incorporated into the report through bold graphics and type treatment.

Novell Weathering **several CEO changes** and as many branding initiatives, Seattle-based **Hornall Anderson Design Works'** longstanding relationship with global software developer Novell Corporation is **rather unusual.**

⊗ Novell's objective for a new corporate brochure was
⊗ to effectively leverage their past while incorporating a
new brand strategy that would solidify the company as
a significant player in the Internet economy.

For yet another large design initiative, Hornall Anderson created a corporate brochure to effectively leverage the past and introduce new brand elements that would make Novell appear more Internet-savvy.

"When we started working together—which was our first attempt at redefining Novell because nobody knew who they were—our goal was to give them a photographic or illustration bent that categorized the different products and services within Novell. That lasted a good three to four years," says art director Larry Anderson. "From there, the momentum started to build, and then it was an opportunity to peel back that complexity and get very simple. You can even see in the photo style we became very simple and straightforward because that was the majority of the inspiration for redefining them.

"A long time ago, when Novell was pretty young, they actually referenced illustration. They had an illustrator back in the '70s who created a look for them that they liked quite a bit and they thought might be a good thing to bring back. Because of international concerns and because they're an international company, they thought they needed something that's a little bit more fluid and flexible. We felt photography might be a little easier to implement, so we moved away from the illustration, although there is somewhat of an illustrative quality to some of the metaphors used in the brochure."

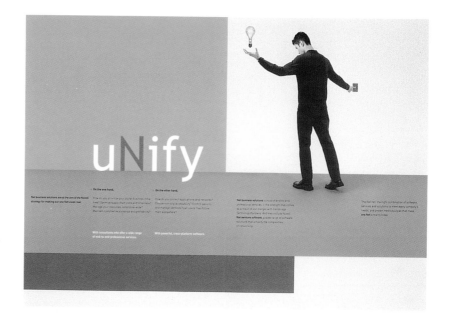

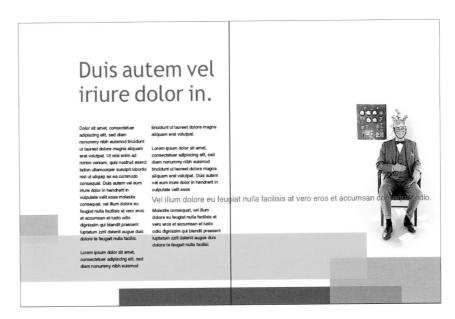

Looking back on the early iterations of the project, Anderson says he started off a little bit too busy. The further into the project he moved, the more he stripped away all of the unnecessary components—a decision that made use of a lot more white space and accomplished a strategic goal of Novell, which was being able to own the color combination of red and white. Ultimately, Anderson says, simpler was much better. The philosophy behind doing the sketches was finding a way to incorporate color blocks, cascading type, and photo metaphors. A bold use of color was also a purposeful choice. Initially, rough illustrations were adopted for the sketches with the understanding that they would eventually be replaced with photography.

"We actually did start off with color clothing (on the models), but then we thought no, maybe it's getting a little bit too much. We decided to do that kind of juxtaposition of black and white and color. It made the methodology behind Novell a little deeper and richer.

"Conceptually, one of the ideas that was used throughout this whole campaign and throughout the company was creating metaphors so all of the strategies were metaphoric in nature. That was the juxtaposition we were trying to achieve. There are a lot of ways to say technology in a metaphoric way, and this actually lightens it up.

"The red cover with the *N* on it is an attempt at being able to say, 'We own red and we're going to own it in a big way, but we're going to be understated about who we are in terms of the visibility of the Novell mark.' That's a nice way of illustrating the company without getting too photographic. It's understated, but it's bold because of the flood of red."

The biggest challenge for Anderson was developing a corporate vocabulary that was in concert with a newly developed strategy and mission. Not all visual and messaging cues were fully developed from a corporate perspective at the time Hornall Anderson created the brochure.

"This was kind of a flagship piece that set the tone for Novell," says Anderson. "It was a huge success for them to have something that really exemplified where they should be and how they should be perceived in the marketplace. From there we developed a whole series of standards and components, which developed into a Novell standards guide, from that one book. It really redefined the company."

In fact, the brochure carried so much weight that the advertising agency picked up on this and later did a pretty extensive campaign, making this metaphor fairly successful. In addition to the impact the piece had inside Novell, the brochure also earned praise from peers in the advertising and design industry. Hornall Anderson won a district Addy and was also recognized in the design annuals of *Applied Arts* and *STEP Inside Design*.

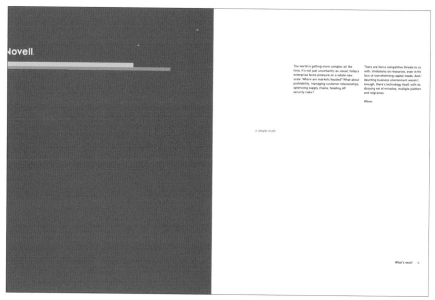

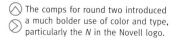
The comps for round two introduced a much bolder use of color and type, particularly the *N* in the Novell logo.

freedom

With Net business solutions, Novell enables people, processes, and systems to work simply and more seamlessly together. We secure and power all types of networks – intranets, extranets, and the Internet; corporate and public; wired to wireless – to work as a single network: one Net.

And free organizations, currently swamped by complexity, to surf above it, to take advantage of the profits and opportunities in this newly networked world.

It's happening right now.

Although Hornall Anderson considered using only illustrations, actual photos of people were used in place of the human sketches for more contrast.

strategy

We know where we're headed. Net business solutions is how.

This unique suite of products and solutions is at the core of Novell's strategy for addressing customers' complex business problems and making our one Net vision real.

→ On the one hand.

Net business solutions consist of technology-neutral [all word here: inclusion or cross-technology] consulting services – the strengths that come to us as a result of our alliance with Cambridge. How does an organization prioritize its digital business initiatives? Optimize its supply chain costs and timeliness? Manage its resources, enterprise-wide? Maintain customer relationships and profitability?

Through Novell's consulting services.

→ On the other hand,

Net business solutions include platform-inclusive Net services software that enables password and identity management, Web security, portal services, delivery services, networked storage and more. How do our customers power and secure networks of all types to work as one Net?

Though Novell's Net services software.

The Net nets a huge continuum of soluti meet the needs of companies, large and and a smooth implementation process place, ready to go.

The promise

In the end, it comes down to giving organizations the ability not just to adapt to—but profit from—the opportunities of a networked world. We do so when we simplify their businesses and speed up their transactions. We do it,

by securing their resources and extending their business processes without bounds. With real products and solutions today, Novell gives people greater freedom to communicate and connect.

And delivers — in a world where change is constant —

the power to change. →→→

Octel Ideas On Purpose was formed in 2000 by three design colleagues from an **award-winning design firm** in New York City. When the firm decided to close its annual report business, the **three art directors set up shop** and negotiated to take a couple of clients with them, one of which was the Octel Corporation.

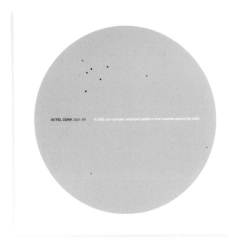

Octel is a specialty chemicals company based in Newark, Delaware, that has been in business for approximately 65 years. Octel experienced incredible growth in 2001, not only from a strategic standpoint but also from a geographic standpoint. Because of a five-year transformation (2001 was year four) to a specialty chemicals company, Octel was now found in unexpected places. As the front cover of the report notes, in 2000, Octel had employees in nine countries; in 2001, it had expanded to 23 nations and four continents.

"I immediately knew that I wanted to represent the different cities in an abstract manner and to tell the growth story in a different way," says art director Darren Namaye. "The idea of movement, bold geometric shapes, fun but retro-inspired colors, and simple, strong typography were my inspirations going forward.

"I wanted the cover to be mysterious in some way," Namaye says. "I knew from the beginning that I wanted die-cut holes to represent the original nine countries that Octel occupied. How the holes were going to be laid out I had no idea. I originally thought of them as a timeline—from left to right—but felt that was not dynamic enough. Then I thought to use the actual positions of the countries, as on a map, to give a more organic, random look to the holes, which added to its mysteriousness."

The designer created intrigue on the cover by using tiny holes to indicate where the company was based prior to 2001. When you open the cover, you see all of the newest locations on the globe. Meanwhile, the full-page photo spreads offer a bolder look in the interior.

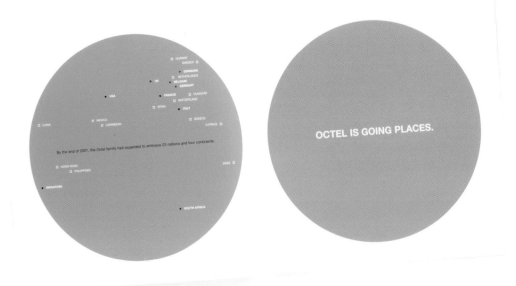

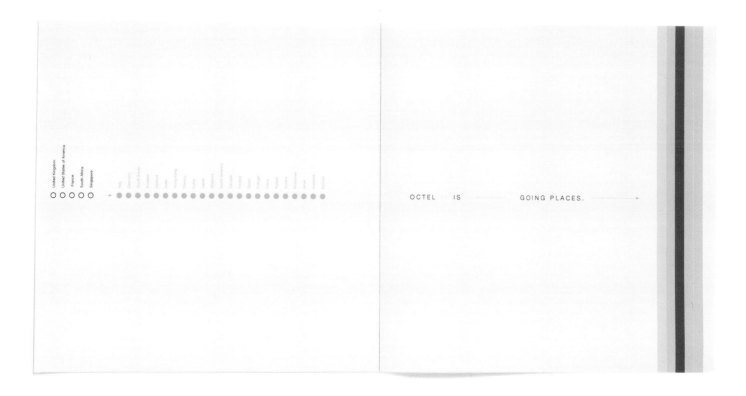

OCTEL — IS — GOING PLACES. →

OCTEL CORP. 2001 ANNUAL REPORT

The earliest version of the Octel annual report cover and inside spread is quite bland in comparison with the final version, but it shows the thought process of choosing a visual vocabulary.

Namaye says he finds inspiration in many everyday things. "Language inspires me greatly. Words conjure up images and feelings. I do not consciously look for inspiration around me. Things pop into my head from deep within the subconscious or memory. From time to time I do thumb through things—mostly fine art books, TV or film, or design language from the past, the everyday vernacular of life.

"For some reason, with this client I subconsciously tried to design something British in tone, look, and feel," Namaye says. "The British aesthetic greatly inspires me: it has understated, elegant typography, no-nonsense layout, with clever wit and subtlety. I don't know if I achieved it, but I tried. I did look at Bradbury Thompson's work and felt that the simple geometry felt right, especially with the perfect square format of Octel's annual.

"Generally, I felt the mockups didn't fully capture the clarity of the message. Something didn't feel right. I kept paring down things to their essence, making sure everything had a function and a reason for being there. Both mockups were really variations on a theme.

"Internally, the book was originally thought of as being single-page examples of where Octel was based coupled with scientific schematics, lines, and boxes knocking out of images to represent movement and fractured spaces. That approach also added a lot of details and intricacy that at the time felt right."

Of course, that idea didn't last, as you can see from the finished piece. Namaye made the decision not to carry through the elaborateness of the first section into the financial area. However, the financial section does mirror the front of the book in typographic style. "The financials would never mirror the front section because there is no room for it," Namaye says. "Due to a tight budget, the financials are printed in one color on fairly inexpensive paper. We spent the majority of the budget on the front section of the book."

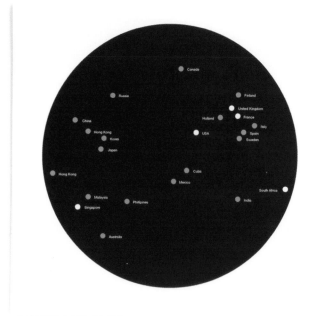

⊘ The second mockup reveals how the initial idea started to become clearer and the layout more polished.

Namaye's design secret is about concentrating on the client's message. "For me, the message is always paramount and should not be hindered by design," Namaye recalls. "Although the client signed off on the design as-is, it just didn't feel right to me. Some things worked very well, but others didn't. I felt the message was not accessible enough and that people who skim should be able to get the idea quickly. I turned the single-page examples into spreads, maximizing the images and turning them into posterlike billboards. I added the strong geometry of the circles on the cover. The first two pages reinforce the world and being global. It was still mysterious and pure in form. In a nutshell, I pared down the book by taking out the extraneous elements and adding impact by maximizing scale and form."

Namaye says that one valuable takeaway from designing the annual report was that simplicity is often better than complexity. "If anything, this project reinforced my belief that one should not overdesign," says Namaye. "If design does not ultimately serve the message or content, then it has failed. Yes, things can be decorative and should be attractive to the eye as well as the mind, but it ultimately aids in understanding. Appropriateness is key, and sometimes that lies within you and comes from your gut and your instincts."

Listening to his instincts paid off for Namaye. The Octel Report found its way into several design annuals and competitions including *STEP Inside Design's* 2003 Annual 100.

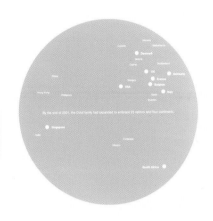

⊘ The third and final comp shows how the design concept came into focus as ideas continued to enhance the structure and appeal of the report. Text was adjusted by using contrast, and images were cropped or enlarged for greater impact.

⊘ This spread from the final shows how Namaye achieved a balance between a full-bleed image and text overlays.

Orivo

Orivo Hornall Anderson Design Works of Seattle is known for creating **something where there is nothing.** But for a new company called Orivo, **that challenge was even harder,** given that their business was **developing new products.**

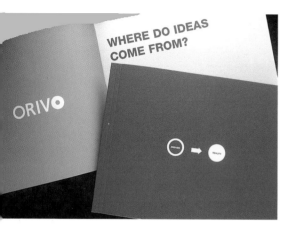

Because Orivo didn't sell a product or service, Hornall Anderson chose a more narrative, big-picture approach and made the brochure almost an ideabook by leaving 96 pages blank.

First, Hornall Anderson created a wordmark that was clean, simple, and had a European flavor—timeless, confident, and established—and didn't look like a start-up company's. Then came the need for a marketing piece that conveyed Orivo in a way people would understand, considering they didn't yet have a variety of personal examples to glean from.

"A brochure was created that played on the theme of 'taking dreams into reality,'" says designer and project manager Andrew Wicklund. "No specific stories were available to share, so the design team developed a sketchbook that displayed vignettes and stories of famous ideas that remind the reader—through pictures of people similar to the client—of others who have had the ability to identify what the market needs are and how to provide it. The book offers exercises to help generate ideas. There is a sense of responsibility about the book while still pushing the limits. The main intent was to create interest and encourage using the exercise to get a dialogue going.

"We used the same metaphor throughout. The hiccup was someone who has never heard of Orivo—he or she gets this thing and thinks it's somehow involved with the food industry or the grocery industry," Wicklund says. "There was some inspiration there, seeing how we could use metaphors and speak abstractly, but what we did there was too specific to produce. What came out of that was the seed and the way we talked about using something from Point A to Point B to Point C—that progression of how ideas germinate, grow, and finally get to the end user.

"At first, it was daunting," says Wicklund. "That's where I wouldn't say that the apples comp was a misstep. It was so open at the beginning. We at least had hit the mark a little bit or were at least in the right ballpark, so it was a good start. It's always nice to have certain parameters, but for the most part no idea was too crazy. That's always a great way to start a project.

ORIVO

- Ideas & Implimentation
- Passion & Practicality

* Genuine
  ↳ don't build up to something he can't live up to

10am / 1200 western ring at entry board
#048   5/8 unit

Bleeding knee → bandaid
mildly → quirky

100 ~ 150

- Build emotional story
- Smaller in size... intimate
- Something to hold on to (keep)

→ Sketchbook / Journal
  ↳ "Ideas" book

- WHERE IDEAS COME FROM
- HISTORICAL REFERENCES

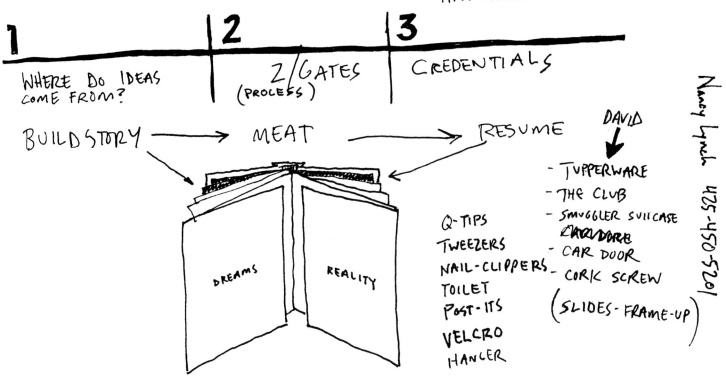

1 WHERE DO IDEAS COME FROM?

2 2/GATES (PROCESS)

3 CREDENTIALS

BUILD STORY ———→ MEAT ———→ RESUME   DAVID ↓

DREAMS   REALITY

Q-TIPS
TWEEZERS
NAIL-CLIPPERS
TOILET
POST-ITS
VELCRO
HANGER

- TUPPERWARE
- THE CLUB
- SMUGGLER SUITCASE
- CAR DOOR
- CORK SCREW
(SLIDES - FRAME-UP)

Nancy Lynch 425-450-5201

Dream.

Deliver.

Opportunities are out there.   Harvest them.   Celebrate their unique qualities...   ...and deliver them to those who are hungry for them.   Tap into it's potential.   Do these things and you will satisfy the consumer's hunger.

◇ For the first round of comps, Hornall Anderson had the right concept and storyline, but the imagery and metaphor might have been too confusing. Orivo isn't involved with the food or grocery industry, but this was not clear from their early comps.

PUTTING PENCIL TO PAPER?

In 1564, graphite was discovered in Borrowdale, England. It put marks on paper better than lead, but was so brittle it broke easily. Wrapping string around the pieces hardly helped. The next year, 1565, the Swiss-German naturalist Conrad Gesler hollowed out sticks of wood to hold the graphite and the pencil was born.

DRAWING ON EXPERIENCE?

David Sinegal is a seasoned veteran of the consumer product industry. In positions of executive leadership at Costco, the fifth largest merchant in America, he turned his talent into valuable skills. He fine-tuned techniques in product and process innovation. He perfected key abilities in risk management, negotiations and partnership. He field-tested best practices and refined a better set of rules. For bright ideas and better ways, draw on Sinegal's experience.

◇ Another example of the original layout shows the introduction stories about the history of innovation. At this stage, a decision was made to create more impact by using larger photos.

"We didn't want to take it to the expected, because a lot of people use the words *idea* and *innovation*," says Wicklund. "There's the obvious connotation with the light bulb. We just thought, 'this guy really needs to stand apart from that general hum of market vocabulary.' Everything worked in harmony—down to the paper stock and color—to say, 'Hey, look at me. This isn't something that you've seen before.'

"We discussed a few directions in which we could take the project: shape, form, size, delivery. When we all agreed on the ideabook concept, we showed only two executions of one concept. Both stock photographs and quick digital photos taken around our office were used to reflect imagery that would best illustrate the message of new ideas, as well as serve as representations of the messages the client was trying to express. Also, we wanted to create a layout for the brochure, where the second half of it served as a journal/sketchbook so people could record their own brainstorming.

"There are two different kinds of spreads in the book. But the visual or graphic presentation is meant to be unslick and almost researchlike," says Wicklund. "Here's a guy [Orivo's founder] who is really in touch with the world and everywhere he looks he sees

opportunities. That was the concept behind it. Kind of leading you to think there's always something new on the horizon."

Measuring the success of the Orivo brochure wasn't easy. However, Hornall Anderson found that the brochure got Orivo in the door early on with many of the kinds of people they wanted to meet. Potential clients took them seriously enough to meet with them. The irony is that most of Orivo is now defunct. The founder has started another company and is focusing on a specific industry rather than casting his net so widely.

Wicklund says the interesting thing is that even though people scratched their heads a little bit about this piece, that was a good thing. "If it gets them to pick up the phone or to talk with me a little bit more, that's a huge win. It didn't sit on their desk and go unnoticed, which was the key."

It didn't go unnoticed as far as design awards and recognitions, either. Hornall Anderson came away with a regional Addy award and an award of excellence at the 37th Annual West Coast Show. In addition, the brochure was a finalist in the 2003 London International Advertising and Design Awards Competition.

There are countless products that improve our lives.

Some are simple, some are complicated.

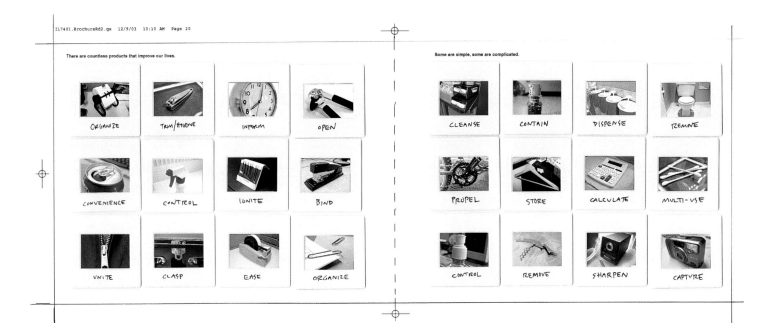

ORGANIZE TRIM/HYGIENE INFORM OPEN

CONVENIENCE CONTROL IGNITE BIND

UNITE CLASP EASE ORGANIZE

CLEANSE CONTAIN DISPENSE REMOVE

PROPEL STORE CALCULATE MULTI-USE

CONTROL REMOVE SHARPEN CAPTURE

Many are multifunctional.

The question Orivo asks, "What is...

CUT CONTAIN COMMUNICATE OPEN

REMIND DRIVE TIGHTEN DELIVER

COOK HOLD HOLD BIND

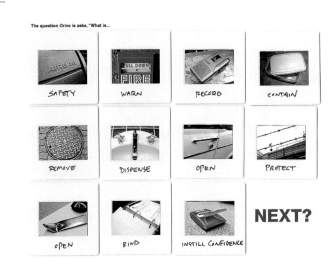

SAFETY WARN RECORD CONTAIN

REMOVE DISPENSE OPEN PROTECT

OPEN BIND INSTILL CONFIDENCE **NEXT?**

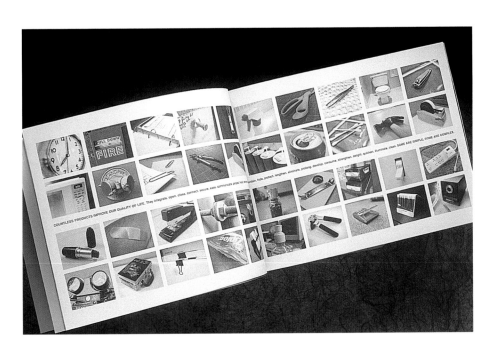

A series of everyday tools and products served as the impetus for showing how problems find solutions. This photo concept spread became much cleaner with text running through the middle of the pages.

This spread from the final shows the balance Hornall Anderson achieved through the series of inside images from the earlier comp (shown above). The approach here was less literal and more open to interpretation.

The Penford Corporation is a developer, manufacturer, and marketer of **specialty-ingredient systems** based on **natural, renewable resources.** Their technology and applications apply to the **global food markets,** papermaking, and textile industries.

The vertical nature of the Penford annual report gave it an unusual format that was meant to emulate the methodical and linear approach Penford takes to their work.

At one point, Methodologie thought about making the report larger with a wrap that would fold out into a poster-size piece.

Penford has been a client of Seattle-based Methodologie for about six years. When it came time for a 2002 annual report, Methodologie was tapped for the task. The overall strategy of the design would be to articulate and reinforce Penford's new brand tagline: "Nature. Science. Solutions."

"The biggest conceptual departure for this book is the way it is read. It opens vertically instead of horizontally," says art director Minh Nguyen. "This layout better emphasizes the linear reading of the book because everything cascades down throughout the book. We hoped to convey the methodical, logical approach Penford applies to their work, from start to finish. The vertical page turning was an idea to help support the linear aspect of Penford's approach to research. It just seemed smoother to lay out the information in this fashion—it helps link the three major sections. Penford is a company that places a high level of confidence in their research-driven philosophy, so everything for them revolves around that.

"The early sketches were explorations of how to organize the message of 'Nature. Science. Solutions'," Nguyen says. "Ultimately, the layout was simplified to devote appropriate space for each of the three topics. For the most part, the early layouts and sketches were used to develop the organization of the content. The visual elements came from that."

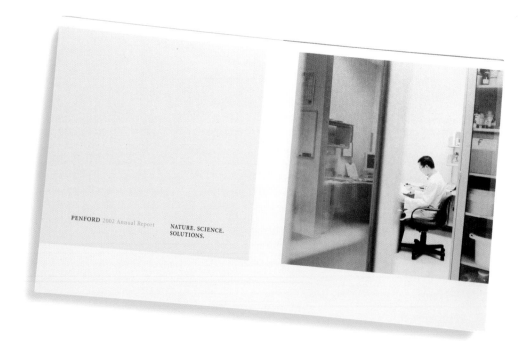

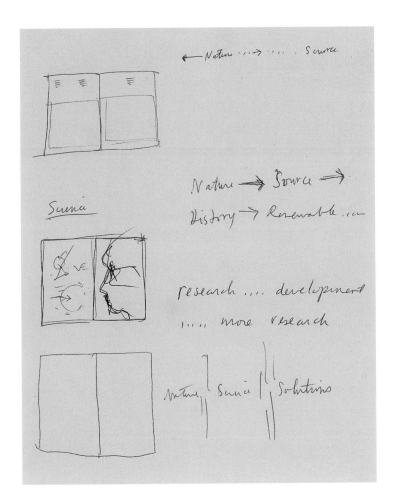

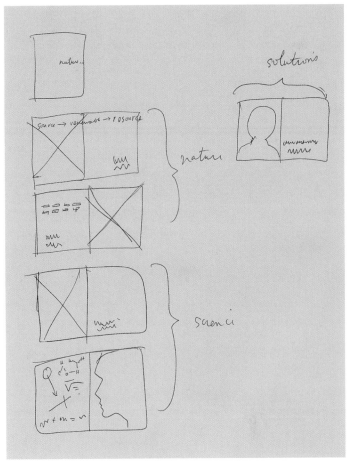

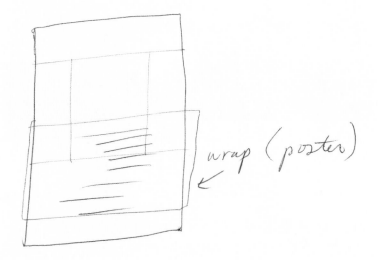

Early on, art director Minh Nguyen sketched out the rough layout and format of the Penford annual centered around the new tagline: "Nature. Science. Solutions."

Nguyen says one cover image came about during the editing process. The choice to feature one image was based on making the complex much simpler. "The one image came about when we edited all of the shots. It communicated all we wanted to say about the company, that they simply cared about their work and their dedication to research. The cover variations partly help us explore different avenues, in terms of formal aspects like color and structure. This image indicates the thought process that goes behind Penford—more than a standard shot of people running around in a lab and pouring chemicals."

Staying away from colors normally associated with science, such as blues, reds, and greens, Nguyen says the process for establishing a color palette was rather lengthy. She wanted a combination of colors that had a warm, organic quality to them, so she chose to incorporate hues of brown and orange.

The overall layout is based on aspects of logic, science, linear processes, and defined structure. "We usually present two options to the client, with a strong encouragement for one of the directions," Nguyen says. "In this case, we picked the more unique format as the final. Again, it supports the idea of calculated thinking and research. It almost seems to be laid out on graph paper coordinates.

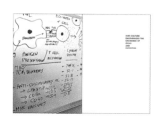

⬨ Methodologie typically presents two options to clients with strong encouragement for one of the directions. This early direction lacked the organic feel or uniqueness the designers wanted.

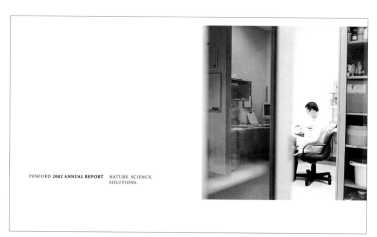

NATURE.

PENFORD 2002 ANNUAL REPORT

SCIENCE.
SOLUTIONS.

PENFORD 2002 ANNUAL REPORT   NATURE. SCIENCE.
SOLUTIONS.

NATURE.

PENFORD 2002 ANNUAL REPORT

SCIENCE.
SOLUTIONS.

⬨ "The cover variations are partly to help us explore different avenues, in terms of formal aspects like color and structure," says Methodologie's Minh Nguyen. The final cover version featuring one image was chosen because it seemed to distill Penford's message into one shot—the care and dedication they bring to their work.

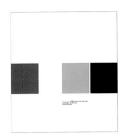

⊘ This series of comps comes closer to the final version of the annual's design. Some slight variations in color combinations and image selection would be made to the final.

"The photography was directed to give a sense of the working environment at Penford without being too literal or clichéd, more like snapshots of what goes on in an average day of work—nothing glamorous."

Nguyen says the challenge was to balance the three themes of the new tagline effectively without detracting from the overall appeal of the report. Or, in her exact words, "how to communicate the message without being boring." Nguyen livened up the overall look and result by telling the stories directly, in a more compelling manner.

She says the secret is often in trusting your own instincts and seeing where they take you. "I think successful design solutions are usually the result of meandering and getting lost," Ngueyn says. "Brainstorming is great for initiating thinking and random thoughts. Start with a problem and from there just wander in different directions Try to find meaningful relationships in completely unrelated things. Writing ability is also crucial; if a designer possesses strong writing sensibilities, then he or she is a step ahead. Writing skills help designers integrate words and stories with visual elements more cohesively, instead of the two realms living independently on the same page," Nguyen says. "Even if you're not a great writer, you should be able to direct copywriters in the same way you direct a photographer or an illustrator. Writing ability also allows a designer to think strategically and more comprehensively."

Despite winning several awards and recognitions by such publications and organizations as *Communication Arts, Print, Applied Arts,* and the *Black Book Annual Report 100,* Methodologie defines success differently for the Penford Report and many of their projects. They'll do it again next year.

project themepark

project themepark Fresh out of school, three enterprising **friends in London** decided to create project themepark, a combination **publication, website, and event planner** to find **new artistic talent** emerging on the scene.

 Part of a system of themed publishing (print, Web, and live events), themepark represents a hybrid publication that falls somewhere between book and magazine. Essentially, it is an experiment of design and content on several levels.

Their company, 20/20 media Ltd., sought help for branding and design assistance. They were put in touch with envision+, a design and branding agency in Germany. Envision+ principals Brian Switzer and Esther Mildenberger saw their collaboration as a perfect match.

Essentially, project themepark is themed publishing in three different media: magazine, websites, and events. "Authors, artists, designers, photographers, or people with something appropriate to say or show are invited to express themselves based on the current theme," says Mildenberger. "The design coherence, cross-linked content, and youthful culture is what makes themepark fresh to the publishing world."

Because of the nature of themepark, envision+ chose to make all three versions stand alone yet remain connected because of their linked purposes and themes. "From the start, we wanted to create a hybrid publication—somewhere between book and magazine. Additionally, we sought to cross-link different events and media, whether print, Internet, or live events.

"The magazine hit the shelves about three times a year and spanned the space between periodical and book," Switzer says. "The format and treatment of the content are conceived to make themepark a collectible exhibition. We determined the sizes by holding books or magazines in our hands—the weight and feel of the paper was very important. Did it feel substantial? Was it a good size to curl up with for a good read? Did it feel collectible? We wanted it to be something you would want to put on your bookshelf."

Switzer says the idea behind the original concept of the publication was to create an interesting narrative to the flow. "I think the biggest inspiration for the publication and project was the London creative scene—artists, poets, writers, photographers, fashion designers, furniture designers, illustrators, architects, and so on. All were gathered in east-central London, working, living, and hanging out in cafes, bars, and clubs. The spirit of the time was that anything was possible, and there was a buzz in the air. To capture that excitement, give it a container, and make it a collectible was our first priority. We wanted to create intriguing yet thoughtful image-and-text combinations and, at some level, integrate the theme of each issue in the design, as well as provide access or links to the other media.

"The development process was to get a design/layout/container that was recognizable, yet also specific to the theme. This was important to us because lots of themed publications really look the same. They are more about one layout idea rather than a set of ideas. This project was more work to develop because we had

Relying on an overall theme for each edition, the inaugural issue was a study on violence. Because it was the first issue, themepark 01 went through multiple layout changes and experiments.

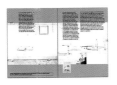

Many preliminary layouts were done because content came in bits and pieces. Plus, there was no specific format to follow because the publication didn't yet exist.

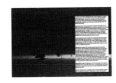

to ask the question, 'What works best?' for every medium, but in the end it was very satisfying and, we still think, unmatched. We always worked closely with the editors—they chose content and said what was important or which ideas should be discussed for the upcoming issue."

Envision+ created approximately three rounds of options for the client. "At least three rounds of designs were done, and each round presented multiple options," Mildenberger says. "Underlying the magazine pages, we developed a flexible grid, allowing for both consistency and variation. Certain elements, such as typographic specifications (size, spacing, kerning, and outline style for headlines, introductory text, body text, and credits) and format were constants. The grid, however, allowed for a great deal of experimentation and play, such as asymmetrical grids, symmetrical grids, turning the layout 90°, and varying numbers of columns. In addition, certain parts of the layout were more consistent. The introduction (the first spread always showed a full-page image interrupted by the table of contents and colophon), table of contents, and subscription info (other than the color scheme) remained similar throughout all issues."

Yet another aspect of themepark's consistency and play was the color scheme. Two colors were chosen for each theme and then applied to all aspects of that issue (whether online, in print, or at an event for that theme). This decision gave each issue a consistent feel, even across the various media, and gave each publication a unique look. For example, the inaugural issue on violence has more split images or pages turned 90°, and even pages with vertical text.

Switzer says envision+ likes to treat each new design project like inventing a game. "I think we try to come up with a game that has rules but is still fun to play," says Switzer. "Each situation or project has different parameters, and these become part of the game. Is the content serious? Is there lots of money or time? It all affects the rules of the game. In the end, it has to be fun for all to play and, at the same time, produce work of which everyone is proud. If we're lucky, it might even be unique. Ideally, it is something that pushes everyone to be a little more than they thought they could be." Who wouldn't want to play that game?

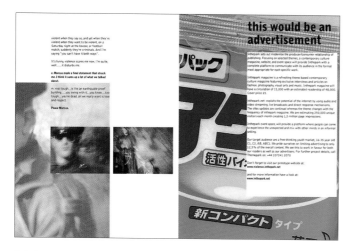

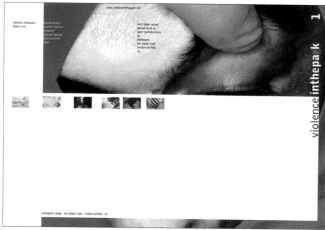

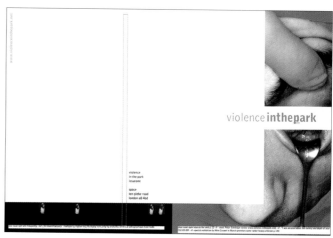

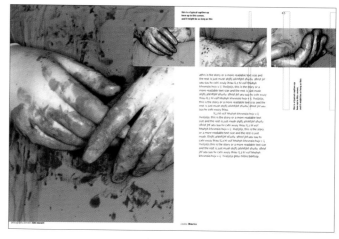

Each stage of the comps got envision+ closer to a final grid, which was slightly different for each issue and would be designed to keep readers' attention.

Underlying the magazine pages, a flexible grid allowed for both consistency and variation. Certain elements such as typographic specifications and format were constants, yet the grid still allowed for a great deal of experimentation and play.

With each prototype or sketch, the process was the same. Envision+ presented their ideas, 20/20 gave their feedback, they discussed their impressions as a group, and the next version would be created.

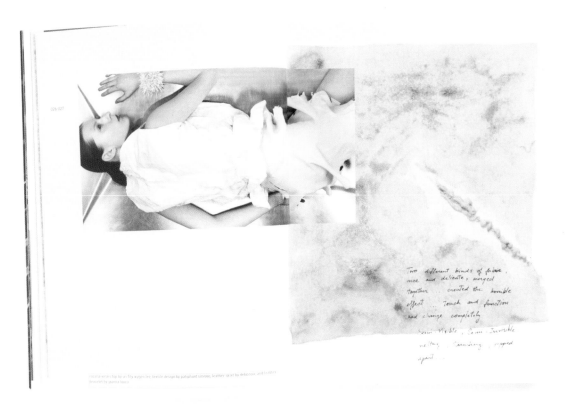

Each spread of themepark is unique, even though each issue focuses on one unifying theme.

The overall size of each book was decided by envision+ simply by holding books or magazines in their hands. The weight and feel of the paper was important: Did it feel substantial? Was it a good size to curl up with for a good read? Did it feel collectible?

Pure Design

Founded in 1994, Pure Design is a Calgary-based manufacturer of **contemporary home furnishings** with **original product designs and collaborations** with international designers.

The cover image reflects the rugged landscape of Alberta and depicts the mountains in a graphic, patterned illustration.

Each year, Pure Design produces a catalog showcasing their most recent collection. For the past five years, Edmonton-based Nine Point Design has collaborated on the design of their catalog.

According to Nine Point founder and art director Denise Ahlefeldt, Pure Design is not a typical client. Pure Design has consistently been creatively involved in defining the theme of their catalogs over the years. "The concept for this particular design was to juxtapose Pure Design's furniture with our Canadian landscape," says Ahlefeldt. "We wanted to show the product as being connected to its surroundings. The cover is a graphic representation of the dramatic landscape in which we live. The interior photo concepts were developed using a combination of stock photos and a number of digital photos shot around Edmonton. Close-cropped images of the products were then placed into the different environments until we achieved the desired effect. The final result was a marriage between the clean lines of the furniture and the natural beauty of the setting."

Because Pure Design produces contemporary items, their marketing pieces must reflect the products and consumers who purchase their furniture. For inspiration, Nine Point turned to contemporary cultural influences. "I looked to current trends in music, fashion, and snowboard/skateboard culture to gain some initial focus," says Ahlefeldt. "I also found inspiration in my surroundings. Alberta is about dramatic changes. In a few hours, you can go from desert to rolling forests to the foothills and then into the Rocky Mountains, and in a matter of days from hot sunny summers to snow-filled winters. The layering of prairie, foothills, and mountains creates depth and substance, which is often mirrored in my design work.

"Because Pure Design's products are so striking on their own, they need to be allowed to speak for themselves. This means creating an interesting style balanced with minimalist design. Design elements set the tone and keep the design interesting and appealing year after year. I like to present the products in two ways. I like the product to stand on its own so that potential customers can appreciate the design and imagine how the product would fit into their lifestyle, but I also like to provide situational photographs to challenge and inspire."

Even though Pure Design collaborates on the catalog's vision, Nine Point still must steer the project and make sure it stays on track. Whatever basic parameters the team defines for the photography, Nine Point must make the production happen. Nine Point designs the layout of the catalog so it matches the photography, decides on the final concepts of the photos, and directs the actual photo shoots.

"The biggest challenge, as always, was to create a balance between minimal design and stylistic elements," Ahlefeldt says. "There is always a bit of push and pull going on. I typically start by adding too many elements, and then the challenge becomes trying to decide what is necessary and what isn't. A lot of adding and subtracting of elements occurs while we determine how to best feature each product.

"The creation of the cover art also turned out to be a bit of a challenge," Ahlefeldt admits. "The cover is a graphical representation of the Alberta landscape. It reflects our layered terrain— from the prairies to foothills to the Rocky Mountains. At first, I was trying to create a pattern using multiples of the same elements, but I was not getting the desired results. I was working with an illustration, created from individual shapes, which then became an abstract pattern. Eventually, I started creating more complex individual shapes. Through a process of layering those shapes, the cover art took its final form."

Ahlefeldt says the overall design was born out of a collaboration with Pure Design, the photographer, and her studio. The idea evolved around an emphasis on situational photographs for various furniture items. Everything else in the catalog had to revolve around this design decision. Ahlefeldt says the ongoing conversation with the client during the design process helped create the final piece.

"My design process always starts with a conversation with my client," says Ahlefeldt. "I sit down with them and talk about their vision and their expectations. It is from this conversation that I decide what is valid and what isn't, what is suitable and what isn't, what will work and what won't. My process is about trying to find the balance between what the client tells me they need and what I feel is appropriate. Sometimes our visions and ideas are quite far apart. In the case of Pure Design, because I've worked with them for so long, our visions usually are quite similar. My job is to make sure that the final piece represents the best of both of our ideas, that it is appropriate for the intended audience, and that it produces the desired effect (which, in Pure Design's case, is to sell furniture). I think my approach works because I understand what end result the client wants."

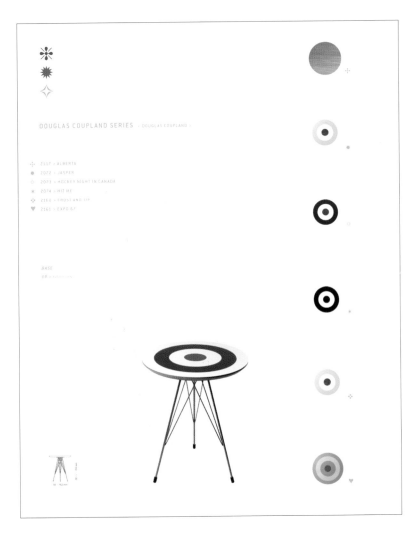

This series of patterns uses multiples of the same elements to represent the Alberta landscape. One of these patterns was chosen for the cover image.

Most of the early sketches focused on developing the cover and bringing those elements into the body of the catalog.

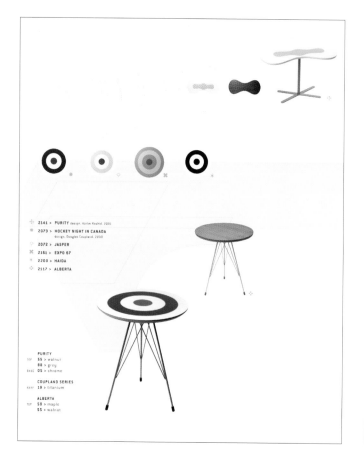

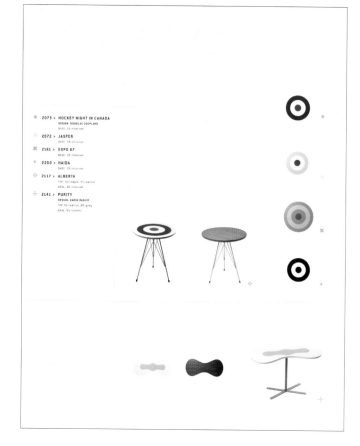

The contemporary furniture designed by Pure Design and their affiliates calls for a marketing piece that is equally contemporary. Nine Point tried different variations that were all clean, edgy, and modern.

While on location setting up for the "lamps in the field" shot, photographer Vicocky O'Grady saw a crescent moon rising into the shot—a fortuitous addition to the photo.

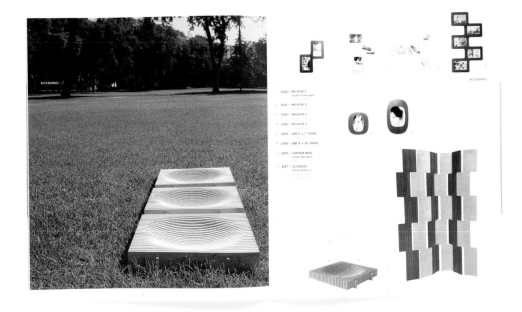

The concept for this particular catalog was to juxtapose Pure Design's furniture with the Canadian landscape.

Raid Gauloises Perhaps most famous for the race

itself, the Raid Gauloises, or Original Adventure Race, is held **once a year in different countries** around the world. However, Raid Gauloises is divided into two **separate entities:**

The Raid Gauloises, better known as the Original Adventure Race, includes a fashion element, too. Austria-based Zooom productions was asked to compete with two other studios for designing the catalog. Guess who won?

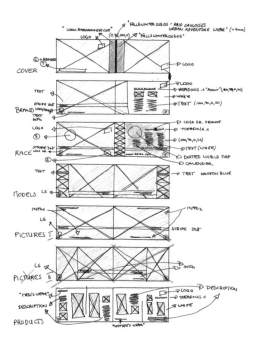

Before getting down to the actual layout, art director Horst Koepfelsberger made a rough template for the entire catalog, including color scheme and copy placement.

Raid Gauloises—Original Adventure Race (a physically challenging adventure race) and Raid Gauloises Fashion.

Austria-based Zooom Productions was asked to compete with two other studios for designing the fashion catalog. The challenge facing each competing firm was somehow to link the fashion products to the race itself, or the urban adventure to the Raid Gauloises race. Zooom won the job based on the merit of their layouts and the presentation of the race.

"We tried to link the two worlds—urban adventure (outdoor fashion) and a tough human experience (the race)—by taking opposite and similar aspects from both," says Horst Koepfelsberger. "You can see pictures of race participants in Vietnam from the same perspective as the two models wearing Raid Gauloises clothes in Vienna. We also added a transparent stripe to add some connection between the pictures on the double pages. The text also had to create a clear relationship between pictures, for example, 'Tested in nature...to survive the city.' In addition, we looked at similarity of movement in different surroundings, similarity of surfaces, difference in light, and many others aspects."

Koepfelsberger says the challenge was to create some extraordinary connection between the race and the fashion, between lifestyle and functionality, and between urban living and a natural experience, all within a two-month timeframe. Zooom showed the client only one concept, which was developed from the pitch and some minor variations to get close to what the client wanted for the final product. Some of Zooom's inspirations included photos of the race, children's books, elements of the race, Ulrich Grill's (the photographer) photos, sleepless nights, and sitting together and 'letting the brain smoke.'

"We mostly show image shots where the clothes are in action, but there is a part with clear fashion shots of the products—shot in a studio—at the end of the brochure," says Koepfelsberger. "We weren't satisfied with static shots, so we had them shot in action as well. The advantage of the neutral background is that your attention is drawn to the product and its details."

Another daunting challenge of connecting the race and the fashion catalog of Raid Gauloises was that they had two different audiences. "We had a completely different target group than the race," Koepfelsberger says. "The race had a tough focus on the participants and the journalists of adventure sports. This catalog was made for the target group of the fashion brand: 25- to 35-year-old consumers, highly educated, living an urban lifestyle. The catalog addressed dealers, consumers, and fashion journalists.

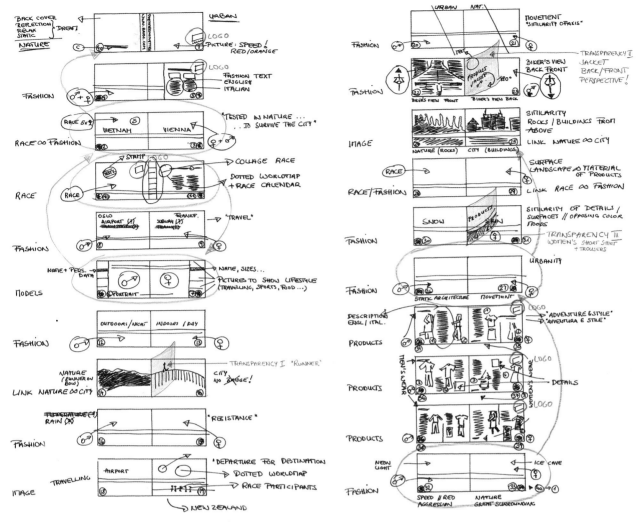

In this sequence of sketches, Koepfelsberger begins the process of maneuvering pages and adding more detail to the photographs and overall layout.

"In this special case, I took a lot of inspiration from the root of the brand—the Raid Gauloises Race—and adventure racing in general," says Koepfelsberger. "I did some research on this topic and thought about the general design in this special field. I looked at pictures taken during the races. I was interested in landscapes, people—both participants and the local population—and the sports disciplines. What do they look like? How do these people feel? What do they use? What are their reasons for taking part?

"Second, I was interested in their tools. What does a GPS or compass look like? How does its interface work, and how is it designed? What kind of manuals do the participants use? What are their personal notes and scribbles? How is their information represented? How do they get necessary information about weather and geographic coordinates?"

Koepfelsberger explains that he purposefully used certain aspects of the design for specific purposes in the catalog. For example, he used graphic elements such as the world map and the logo to represent freedom and travel; descriptions of the location and its weather conditions to support the aspect of traveling and show the advantages of the products (for example from 21°F to 95°F [-6°C to 35°C]); stamps to show the locations of the race; and pagination as barcode to create some movement through the pages.

"We were looking for extraordinary ways to present the products and the connection between the two worlds (urban and natural),

so we inserted transparencies, which gave us many possibilities. In the end, we decided to use the transparencies for three aspects: as a connection between the two worlds (a runner in the desert and in town); to show the product from back and front; and to support the similarities and differences of the products' surfaces."

The secret Koepfelsberger brings to each design challenge is to compare his work to that of a conductor. "Every piece of design work for me is comparable to a piece of music—some kind of music for the eyes," Koepfelsberger says. "I try to pack every bit of content into a piece of music. It is always necessary to have some rhythm within a piece of design—it could be a story, the format, or the page sequence. This rhythm is the basic line of the story, the presentation of content. I use graphical elements as different instruments—some for rhythm, some for lead, some for solos."

In the end, Koepfelsberger and his team proved that Raid Gauloises Fashion selected the right studio to design their catalog. "The catalog was really successful because it was the first catalog to integrate all aspects of the brand. It was well received by the client, and we had good feedback on the message provided. Unfortunately, we do not have clear figures of the number of products sold, but it definitely made the brand more known to the target market. As a whole, the catalog was appealing to many people. But we got great feedback on special elements such as the transparencies, because they made the catalog somehow more unique."

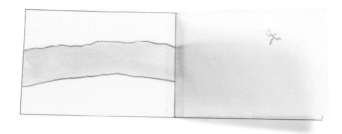

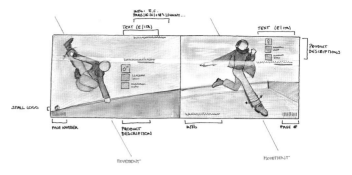

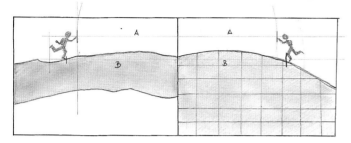

Here, an action shot is overlaid onto a static photograph. First, Koepfelsberger sketched the overall layout; second, he moved into actual overlay; then, he decided on appropriate page location and, ultimately, the final placement.

This sequence shows how a two-page spread in the catalog came to life. Notice how the subtle changes in copy placement and design elements added to the interest and overall movement of the catalog.

A more refined comp still gets the art director's treatment to match the rest of the catalog, not only in typography and action photography but also in movement and consistency.

The final Raid Gauloises catalog captures the active urban appeal of the product line and places it amid landscapes that evoke the environment and conditions of the race itself.

RGD Every year, the Association of Registered Graphic Designers (RGD) of Ontario, Canada, selects a **well-recognized** design firm known for **doing great work** to be considered for designing **materials for their annual conference.**

DESIGNTHINKERS 2003

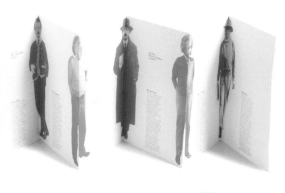

The theme of the 2003 RGD Conference was "Think Innovation." After wading through sad and clichéd images, Toronto-based Pylon Design chose a well-known icon to represent the conference materials. Pylon also incorporated the branding of RGD by emphasizing the color red.

Opposite page, top left: After art director Scott Christie pores over the creative brief and client materials, he often escapes to a coffee shop where he brainstorms and begins to sketch out ideas, such as the originals seen here.

Opposite page, top center: Christie usually comes up with an idea, but when he doesn't, it is often because he doesn't have enough information about the project and must ask more questions.

Opposite page, top right: Once Christie had the idea to use an icon to represent innovation, he began to lay out the possible elements to the conference materials.

Opposite page, middle: Christie's original idea was to put the names of the conference speakers on top of the Einstein photos, but the agency that owns the rights to the photos wouldn't allow it.

Opposite page, bottom: Because there were so many elements to the conference materials, Christie had to make sure his idea would translate to each piece.

Some of the early outtakes from other designers at Pylon show a completely different direction for the conference theme. Pylon believes strongly in competition, so each designer gets a shot at coming up with ideas for projects.

The company name is submitted and voted on by the RGD board. In 2003, Toronto-based Pylon Design was submitted and won the job.

"The theme of the show was innovation," says art director Scott Christie. "As you can imagine, lots of sad and clichéd images come to mind. Our take on the theme was that the speakers themselves were the innovators. Why else would they be invited to talk? However, showing the speakers would have been dull and a complete cop-out. I thought along the lines of great innovators of our time: Lincoln, Gandhi, Franklin, Earhart. The only catch was no one would recognize these people. If, for example, I had put Paula Scher's name with Earhart's photo, people might have thought it was Paula.

This line of thought led me to Albert Einstein, who is recognized worldwide as a great innovator. The usual silly headshot wasn't going to work, hence the use of the full profile or somewhat less-than-expected images of Einstein. The other task this design had to address was the RGD branding. Previous years' materials had ignored the RGD visual brand. We embraced it. The red and black color scheme and the font usage is completely RGD."

Christie is a strong believer in the sketching phase of the design process. "Every project I tackle starts with drawings," Christie says. "They are very rough and in some cases legible only to me. They do, however, lay out each item the conference required, including a bag. From here I went straight to blowing up one image of Einstein to 12" x 18" (30.5 cm x 45.5 cm). This is the only layout I did to sell the job."

Meanwhile, other designers created mockups for the conference because Pylon believes that competition produces the best results. Each idea is judged internally first, then a shortlist is presented to the client. RGD chose Christie's concept to be developed further.

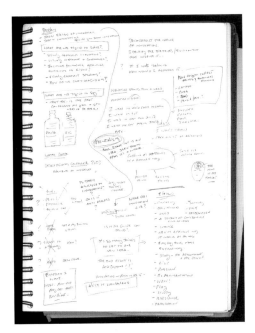
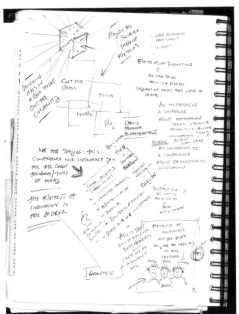
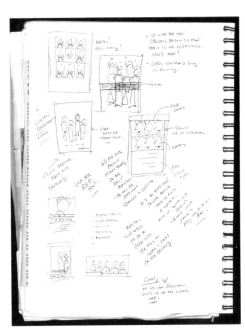

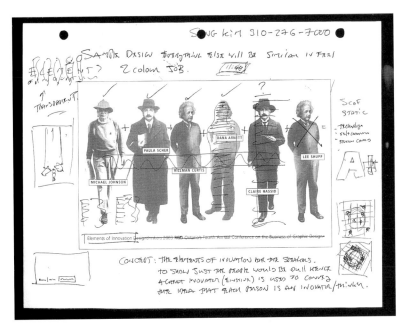

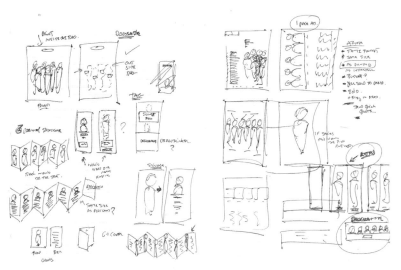

"I approach projects by reading all of the available information, seeking out competitor materials, then letting all of the information digest over a week or so," says Christie. "Then I usually escape to a coffee shop somewhere and start brainstorming by myself. In most cases, something comes to me. If not, I find it is because I don't know enough about the project and need to ask more questions. Questions are very important in developing and choosing a solution.

"The design solution is often found in the words," Christie says. "That's why I always read and always sketch. I think the biggest secret I have about layout is to not design with the grid in mind. I usually design my layouts first, visually, by eye, then later, if needed, I will develop a grid."

Christie says he never dreamed how much the decision to use Einstein in the materials would affect the project. "The biggest challenge—and most frustrating point—in the design was getting approval to use the Einstein images. I had no idea that the Richman Agency would be allowed to have a say in the design. They would not allow us to place the speakers' names on top of the Einstein images. Therefore, all of our designs had to work around this one obstacle."

In addition to their design demands, the Richman Agency got Pylon's entire budget just for the rights to use Einstein's image.

Christie says most of his inspiration comes from magazines and the occasional book. He says it was a recent book called *The Art of Innovation: Lessons in Creativity* by Tom Kelley that inspired the ultimate solution for the DesignThinkers conference materials because of its unorthodox approach to finding creative inspiration in unusual places and things.

Perhaps the biggest and most surprising impact the conference materials had was on one of the scheduled speakers, Elsie Maio. She originally had cancelled her appearance, but when she received the postcard announcing the conference, she changed her mind. It turns out she is a huge fan of Einstein and brought up the conference materials on numerous occasions—proving that you never know who will be impacted the most by a project. Naturally, Pylon gave Maio a conference poster as a keepsake.

Solutions at Work (S.A.W.) is the nonprofit partner of the Cuyahoga Board of Mental Retardation and Developmental Disabilities, the largest employer of people who have disabilities in Ohio.

Enspace ultimately added a belly band to the S.A.W. annual report when they were told there was extra room on the press sheet. The budget limited the cover to one color, but the band adds a welcome punch.

Cleveland-based design firm Enspace, Inc., has a history of community involvement and actively pursued a creative partnership with S.A.W. that has lasted for the last five years.

"In 2001, S.A.W. was undergoing structural and ideological changes," says art director Jennifer Visocky O'Grady. "It was important for the annual report to present the positive energy fueling these transformations. S.A.W. has dual responsibilities, serving both as a corporate entity servicing the Cleveland and Cuyahoga County business communities, and as an outlet of growth and social exchange for individuals with mental retardation and developmental disabilities. By focusing on the name of the company, Solutions At Work, and using 'we' statements that speak directly to the viewer, we were able to illuminate the myriad ways S.A.W. is a valued community partner.

"Our process for every job consists of several phases," says Visocky O'Grady. "We start with loads of research, including in-depth client interviews. We then distill that information while brainstorming on concepts. When we've got a solid idea, we take a big-picture approach to the project—in this case, information architecture before aesthetics. When we've got the content and pagination worked out, we jump into the design. Our design team still uses plain old pencils and graph paper when we tackle the sketch phase of a project, which allows us to prototype quickly, share rough visual concepts, and determine what directions to pursue in more detail."

The initial concepts and sketches presented the information visually. To get the right combination of information and graphics, Enspace spent a lot of time inside S.A.W. "Our designers have toured a number of the S.A.W. facilities and work enclaves and have spent a great deal of time interviewing management and staff," notes Visocky O'Grady. "There is a wealth of positive energy and empowerment running through every level of the organization."

Despite their history of working together, Enspace still faced the challenge of communicating important aspects about the nonprofit organization. "S.A.W. is simultaneously a human services provider and a business entity," says Visocky O'Grady. "This single marketing piece needed to reach a business audience that focuses on numbers, efficiency ratings, and cost, as well as communicate the life-changing individual opportunities generated each working day. With every annual report that we design for S.A.W., we are challenged with shifting a paradigm and presenting the extensive abilities and strengths of the disabled public."

The contrast between the visual background and the focus on numbers was an idea that came about after the team sketched

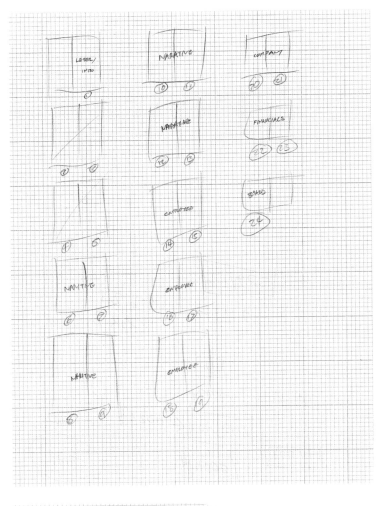

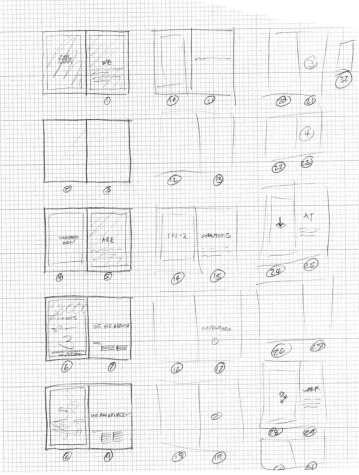

potential page designs. "We wanted to show the numbers in some sort of abstract context—something that may not make a complete connection until the captions at the bottom of the page are read," Visocky O'Grady points out, "An idea that is slightly out of context can make a lasting impression on viewers, as well as force them to make connections. This approach works well for S.A.W. because it fits in with the overall theme of showing the ability of the disabled. It shows readers new connections, maybe changes their impression of the community S.A.W. assists."

Another reason Enspace chose to emphasize numbers was the timing of the annual report's publication. "We wanted to show concrete, definitive examples of how S.A.W. is a solution for persons with mental retardation and developmental disabilities, as well as a solution in the business community," Visocky O'Grady says. "Focusing on these impressive numbers allows S.A.W. to show off their strengths as a human service and business entity. Also, by using the large numbers and the statements about what they mean, the narrative functions at a quick glance. As you progress into the narrative, each one of the 'We are' statements is expounded upon in greater detail. We felt that this approach was effective for a sales presentation or as a marketing piece, which are the primary roles for this annual report. In addition, we emphasized positive numbers because the financial performance for S.A.W., as well as many other businesses, was down in 2001. By creating an association with numbers not related to money, we shifted value to positive occurrences in a year when everyone's bottom line was hurting. Furthermore, the addition of the arrow was important to show growth in each category. It shows stability for both the businesses that S.A.W. works with, as well as the families of the people they employ.

"The cover is always the last thing we design on a project like this," says Visocky O'Grady. "After designing the narrative and the rest of the report, we wanted to do something that would contrast sharply with the large images and fields of text. Also, our budget dictated that we print the cover 1/0, so we were limited in what we were able to do. That said, we decided to focus on the title and the full name of S.A.W. with a simple typographic treatment."

One way Enspace added color and a more dynamic feel to the annual report overall was by using a belly band. "From a production standpoint, we had some room left over on the press sheet, and we wanted to use it," says O'Grady. "S.A.W.'s budget allowed for the cover to be printed 1/0. We thought the belly band would be a good way for the narrative and colors to be incorporated onto the cover."

Although a good choice for the cover, the belly band would come back to haunt Enspace in the end. Due to a combination of budget woes and miscommunication between service providers, Enspace was left with belly bands that weren't glued together. The studio bribed relatives and friends to help them apply 5,000 bands over a weekend. Thanks to their commitment to go the extra mile, the annual was sent on time and was a big hit.

◁ Enspace still uses pencils and graph paper when they tackle the sketch phase of a project. Notice how each sketch phase gets more and more detailed. Each new sample shows the layout getting more specific.

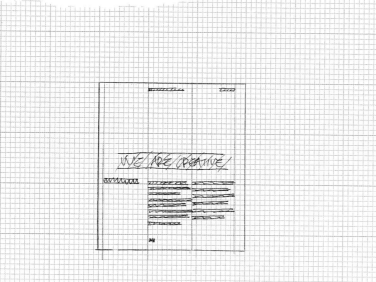

WE ARE!

WE ARE CREATIVE — PLUE PRINT, BUBBLE GUM, MACHINE, ART

WE ARE GROWING — GRASS, FLOWERS, TREES

WE ARE RELIABLE — .....?

WE ARE ACHIEVERS — HANDS, WORKERS

WE ARE PARTNERS —

Finally, the look and feel of the report began to take shape as copy came into play to balance the visual emphasis of the piece.

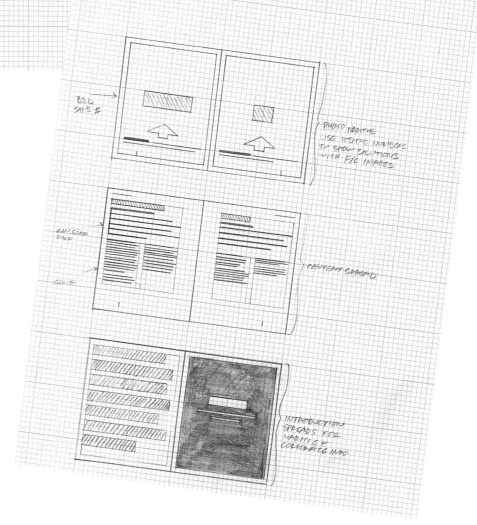

A miniature mockup of the annual report shows the design concept coming into view. Last-minute changes are often made at this stage, before the final product goes to print.

Because S.A.W. was experiencing both structural and ideological changes, Enspace used dramatic photographs to capture the positive energy behind the transformations.

Sequoia Hospital

Joshua Chen, of Chen Design Associates in San Francisco, **jumped at the chance** to revamp the **entire brand** of Sequoia Hospital, which is based in Redwood City, California. The process **called for a total redesign**

The newsletter is purposely designed to stand out in the mail because the front side, rather than just the back, is exposed.

of the brand's marketing materials, including media kits, brochures, newsletters, and fact sheets.

"The bulk of the initial marketing plan was to create a newsletter that the hospital could send out to the community," says art director Joshua Chen. "But as we met and talked about the strategy and their needs, it became evident that a media kit was something they could really use. We looked at some of the foundational challenges that they were facing and what we could do to overcome those. We pretty much started from the ground up again. We did a communications audit and audited all of their print materials and collateral, as well as their signage and the on-site look and feel. We did the same with their competitors and came up with a systematic way of rating what images were presented. Then we presented this analysis in a report with our recommendations and idea for what needed to happen to move forward."

The first design solution was to create a new logo for the hospital as a whole. However, due to complications with the parent company, Sequoia decided at the last minute not to roll out the branding for the hospital and opted simply to use the logo that was selected for the newsletter throughout the media kit.

"Among competing hospitals, we found an overuse of red and bright blue. We concluded that a more refined color palette would better speak to the overall level of quality that Sequoia has to offer," notes Chen. "Accordingly, we used more muted and cross-processed photography. The limitations—if we had to call it that—were mostly in the client's general resistance to something new and unfamiliar, but that's where concept comes in. If an idea solves the problem well enough, the client will often come around."

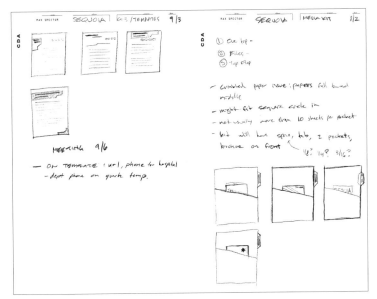

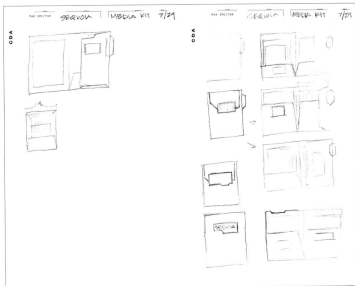

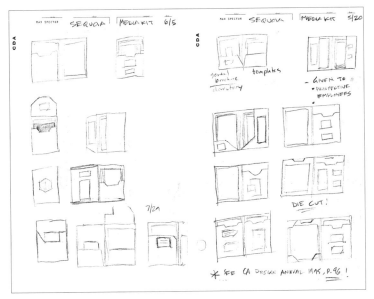

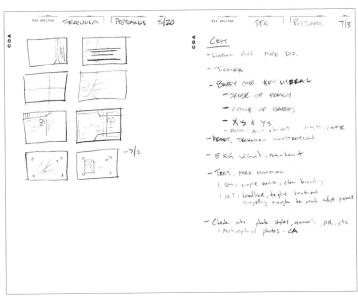

⊗ Early sketches show the progression of concepts for both the postcards and the structure of the media kit folder and how the media kit's elements would fit together.

Like many hospitals, Sequoia wanted to be perceived as "high-tech/high-touch"—highly technical but also highly attentive and caring. When researching the visual identities of competing hospitals, Chen saw a noticeable trend toward overstating the high-touch aspect while disregarding the high-tech. He wanted to implement a more fine-tuned and contemporary balance of the two ideals while being careful not to repeat the clichéd and trite imagery that so many hospitals use. Instead, he opted to use more dynamic crops, unusual angles, and sophisticated composition.

"In all of the Sequoia Hospital pieces are a lot of places where that high-tech idea is expressed through graphical elements, such as lines and geometrical shapes. The high-touch concept is expressed not through traditional hospital photography where everyone is happy but through photography that is a little more engaging and a little more emotional. Those are the two main ways visually that we wanted to launch," Chen says. "In terms of the flexibility of the typefaces and the color palette, that was another thing where we set up a visual toolbox. We could mix and match within the toolbox and still give the client something that was consistent across the board and would continue to be fresh

and able to evolve. The other thing we needed to create—because there are so many different departments with so many different needs and emphases—was a visual toolbox. It needed to allow flexibility, for instance to be able to use one color more prominently in a piece for radiology versus using more text-driven elements for another area, yet still making sure everything felt like it was part of a family.

"We presented three different directions for the folder, and this one went through. Structurally, it didn't go through many revisions, but in terms of color and design, it went through several more," says Chen. "I think structurally they were really happy with something that stood out from everyone else's stuff. They liked the tab on the side so people could file it and find it easily. They liked the unusual opening factor because you have to think about it to use it. Designwise it was more of a challenge in terms of color and the layout.

"The newsletter actually had more constraints on its own, apart from the folder," Chen says. "Because it was being sent to 90,000 people—a huge mailing—it was absolutely necessary that we stay

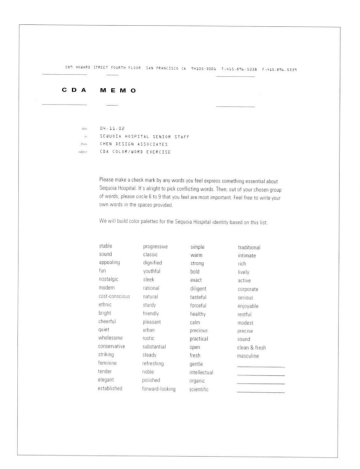

CARE

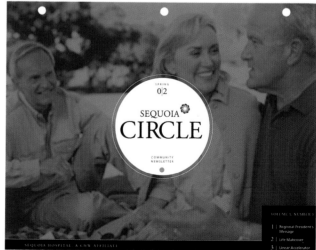

SEQUOIA ⬡
CIRCLE
SPRING
0|2
COMMUNITY
NEWSLETTER

SEQUOIA ⬡
CIRCLE
SPRING
0|2
COMMUNITY
NEWSLETTER

⊘ A visual toolbox consisting of a color palette and type treatments was developed so consistency could be maintained throughout all of the Sequoia materials.

⊘ Initially, Chen was hired only to redesign the newsletter, but as the project unfolded, he saw that a media kit would better serve Sequoia's needs.

within postal regulations. But even so, we were able to push the regulations a little bit in a more unconventional way. You'll notice that the mail panel is actually on the side of the front cover. That placement really allowed us to fold the newsletter out instead of in. With most mailed newsletters you see the back page first. The way we did it, the front side was out. Visually, that was something we really wanted to ensure it stood out from all of the other mail people get."

Chen notes that his approach to design projects begins with laying the groundwork before any concepts are created. "We definitely have a process that we follow, and although it varies from client to client, there are definite phases that we go through," says Chen. "Visually, what we'd like to be known for is that we don't have a specific style when we go into a project. We really believe that the style should inform and support the objective at hand. We don't go into something with preconceived ideas. We do a lot of research—looking at competitors and then looking at their audience and who they need to communicate with, coming up with visuals. When we have that groundwork, the rest is pretty straightforward."

Sequoia's press kit was a huge success that still garners a lot of attention, even after the fact.

⊘ Early versions of the newsletter emphasized the community connection by using a larger number of full-color photographs of individuals. The photos later were reduced in number and muted to match the rest of the marketing materials.

Chen shied away from traditional photography found in most hospital brochures and materials and instead chose more emotionally engaging photography, which was muted and cross-processed.

The Sequoia Hospital postcards were formatted to make an impression on the recipient by using ample white space and perforating a small portion of the card.

SGF The Société générale de financement du Québec, or SGF— a Canadian **investment firm and financial partner** with **technology-based businesses**—needed a dual-purpose publication for their **annual report.**

◈ Four different versions of the annual report were printed in four different colors. The report was also printed in two languages, French and English.

◈ The inside full-color spread stands out from the rest of the annual report because the section highlights the variety of the Quebec landscape. The section is flanked by a financial breakdown.

They wanted something that would serve not only as an annual report but also as a promotional brochure to entice foreign investors. For the fifth consecutive year, SGF tapped Montreal-based Gauthier Associés Designers to create the document.

"Our challenge was to create a product that was both high-tech and understated," says art director Paulo Correia. "A judicious choice of visual elements helped us achieve our goal and impart a modern and avant-garde look—two sought-after qualities on the international market. The contrasting textures (metallic and offset paper), the association of media (printed and electronic), and the use of nonconventional materials (vinyl sleeve) create a stimulating visual environment."

In addition to the important mandate to present the advantages of investing in Quebec, Gauthier set out to change misconceptions about the province. For instance, contrary to popular opinion outside of North America, winter is not a year-round season in Quebec. With this in mind, Gauthier purposefully chose a seasonal theme to showcase the changing seasons of the province.

"The regions of Quebec served as the basis of our inspiration," Correia says. "The vastness of the territory and the changing seasonal landscapes are rich in imagery and great sources of inspiration. The annual report shows off Quebec as if readers were on a trip through the province.

"Because the SGF is a government agency, we opted for a streamlined page layout," says Correia. "Counterbalancing this simplicity are varying color covers, a central spread rich in color and images, and vertical stripes that accentuate the SGF's dynamic nature. It's the combination of this mix that produces a unique publication. Two-page spreads of black-and-white photos start off each section of the annual report and balance the color elements.

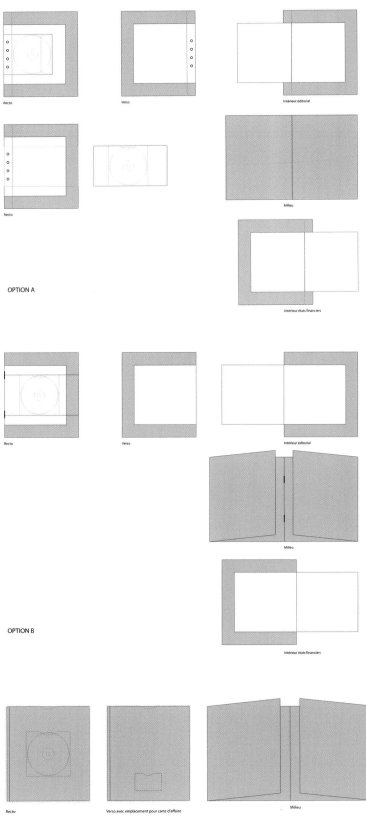

Recto

Verso

Intérieur éditorial

OPTION A

Milieu

Intérieur états financiers

Recto

Verso

Intérieur éditorial

OPTION B

Milieu

Intérieur états financiers

Recto

Verso avec emplacement pour carte d'affaire

Milieu

OPTION C

Gauthier developed several different options for incorporating the CD-ROM into the annual report and having it fit into the overall design.

These frescos conjure up notions of strength and solidity—qualities embodied by the SGF.

"Although multiple elements had to be considered for both print and electronic formats, it is the sleeve that packages all of the elements into a whole," Correia says. "The report also serves as a valuable tool to stimulate interest during international exchanges."

The report's unusual format hints at the rest of the document's originality. Beyond the uncommon binding, with the center spread in cover stock, the report is flexible and easy to consult—an important feature given the twofold purpose of the publication. The original packaging sleeve houses the different media (a printed report and CD-ROM) and their complimentary information.

"We proposed a document that would showcase Quebec's uniqueness," says Lisa Tremblay, Gauthier's president. "By using four covers in different colors and four landscapes, we evoke each season's distinctiveness. The originality of the document and its packaging reflects Quebec's inherent creativity and diversity. The colors were chosen to represent the distinct seasons in Quebec (blue for winter, yellow for spring, green for summer, and orange for fall). The central insert, continuing the seasonal theme with full-color photos, illustrates the diversity of the landscape. This insert draws attention to an important part of the annual report—the SGF's portfolio of partner companies found on the CD-ROM."

"The challenge was to infuse originality into a corporate document on investments," says Correia. "The document attracts attention with its unusual format and packaging. Managing the information and balancing the visual elements for different media (printed and electronic) proved to be a challenge of a different nature.

"For the review of activities, we chose to illustrate the SGF's sectors of activity with concrete representations of those sectors," says Correia. "These visual elements also serve to structure the interactive portfolio of partner companies on the CD-ROM. An interactive CD-ROM complements the review of activities with additional information. The disk contains the SGF's portfolio—an indispensable tool for business development."

Ultimately, the balance between the two functions—annual report and promotional brochure—is found in the difference between page spreads. Like postcards, the landscape spreads evoke travel and discovery, with their inherent value being promotional. In contrast, the report spreads are pared down and simplified to their factual and informative basics, to keep investors focused on economic realities.

Gauthier got some unexpected reactions the day the report made its debut at an annual meeting of SGF's employees. Thinking there was some difference in the reports, people wandered about, curiously finding out what color document others had received. However, once employees understood the reason for the differently colored covers, they breathed a sigh of relief and applauded Gauthier's creative effort.

Another unexpected surprise of the SGF annual report is its importance within Gauthier Designers. The document has become somewhat of a benchmark at Gauthier. Designers and agencies in the Quebec design community ask Gauthier about the publication on a regular basis. No wonder it has received both a *HOW Magazine* Award and a Summit Award.

PRINTEMPS Lorem ipsum dolor sit amet, consectetuer adipiscing elit, sed diam nonu mmy nibh euismod tincidunt ut laoreet dolore magna aliquam erat volutpat. Ut wisi enim ad minim veniam. Quis nostrud exerci tation ullamcorper suscipit ETE lobortis nisl ut aliquip ex ea commodo consequat. Ut wisi enim. Lorem ipsum dolor sit amet, consectetuer adipiscing elit, sed diam nonu mmy nibh euismod tincidunt ut laoreet dolore magna aliquam erat volutpat. Ut wisi enim ad minim veniam.

AUTOMNE Euismod tincidunt ut laoreet dolore magna aliqua erat volutpat. Ut wisi enim ad minim veniam. Quis nostrud maela exerci tation ullamcorper suscipit lobortis nisl ut aliquip ex ea commodo consequat Ut wisi enim. HIVER Lorem ipsum dolor sit amet, consectetuer adipiscing elit, sed diam nonu mmy nibh euismod tincidunt ut laoreet dolore magna aliquam erat volutpat.

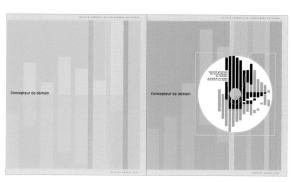

⊘ Top: The breakdown of clients or investors and their respective locations proved to be a challenge to lay out. Because the CD-ROM contains most of the data, referring to the CD was a necessity.

⊘ Above: A color scheme for the covers was chosen to reflect the changing seasons as it pertains to the environment in Quebec. The scheme is broken down by CMYK combinations.

⊗ Gauthier tests different color combinations and CD-ROM sleeves for the cover and back, respectively.

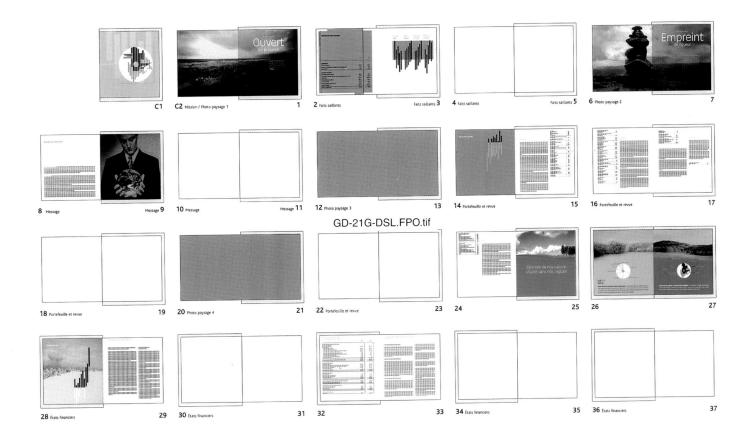

GD-21G-DSL.FPO.tif

⬡ Top: A thumbnail of the annual shows the placement of each color photograph and a breakdown of page structure, including the financial sections.

⬡ A combination of images depicting the landscape
⬡ of the province was considered for the four-color spread at the center of the report. Eventually, Gauthier selected the spring and winter combination for the front and back of the center section.

Song (Delta Airlines)

Song (Delta Airlines) For their new low-cost, spin-off carrier, Song, Delta Airlines wanted **a teaser campaign** designed to **pique employee interest** through a series of posters. Delta turned to **Leo Burnett,** their ad agency of record, for assistance in **conceiving the campaign.**

Leo Burnett art directors and staff members had never seen cross-processes (multiple color processes) work before and were enamored with how Templin Brink achieved the effect.

Leo Burnett took the campaign as far as they could and called on Templin Brink Design, in San Francisco, for help. At that point, Templin Brink had only one week to design the posters and one week to have them printed before their nationwide debut in airports and Delta headquarters.

Working under a tight deadline is a way of life for most design firms, but this turnaround was unusually tight for such an important project, says art director Joel Templin. "We had the basic concept, for which they had written the copy. The posters were meant to be a teaser, so if you worked for Delta and found them humorous, then you were the right person to switch over to Song," says Templin. "Leo Burnett did lay the groundwork with the copy, so we didn't have to create the whole concept—a big time-saver for us."

Despite the time limitation, Templin Brink came up with two different directions that they presented to the client. "We went the illustration route because we immediately thought of old in-flight safety cards and how they were illustrated. We thought it might be interesting to do a graphic approach that way," Templin says. "One concept didn't have all of the illustrations in it, so it was even more graphic. In a way, the timing might have worked to our advantage because they didn't have a lot of time to think about it.

"We decided to create engaging, fun posters to set the tone of this new 'no frills' airline and capture people's imagination," says Templin. "For example, the copy for one of the posters was the question *Can you tell the difference between people and cattle?— If you can, you are clearly the right fit for Song.*"

To create the poster illustrations, Templin improvised and had his wife pose as the flight attendant. Another designer's spouse had an uncle who posed as the pilot. No one posed as the cow, of course, but the cow they did use in the illustration wasn't even real—they took the head from one cow and put it on the body of another. For the rest of the illustrations, Templin says he pulled photography to trace from because neither he nor his staff members are illustrators.

For the color scheme, Templin chose a bold mix that would be sure to capture employees' attention. Templin says the bright and cheery colors were chosen to compete directly with JetBlue and Southwest. He wanted to "pump up the volume a little bit."

⊘ Inspired by early flight-safety cards and airline memorabilia, Templin Brink tried to capture the nostalgia of the early days of commercial flying.

Although Templin Brink was originally asked to work only on the internal teaser campaign, their work really struck a chord at Delta. In fact, the posters were such a big hit that Delta asked for a series of follow-up postcards to send to prospects and current employees. "Some people felt that we captured the essence of the brand much better than what they were seeing from their branding agency," Templin says. "To make a long story short, we ended up branding the entire airline to illustrate our interpretation of how dynamic the Song brand could have been. Unfortunately, due to political reasons beyond our control, Delta never saw this work."

Templin says that he typically approaches projects without any preconceived ideas; he prefers to let the material be his guide. "We try to generate as many ideas as we can internally, but as far as always having a specific number that we present to the client, we present only what's for sale and what truly addresses their problem, who they are, and who their target audience is," says Templin. "If we have only two solid directions, that's what we present. m

"The first thing we do is peruse our resources here in the office—old books and magazines," says Templin. "We've got these radiology file cabinets filled with scrap and things like that. We page through things and pull out materials we feel might hit the mark or present the right tone. When we work with big clients on a large scale and we have a lot of time, we compile everything into a book that we call the 'design precedent book.' If we have time, we actually organize this material according to typography, layout, color, photography, illustration, and so on. It's a way to walk a client down several different visual avenues without actually doing design work. It's a huge visual world, so this book is a way to focus on a couple of different areas really quickly and show them to the client so they can be part of the process, too. This way, when we present design concepts and visuals, it's not just coming out of left field. The client feels more comfortable with it."

Templin says the response to the Song campaign was, in a word, incredible. If it hadn't been, he never would have had the chance to design the overall brand identity, despite the fact that Delta didn't see their efforts. However, Templin says the response that mattered the most was the one by current Delta employees. The turnout far exceeded expectations.

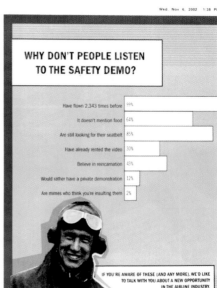

⊘ Leo Burnett sent Templin Brink their original concepts for the poster series for reference. The copy concept didn't change much, but the end result was a dramatic shift.

⊗ For most of the illustrations, Templin pulled photography to trace because none of his designers are illustrators.

⊘ Because Song is going to compete with low-cost carriers like JetBlue and Southwest, Templin Brink chose an attention-getting color scheme that communicates a high level of energy.

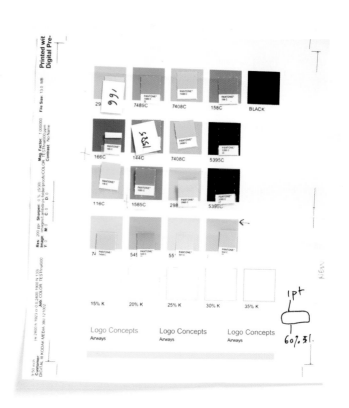

Can you tell the difference between People and Cattle?

These are People

These are Cattle

People carry Luggage

Cattle carry Milk

If you can...
...we'd like to talk with you about a new opportunity in the airline industry. Info available thru 12/20 at dalweb.delta-air.com/treshair

Do you know why passengers don't listen to the Safety Demo?

03 ENTRY EXAM

99% Have flown 2,343 times before

84% It doesn't mention food

85% Are still looking for their seatbelt

30% Have already rented the video

43% Believe in reincarnation

12% Would rather have a private demo

2% Are movie who think you're insulting them

If you do...
...we'd like to talk with you about a new opportunity in the airline industry. Info available thru 12/20 at dalweb.delta-air.com/freshair

Although they had only one week to create the teaser campaign, Templin Brink later was asked to do a series of postcards for the same campaign due to the success of their posters.

Sun Ice

Every year, **Gemini Fashions** of Winnipeg, Manitoba, designs and manufactures **a new line of snowboard and skiwear** under the brand name Sun Ice. An extremely popular brand in the 1980s, Sun Ice was **struggling to regain** some of its previous popularity.

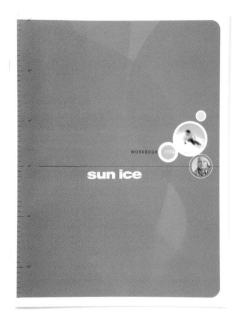

Attempting to revive a once-popular brand, Tétro Design applied a utilitarian feel to the new workbook for the upcoming selling season.

A workbook or catalog is produced once a year for retailers to place orders for the upcoming selling season. Tétro Design got the job because someone at Gemini had worked with them previously when working at a different apparel manufacturer.

"We stepped back and took a good look at the competition," says Tetrault. "Pages and pages of blue sky, perfect powdery snow, and some dude 25' (7.5 m) in the air performing a slick freestyle move surrounded by appropriately cutting-edge graphics and illegible type. What was truly remarkable was how much it all looked the same. We started to think that to really get noticed, we should buck the trend, go low-tech, low-fi, and clean. Thus, what had started as a problem actually became our solution.

"When we learned no actual garments were ready to photograph, we started to panic. What we were trying to sell is such an emotional product, how on earth was that going to come across without slick images of hot models in Sun Ice skiwear? How do you make a CAD drawing of a jacket and ski pants look cool and sexy? And what did we know about skiing and snowboarding, anyway? We're from Manitoba, the Canadian equivalent of Nebraska—flat as a pancake."

"The natural reflex for presenting a product accurately would have involved photography, especially with something as emotional as a fashion product. Unfortunately, the timing for this project did not allow for photography. The manufacturer was extremely behind schedule in developing that season's line of skiwear but faced an immediate need to unveil the entire line at the industry trade shows. On the positive side, the flat graphics did lend themselves to our no-nonsense approach and happened to shave off the expense of product photography and scanning."

Taking Gemini literally when they referred to the publication as a workbook, Tétro achieved the overall quality of the catalog by looking at old documents and books—things that were utilitarian in nature. Little touches of this aesthetic show up throughout the book but have been modernized to suit the product and market.

"Our intention had been to print the book on newsprint," Tetrault says. "We sent a sample of a European newsletter that had the tactile quality we wanted to the client. Then we searched for a fine paper that would perform to suit our needs but with a similar feel and color. What we found just so happened to be made from hemp.

"Initial thumbnails were all about establishing the fit and flow of information. Fitting an enormous amount of content to be digestible

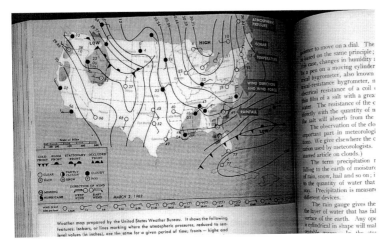

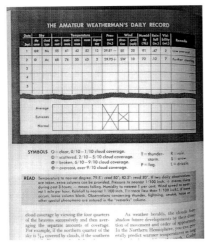

yet budget conscious—this was the most critical part of the project. The look and feel followed. Due to the time restrictions we presented only one option. Thankfully, the client really liked it. If you look at the original design presentation, it is virtually identical to the finished layout, other than some space-saving adjustments made on our part."

An early sketch for a cover concept shows wavy lines that represent hills, moguls, or snowdrifts. The final cover design and some internal spreads use a similar pattern rendered vertically in hot colors. The design was another way of standing out from the sea of blue and white materials in the market.

"Our biggest challenge by far was making sense of the huge amount of content supplied by the client. In total, there are about 150 garments represented in a 24-page book. In addition, the images we were given were produced in Autocad, in RGB color, which made for some production challenges." For example, many of the items looked the same, so after being converted to a different format had to be labeled accurately so the names corresponded with the correct garment.

Tétro took the word *workbook* literally and looked to old documents and books that were utilitarian in nature.

Tétro's initial brief contained specifications and decisions about the parameters within which they would have to work, including a grid design for the products.

Rather than wait for a call from Gemini when the workbook was printed, Tétro decided to call Sun Ice themselves. What they heard was silence. "After the book was delivered, we were really happy with the result and waited anxiously for a call from the client praising our superior talent and design prowess. When we finally called the client, he admitted that he had assumed the book was going to be on a glossy coated paper and didn't like the way it looked on the hemp stock." All Tetrault could do was shrug it off as a matter of personal preference. He says they're still trying to get the client over his fear of uncoated stock.

After the workbook was completed, Tétro Design received several awards and recognitions, including being featured in *Applied Arts* Awards Annual 2002, *HOW International* Design Annual 2002, and *Graphis* Magazine.

In this case, although the workbook itself got some distinction, the product itself did not fare as well. As with any project, many factors affect the outcome. The initiative to resuscitate the Sun Ice brand, although suitable in theory, turned out to be underfunded and not adequately supported by the parent company. Eventually, Gemini dropped the brand entirely.

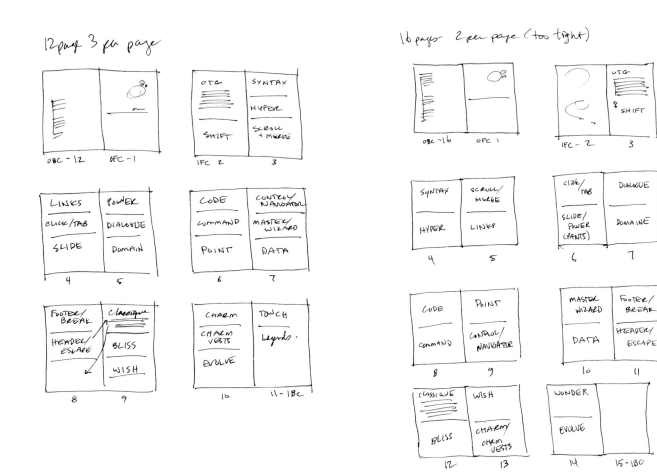

⊘ Thumbnail sketches of the pages accounted for different layout schemes featuring two and three products per page.

⊘ An early sketch of the workbook cover showed wavy lines representing hills, moguls, or snowdrifts. The final design used this same pattern rendered vertically in hot colors, creating flame forms.

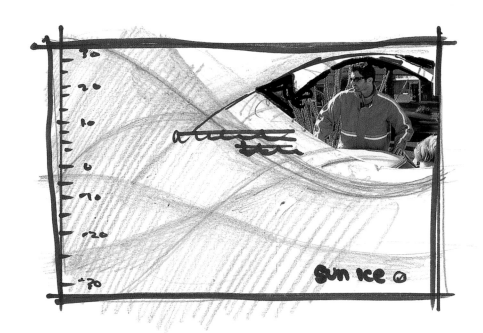

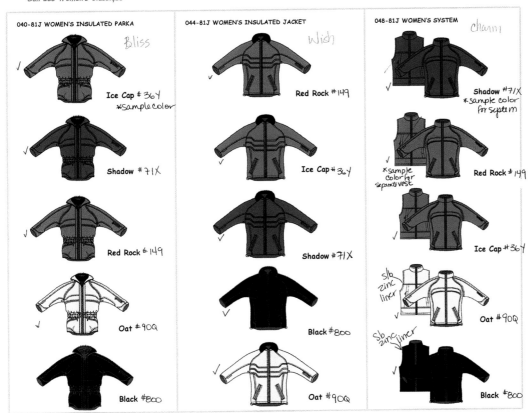

040-81J WOMEN'S INSULATED PARKA

Bliss

Ice Cap #364
Sample color

Shadow #71X

Red Rock #149

Oat #90Q

Black #800

044-81J WOMEN'S INSULATED JACKET

Widh

Red Rock #149

Ice Cap #364

Shadow #71X

Black #800

Oat #90Q

048-81J WOMEN'S SYSTEM

Charm

Shadow #71X
sample color for system

sample color for separate vest

Red Rock #149

Ice Cap #364

s/b zinc liner
Oat #90Q

s/b zinc liner
Black #800

Tétro had only CAD drawings to work with for the product images. There wasn't time or money to shoot the products, but the technical appearance contributed to the overall workbook quality and lent a fresh look in the final spreads shown below.

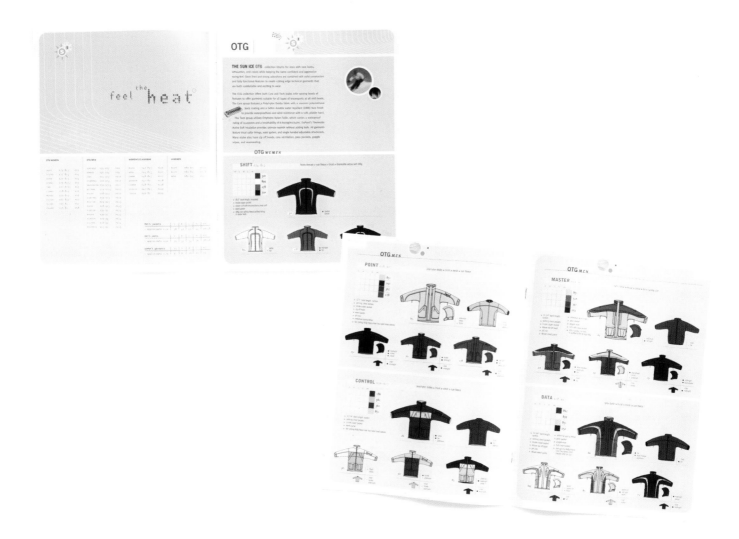

Taylor Guitars is one of the finest instrument makers in the world. Every two years or so, Taylor develops **a new line of acoustic guitars.** Their catalog and website are the key communication vehicles for the release of the new lines.

⊗ Even after 10 years of working together, Mires Brands
⊗ still loves tackling a new Taylor Guitar catalog. This
⊗ particular version captures a "day in the life" of
Southern California musicians and performers.

Mires Brands has collaborated with Taylor almost 10 years, so when a new catalog was needed for the 2002 line, Mires got the call.

"In addition to showcasing the full line of Taylor Guitars, we wanted to connect with the Taylor experience, highlighting the deep connection between people and their guitars," says creative director Scott Mires. "It was also important to create an educational resource that brought to life what it takes to develop an exceptional acoustic guitar. Ultimately, we wanted a piece that musicians would covet and refer back to as they prepared to purchase a Taylor.

"The sketches and early layouts were used to convey the essence of the story," Mires says. "They allowed the client to understand where we were heading and steered that process to ensure it met their needs. The sketches formed the roadmap and springboard for the efforts of everyone involved—copywriter, designer, photographer, client, and printer."

For inspiration, Mires talked with actual Taylor owners in the Southern California area about their unique and compelling stories. "We identified 30 to 40 musicians, and out of those we interviewed more deeply between 20 and 25 of them. We spent a day with them to capture their life and how Taylor played a part in it," Mires says. "For each person, we shot at two or three different locations. That whole body of work from the photo shoot ended up being the brand visuals for Taylor, so their print collateral, price lists, website, and a lot of the key touch points for their brand were represented by that lifestyle imagery.

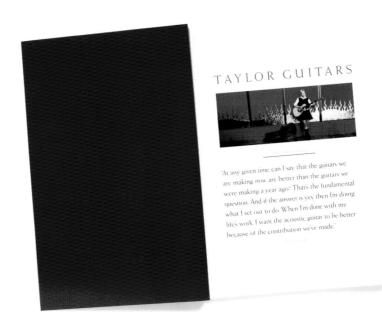

(SIG. SERIES)

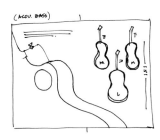

(ACOU. BASS)

#1 = A COUPLING OF 2 GUITARS
(LARGE AND MEDIUM) CLOSE
TOGETHER OR ONE IN FRONT
OF THE OTHER ... A SEPARATE
MED-SIZE AT TOP

CHART INFO TO RT OF NECKS

#2 = 2 MED-SIZE GUITARS AT TOP
1 LARGE GUITAR CENTERED BELOW
CHART INFO TO RT. OF NECKS

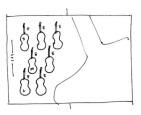

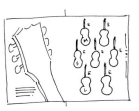

#1 = 3, 2 + 2 GUITAR GROUPINGS
SML, MED, LRG RESPECTIVELY
CHART INFO TO RT. OF NECKS

#2 = 2, 3 + 2 GROUPINGS
MED, SML + LRG RESPECTIVELY
CHART INFO TO RT OF NECK OR BODY

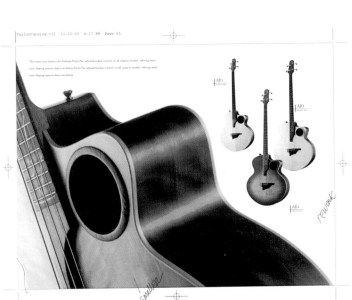

⊗ First, the designer tackled the task of sketching out spreads with varying numbers of guitars. Given that the catalog would be 71 pages long and feature nearly a hundred different versions of guitars, this was a crucial step in the design process.

⊗ With as many as seven guitars to show on each page, Mires sketched several possibilities of different product groupings. The effort was truly collaborative because ideas were taken from all team members.

"Originally, we had three concept options for the direction of the catalog," Mires says. "When a concept was selected, we continued to refine that concept through multiple iterations. It's a living, breathing process that is flexible and allows the design to be refined and improved every step of the way. The piece is not done until it comes rolling off the press—we produce press proofs to refine at that stage as well.

"It wasn't like we completely worked out three different ways. Usually, it's rougher than that. One approach might be more lifestyle driven with a certain kind of a layout. Another approach might be more product driven with a different kind of a layout. A lot of clients want to feature their product, prominently in a catalog, and we did that in this piece. We worked on the still-life product photography very carefully. But at the end of the day, shouldn't one approach be more important than the other? Well, with Taylor, they wanted a nice balance between the two."

Capturing the nuances and brilliance of a product for a catalog usually isn't difficult if you have a great photographer. However, with the Taylor catalog, Mires found it challenging to capture the beauty and craftsmanship of the guitars because of their finish. "It's almost like photographing a mirror. Guitars are so shiny they reflect the light," Mires says. "It's a very tough assignment. Optimizing of the final guitar images required an incredible amount of time and effort, everything from working on the definition of the strings and frets to maintaining the incredibly faint detail of an Engelmann Spruce guitar top. Trying to print what the eye sees—when it comes to a beautiful acoustic guitar—is part art, part science, and lots of blood, sweat, and tears."

Given this requirement for attention to detail, Mires encountered a rather frightening obstacle when he lost his scheduled photographer to a family emergency two weeks before shooting. Fortunately, another talented photographer was in the area and agreed to do the project on the same budget.

When it comes to design philosophy, Mires says he believes less is usually more. "I like reducing things to their essence," says Mires. "I'm also in tune with touching people in a more emotional or personal way. I like visual imagery that connects with people and their lifestyle—not necessarily what you are marketing but how it affects your life. I like to create tactile pieces that you just couldn't throw away and that have enduring value. Sometimes it's hard skirting that issue of art and commerce."

Mires says one of the most rewarding aspects to designing the Taylor catalog is the feedback from actual buyers, passed on to him by the marketing director. Over the years, Taylor has discovered that the dealers have firsthand experience with how well the catalogs sell the guitars. In fact, their research shows the dealers repeatedly say they view the catalog as the most important tool that Taylor uses to sell guitars and grow the brand.

"The takeaway is that if the process is successful, the job was successful," Mires says. "If the client wants to repeat that process, you did a good job." Considering Taylor and Mires are in their tenth year of working together, Mires can rest easy that his work speaks for itself.

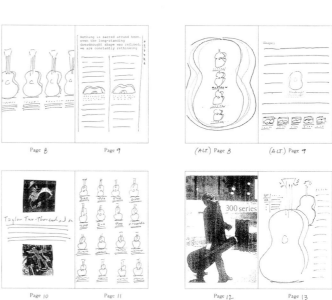

⬡ The entire catalog was created in thumbnail size before the team agreed on a final layout. Photography played a critical role in deciding what guitar models to match with various performers and musicians.

Cover – Option A

Cover – Option B

Cover – Option C

Cover – Option D

Inside Front Cover

Page 1 – Option A

Inside Front Cover

Page 1 – Option B
Fly Sheet

Several different cover ideas were sketched out and thumbnail versions were pasted up so the design team and client could come to an agreement. A photograph from the photo shoot was eventually chosen for the cover image.

The final catalog beautifully illustrates the lifestyle and product combination for Taylor Guitars that Mires was trying to achieve.

University of Illinois

As for many of their other design projects, Chicago-based **Faust Associates** got the job to **create** the University of Illinois at Urbana-Champaign's Master of Fine Arts in Art and Education **exhibition catalog** through an existing relationship.

⊗ Can a Midwestern institution's art and design program strike a balance between the regularity in the landscape and irregularity of the work product? It helps when a former alumni is designing the project.

Principal and art director Bob Faust had maintained a friendship with his former professor, Ken Carls, who was promoted to interim director at his alma mater. When Carls asked Faust about the possibility of working together, Faust jumped at the chance.

Every year, the University of Illinois at Urbana-Champaign, MFA candidates have an exhibition featuring their work created during the course of their studies at the university. A catalog traditionally had been produced to document the exhibit, which assists the graduates in their postgraduate employment and representation search. In the past, the program had used the limited general school funds to create the exhibition catalog, which always had hindered their ability to be more experimental or conceptual in design. As a result, an outside designer never had been hired to produce the catalog.

This particular year, however, Carls found that a restricted grant had been overlooked—one that would assist in covering both the production and design costs associated with creating a more captivating catalog. Moreover, these funds had accumulated for two years and had to be used, according to their restrictions, within a specific timeframe for this specific purpose.

"With the grant, we now had the flexibility to produce something that had serious potential to market these students in a format that almost surpasses the exhibition catalogs that galleries produce," Faust says. "First we addressed the issue of establishing a visual vocabulary based on their location. There was some question of whether to upstage their location, because it is a barrier for some who cannot believe that credible artists can thrive in the Midwest. The fact is they can and they do, so we really played it up by asking for editorial copy that showed parallels between the fertile landscape of the Midwest and the 'fertile' ground for nurturing artists at the University of Illinois. What resulted was a visually amazing catalog with compelling content.

"We talked through three or four forms that the book could take on and then pursued one wholeheartedly," says Faust. "Most of the early exploration was to decide how the programmatic information would be treated: Would it be integrated or separated or some combination of the two. Ultimately, we did both."

After getting a firm grip on the main purpose of the catalog, Faust began to think about a possible secondary purpose for the catalog. The program had never had a marketing piece created, so Faust saw the opportunity to have an impact carry beyond promoting graduates to attracting prospective students to the school.

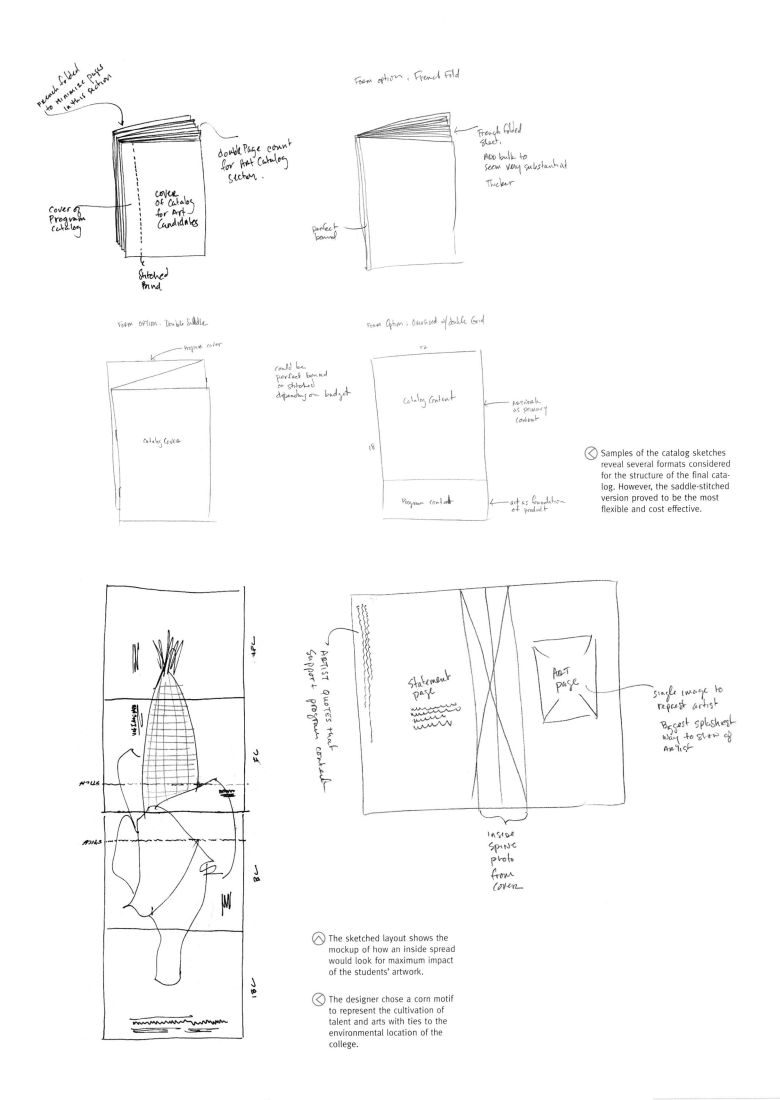

French folded pages to minimize pages in this section

double page count for Art Catalog section.

Cover of Program catalog

Cover of Catalog for Art Candidates

Stitched Bind

Form option: French Fold

French folded sheet. Add bulk to seem very substantial Thicker

Perfect bound

Form Option: Double Saddle

Program cover

Catalog Cover

Form Option: Oversized w/ double Grid

12

Catalog Content

18

Program content

Artwork as primary content

act as foundation of product

could be perfect bound or stitched depending on budget

⊘ Samples of the catalog sketches reveal several formats considered for the structure of the final catalog. However, the saddle-stitched version proved to be the most flexible and cost effective.

STITCH

STITCH

Artist quotes that support program content

Statement Page

Art Page

single image to represt artist

Biggest splash/best way to show of Artist

Inside Spine photo from cover

△ The sketched layout shows the mockup of how an inside spread would look for maximum impact of the students' artwork.

⊘ The designer chose a corn motif to represent the cultivation of talent and arts with ties to the environmental location of the college.

"Many concepts were discussed that largely revolved around pre-conceived notions about a valid art education coming out of a Midwestern institution," says Faust. "Would using Midwestern icons turn off potential students who might mistakenly label the school as conservative? The question became whether to celebrate or avoid the context of the work product in the school's immediate surrounding environment—vast fields of corn."

When Faust got the opening "fan" letter from Los Angeles–based artist, writer, and educator Christopher Miles—the content of which emphasized the surprising lack of regional influences in the work of the graduates—he felt he could turn up the volume on a regional concept. That's how an enormous ear of corn landed on the cover.

"We did some word association and came up with fields, fertile plains, growing, cultivating, corn hybrids, and crops," says Faust. "Soon we developed a more romantic perspective of the students' work product in relationship to their exterior environment. They weren't a body of students. They were a crop of students. While at the school, this crop was being nurtured by the fertile ground upon which they landed. At the school, they were growing from art students into artists through a visionary liberal arts program, one-dimensional in its locational perspective but multidimensional in its educational perspective."

Ultimately, Faust found a way to insert the marketing aspect into the catalog by using the spine for information about the school. "Formally, the program information is housed as a separate brochure in the spine," Faust says. "Conceptually, this structure reinforces the idea of the school being the support system for the artist as well as the linking device to the world and each other. We also added quotes running vertically from the students about the program on all of the exhibition pages. The vertical alignment references the orientation of the program catalog while remaining true to the student content found on the exhibition pages."

Faust prefers to approach each project with imagination and creative freedom so he doesn't get stuck with limitations. "When I start out, I like to think about possibility without worrying too much about usability," says Faust. "Much of the time, what you know gets in the way of what can be. If there is a great idea, figuring out how to do it is the next step, not looking for a reason to kill it."

Faust says he's glad he didn't allow himself to kill the idea for the MFA exhibition catalog. He felt he had to come up with a great concept because he basically was designing for his old college professor—an unfamiliar place for most designers. Ultimately, it was their collaboration that made the project so rewarding and successful.

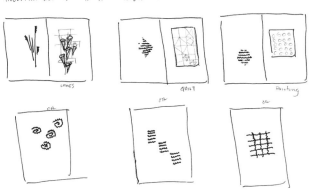

A sample sketch shows three spreads and how the text would counter the artwork. Notice the alternate copy design underneath each spread.

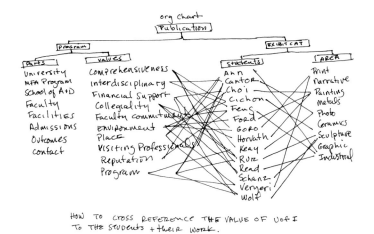

Faust used an organization chart to draw a visual correlation between the programs offered at the university and their value to the students. The student section on the right was used on the cover and the invitation for the exhibit.

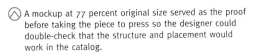

A mockup at 77 percent original size served as the proof before taking the piece to press so the designer could double-check that the structure and placement would work in the catalog.

The spine serves as the marketing aspect of the brochure by inserting details about the university's programs. It's also a graphic representation of how the school is a support system for the artists.

Faust's final layout of the catalog combines both vertical and horizontal type juxtaposed with student work.

Virginia Zoo
Sometimes, tackling a pro bono project can be a real bear. Between **juggling paying clients** and important—but free—work, **pro bono projects** often get the raw end of the deal. **That's not the case, however,** with the Virginia Zoo's annual report.

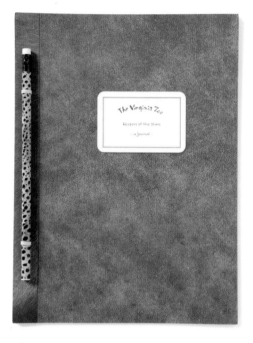

The Virginia Zoo annual report was a labor of love for art director Jeff Ringer. Despite doing the report entirely pro bono, Ringer put everything into the project and made it come alive, thanks to his personal touches.

Ringer Creative in Virginia Beach, Virginia, truly made it a labor of love—even after the budget was slashed midway through the project.

Creative director and senior art director Jeff Ringer was thrilled to work with the Virginia Zoo because they were such grateful clients and generally approved everything he presented. (Who wouldn't love a client like that?)

The zoo's director of development asked Ringer Creative to do an annual report for them with what was originally a reasonable budget for production. She showed Ringer several examples from zoos around the country and had confidence Ringer could do something just as creative.

"The first thing I did was sit down with the production manager to create a loose timeline," says Ringer. "We worked back from the client's deadline, allowing for printing, production, art direction, copywriting, concepting, meetings, review, proofing, and approval.

"Second, I met with the client to review the details of the project and to fill out the agency Creative Work Plan (CWP) with the client. The CWP asks specific questions such as target audience, project goals, and challenges it needs to solve, as well as what mandatory information must be included. Filling out this CWP with the client ensures that we have client buy in from the beginning, and that no surprises arise along the way."

With about a week to come up with concepts for the report, Ringer found his inspiration at, of all places, the zoo. He had spent nearly every weekend there because it was his youngest son's favorite place to go. Another major source of inspiration was paper samples. Ringe always has admired the creativity, the seemingly endless creative freedom, and the unusual processes used to bind, enclose, and print promotional items. He wanted to capture that creativity somehow in the annual report. In addition, Ringer discovered in a bookstore a re-creation of a journal written by a young Reuters photographer who had been killed tragically in Africa.

"I presented several concepts to the client," Ringer recalls. "I had created thumbnail mockups of each concept to help explain my concepts to the client. All of the concepts fit the strategy and the clients' goals, but for the two that I really wanted to sell—the

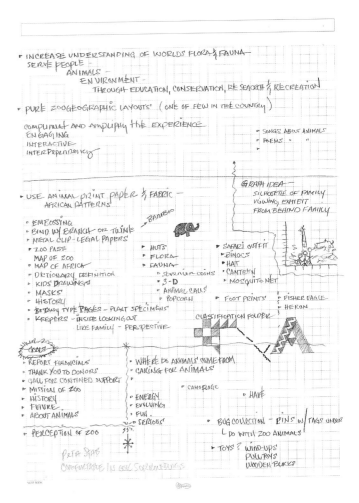

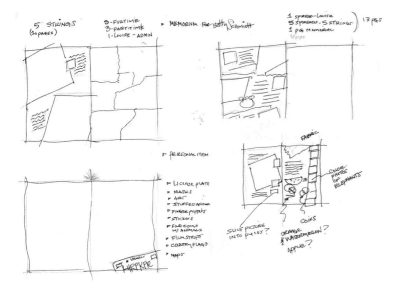

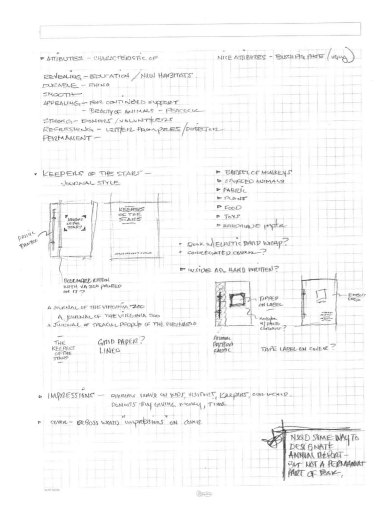
Top, left and right: Early brainstorming logs of meeting notes and inspirations included animal sketches and illustrations.

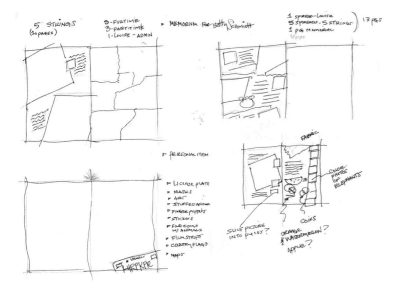
Above: After the budget was cut midway through the project, Ringer had to scrap more lavish ideas, such as binding seeds and materials into the report.

journal concept—I went a step further and created a typical spread layout. The client chose it on the spot.

"The toughest part was scheduling interviews and photo shoots with the zookeepers," Ringer notes. "I treated each interview as a new adventure. I brought an instant camera and self-closing plastic bags for found objects. I nosed around each of the keepers' offices looking for objects that I could use to portray some interesting fact or personality trait of each person. The copywriter and I were welcomed behind the scenes and at times were a lot closer to the animals than we wanted to be. After each interview the copywriter emailed the text for review of facts and content to the keeper and the client, who returned the copy with revisions and/or approval in a day.

"About three-quarters of the way through the project, the client informed me her budget had been cut significantly. We were too far along to change concepts, so I had to beg, barter, and call in favors from a printer, a photographer, and a paper company, which added several days to the process."

The budget constraints almost endangered the overall production quality of the report. "Because the budget was slashed, there wasn't time or budget for me to attend the pressrun," says Ringer. "Thankfully, the pressman running the job noticed that the paper was soaking up the ink, making the job look very

Above and top right: Ringer also found inspiration in the published journal of a young Reuters photographer who was tragically slain in Africa.

One of Ringer's early pitches, the journal idea, was quickly accepted because he went the extra mile to show how it would work.

washed out. He took it upon himself to stop the press, explore some alternatives with his team, and come up with a solution of a touch plate of fluorescent yellow, which made the images pop. The solution made all the difference in the world."

So how is it possible that Ringer pulled off this beautiful piece with a slashed budget? "I began by downsizing the report," Ringer says. "Originally, it was going to be 11" x 14" (27.9 cm x 35.6 cm)," Ringer says, "but I consolidated information and pages into a smaller format. I couldn't bind in the found objects and envelopes, so I scanned the items and used Photoshop to work them into the pages to add dimension. I handwrote most of the copy—luckily I have very legible handwriting—and I did all of the little spot illustrations. I called the paper company and got the

paper at cost. I called the printer and asked them to reduce their price. Finally, my 13-year-old son and I bound all of the annual reports by hand."

Ringer says this attention to detail ultimately saved the annual report from becoming a huge disappointment, given the obstacles he had to overcome. In the end, though, Ringer found that people will rally behind good design and creative direction. Ringer says the unusual concept for the report allowed him to get the desired paper at cost, hire an A-plus photographer, boost excitement at the zoo, and achieve extra attention on press.

Quite an achievement for a pro bono project.

YOUR MEMBERSHIP IN THE VIRGINIA ZOO WILL ENHANCE YOUR ENJOYMENT OF AN AMAZING VARIETY OF ZOO EXPERIENCES. YOU'LL ENJOY UP-CLOSE ENCOUNTERS WITH FASCINATING ANIMALS IN STATE-OF-THE-ART HABITATS DESIGNED TO RESPECT THEIR EXISTENCE AND ENCOURAGE NATURAL BEHAVIORS. YOU'LL SUPPORT FUN FILLED EDUCATIONAL PROGRAMS FOR BOTH CHILDREN AND ADULTS. AND YOU'LL MAKE IT POSSIBLE FOR FUTURE GENERATIONS TO ENJOY THIS REMARKABLE COMMUNITY ASSET.

BONGO: TRAGELAPHUS EURYCERUS THE LARGEST, MOST COLORFUL AND SOCIABLE AFRICAN ANTELOPE.

THERE ARE A NUMBER OF SUPPORT LEVELS AVAILABLE, EACH OF WHICH IS DESIGNED TO FIT YOUR PARTICULAR INTERESTS AND BUDGET. WE INVITE YOU TO INQUIRE ABOUT BECOMING A MEMBER, A VOLUNTEER OR EVEN A CORPORATE SUPPORTER. THE EXPEDITION PROMISES TO BE EXCITING, REWARDING AND PERSONALLY FULFILLING. NOW THAT YOU KNOW WHAT LIES AHEAD, THE NEXT STEP IS YOURS TO TAKE.

BE A REAL MONKEY'S UNCLE! ASK ABOUT OUR ZOO DOPTION PROGRAM

⊗ Ringer handwrote all the text, except for the financial data, and drew all the small animal images interspersed throughout the report.

⊗ The journal concept was particularly challenging because time was short and Ringer had to create and collect materials on his own.

"The Writers' Theatre wanted to increase the connection between its subscribers and the theater," says Tim Bruce, art director at Chicago-based **Lowercase, Inc.** "They wanted to extend the experience beyond attending performances.

The designer emphasized the written word over other images in the publication because the productions of the theatre are scaled back to accentuate the writing.

We determined that *WT,* a literary-driven magazine, would help patrons better understand the works being presented as well as the theater's approach to that work. We also noted that this project would be a good way to keep everyone familiar with the breadth and depth of programs being developed."

Bruce had the luxury of working with the Writers' Theatre when they were just a small theater working from the back of a bookstore nearly 15 years ago. The mini-magazine was simply another step in establishing their presence in the city's artistic community. Bruce says much of the inspiration for the layout came from the theater itself.

"It's intimate, small, and unexpected, and changes constantly, so we thought the pages should capture that," Bruce says. "We focused on what we know about the theater because we have been working with them a long time. We know how they stage their productions: They cut out a lot of unnecessary things and focus on a point of view about the written word. Therefore, they may take a production that has been done many times by other theaters and strip it down to something that's really essential and unique."

One of the early comps was a tabloid that folded out to a larger piece. Although Bruce was partial to this size, both he and the client agreed that it didn't match the theater's image or personality. "Although they really liked the scale and the impact of the tabloid, they felt it wasn't the theater and how they wanted to position it—their space is really intimate, and they are working their way to the very top of the Chicago theater world," Bruce says. "It was easy for them to say, 'We love the energy of this, but we need a small, intimate book that reflects our space.'"

Like a lot of designers, Bruce had limited resources for images and limited time to create the magazine. He focused on images that he could make work, no matter the level of quality—hence, the emphasis on black-and-white images and two-color processing. "Pretty early on, we made two design decisions: one, we were always going to do it in two-color, and two, we had a range of image quality that we couldn't control, so we had to find a way to make that imagery interesting as well as practical from a production standpoint. The inconsistent image quality allows you to mask some of the weaker images and also tie it together so it seems as if it's all from one place."

Type treatment plays a significant role throughout each issue of the Writers' Theatre publications—an influence directly from the theater's emphasis. "The type treatment is a direct reflection of the theater's concentration on the written word. They are the *Writers'* Theatre—their focus *is* the written word—so it just makes

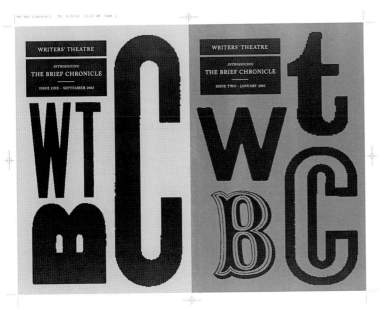

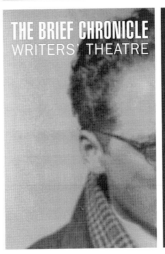

⬡ The inspiration for *WT* magazine came from vintage theater programs and the theater itself, says art director Tim Bruce. These mockups were rejected because of their size and inconsistency with the intimacy of the Writers' Theatre.

⟩ The designer was partial to one of the early tabloid-size comps, but when the client said it didn't match the theater's intimate personality, he had to agree.

perfect sense to reflect that emphasis. As a result, the designers have crafted the type on the page to speak a little bit like the actors might speak."

Bruce says the trick to creating a successful layout is to work quickly from the start. This method allows time to step away from the project and come back with a fresh approach. "What that does is allow us to get a lot of those ideas down as they come. We then have the benefit of setting it aside and coming back to it later to evaluate the ideas. I think we get better stuff in the end because we keep the freshness of an initial rush, but we refine the concept so everything ties together really well. The other thing about setting it aside is that it sort of frees your mind because you've gotten all of that stuff out that you first thought of but you have time to think about everything that's done. In this way, you have a new freshness that you can take in different directions, which is harder if you don't have that break."

"Typically, we work in opposites; each idea is a character foil for another idea. Therefore, we present as many good characters as come out of our design process, whether it be one, two, or five. We change everything all of the time. We dig deep into the subject and adapt accordingly; we would approach a book for the Milwaukee Art Museum far differently than a cookbook for Charlie Trotter. The subject drives our process."

As a recurring publication, there are a number of consistent design elements in *WT* that hold each issue together: a two-color approach, format, masthead, grid, table of contents, and typefaces.

Thanks in no small part to their collaboration with Lowercase, the Writer's Theatre has emerged as a premier company in the Chicago area. Reviews of their productions appear regularly in the *Wall Street Journal*.

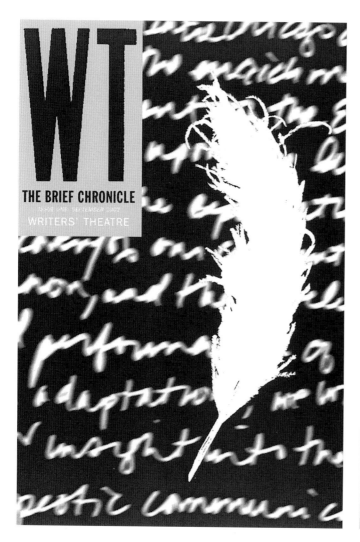

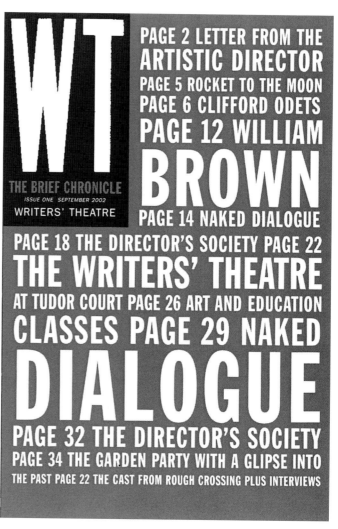

◇ Early cover iterations narrowed down the magazine's size and began to show the combination of type and image on the final pieces.

◇ Opposite page: Bruce had a variety of images of varying quality, so he made everything black and white. To tie it all together, he cross-processed each image.

...IT WAS ODETS' OWN TURBULENT MARRIAGE

for a "dentist play." Regan took the idea as her own and wrote *Every Day but Friday*, a forgettable first play about the plight of the working man. (Regan would later write the acclaimed play *Morning Star*.)

Odets, however, would use the same setting to explore a more personal story. The cramped dentist office in *Rocket to the Moon* became a metaphor for his own crumbling marriage. Belle and Stark were surrogates for Ranier and Odets, with the young secretary representing Odets' ideal woman.

The first two acts of *Rocket to the Moon* were written rather quickly

and contained some of Odets' most powerful (and personal) dialogue. But the third act, the play's resolution, proved more difficult to write. Odets was unsure of how the triangle should resolve itself. Should his protagonist stay with his wife or find new love with his secretary?

After many drafts and multiple endings, Odets finally completed the final draft of *Rocket to the Moon* only ten days before opening night. His marriage to Ranier was also given its final ending when the couple divorced in 1940.

Right: Clifford Odets and his wife Luise Rainer, 1937

THAT INSPIRED THE PLOT...

IN OUR TINY SPACE THERE IS NO ROOM FOR LYING OR PUMPED-UP THEATRICAL TRICKS

Back to the North Shore, William Brown prepares to charm the Writers' Theatre audiences once again

Writers' Theatre is delighted to welcome William Brown back to the North Shore to direct *Rocket to the Moon*. Bill has been charming Writers' Theatre audiences for years, both as a director and an actor. His directorial debut for Writers' Theatre was the critically acclaimed, Jeff nominated *The Glass Menagerie* in 1998. Richard Christiansen of the Chicago Tribune called it *"one of the very best shows of the current season...a jewel."* Bill went on to direct the electrifying *Incident at Vichy* in 1999 and, most recently, *Misalliance* which concluded our 2001/2002 Season.

Mr. Brown spent his summer at American Players Theatre (APT) in Spring Green, Wisconsin directing *Antony and Cleopatra*. At APT he also directed *All's Well That Ends Well* and *You Never Can Tell*. Other directing credits include *Halcyon Days* and the Midwest premiere of Tennessee Williams' *Not About Nightingales*, which won six Joseph Jefferson Citations, including Production and Director, at TimeLine Theatre. Last season Bill directed *Pygmalion* at Apple Tree Theatre. He is also the associate artistic director of Montana Shakespeare in the Parks, where he has directed *Much Ado About Nothing*, *The Winter's Tale*, *Love's Labour's Lost*, *The Comedy of Errors*, and *The*

Country Wife. He directed *Macbeth* for Chicago Shakespeare Theater's outreach program, and at Peninsula Players in Door County, he directed *Tons of Money* and *A Funny Thing Happened on the Way to the Forum*.

Also an accomplished actor, Bill won a Joseph Jefferson award for his stunning portrayal of Henry Kissinger in Writers' Theatre's *Nixon's Nixon*. Other roles at Writers' Theatre include Reverend Morrell in *Candida*, Elyot in *Private Lives*, Flaubert in *Dear Master*, and, most recently, the title role in Simon Gray's *Butley*. Bill has been seen at the Court Theatre as Falstaff in *Henry IV*, Jack in *The Importance of Being Ernest*, Almady in *The Play's the Thing* (Jeff Nomination), Dr. Bartolo in *The Barber of Seville*, and many roles in *Travels with my Aunt* (Jeff Nomination). At the Goodman he appeared in *Light up the Sky*, *Sunday in the Park with George*, *The Misanthrope*, and *Wings*. Bill created the role of Jody in Steven Dietz's *Lonely Planet* at Northlight and was Kenny in *Laughter on the 23rd Floor* at Briar Street Theatre.

The diversity and depth of William Brown's work continues to thrill and captivate audiences throughout Chicago. We are delighted to, once again, share his talents with you.

The Young & Rubicam Group of Companies

Every year, the Young & Rubicam Group of Companies in San Francisco hosts a **client appreciation event.** The 2002 event was held at Le Colonial, **a popular Vietnamese restaurant,** a location that **largely determined** the theme of the invitation.

⊘ Before starting to design the invitation, Rooney determined that the format would be roughly the size of a passport. Designing the envelope to encase the invitation was much more challenging.

The restaurant's decor and menu evoke the tropical elegance of Southeast Asia during its French colonial days in the 1930s.

"A quick tour of the eloquently appointed restaurant gave me the initial inspiration for the tone of the invitation," says art director Chris Rooney. "The vintage photos on the restaurant walls depicting early twentieth-century Saigon inspired the idea of taking the invitees back in time to another world. No initial budget was assigned, but the idea to use letterpress was decided from the beginning. The size of the invitation would be similar to that of a passport—everything else had to work around that."

Invitees were indeed transported back into this 1930s world when they received the invitation, with its illustrated directions to the event; a hand-stamped, letterpressed passport; and a response card displaying actual currency of the period. The vital statistics section of the passport is written in three languages: English, French, and Vietnamese. The passport also explains the rich history of food and culture in Vietnam and contains a detailed map of the region in 1930. For accuracy, Rooney used a circa 1930s map he found in a history book.

"Determining the shape and size of the passport part of the invitation was the easy part," Rooney says. "Deciding how to encase it was a difficult decision I had to make early on. Providing a resealable envelope with the inside showing a map with directions was an issue that we had to solve at the beginning."

To achieve the historical accuracy of the piece, Rooney embarked on a search for authentic passport stamps and vintage postage stamps from Indochina, which he found on eBay. "This project offered a lot of leeway, allowing to me to decide the content of the invitation," says Rooney. "After I had done thorough research, purchased some ephemera from early twentieth-century Indochina to influence the look and feel of the passport, and worked out some sketches, it just was a matter of executing the idea."

When a Vietnamese colleague at Young & Rubicam agreed to translate the invitation copy into Vietnamese and French, the invitation began to fall into place. Later, a seamstress friend of Rooney's volunteered to saddle-stitch the 250 passports. Despite this hands-on assistance, Rooney still spent several evenings stamping, folding, and stuffing to pull off the project in the end.

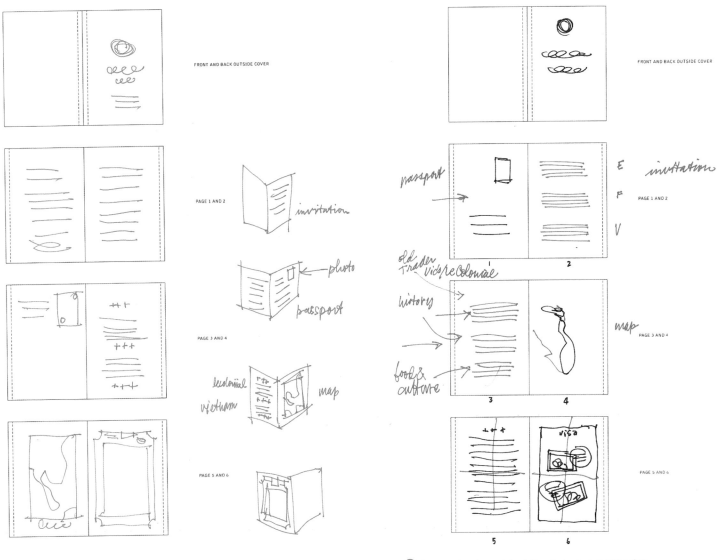

FRONT AND BACK OUTSIDE COVER

PAGE 1 AND 2

PAGE 3 AND 4

PAGE 5 AND 6

invitation

photo

passport

lecolonial vietnam

map

FRONT AND BACK OUTSIDE COVER

passport

invitation

E

F

V

PAGE 1 AND 2

2

old Trader Vic's Le Colonial

history

food & culture

map

PAGE 3 AND 4

3   4

visa

PAGE 5 AND 6

5   6

◯ Preliminary sketches of the passport show how Rooney would incorporate the overall feel of the invitation inspired by the Vietnamese restaurant for the venue, Le Colonial.

◯ Rooney takes the early invitation design in a direction that captures the historic authenticity of the time period.

Rooney's font choices—the art-deco Bakerscript and regal Avenir—reflect the time period appropriately. Finally, to give the passport a more authentic look, Rooney used Dingbats for the borders on the front and back covers.

Rooney says layout is the part of the design process he enjoys the most because of the variety of directions in which he can go. "The most difficult portion of the whole design process for me is not so much coming up with ideas as deciding on a direction when I have several good concepts," Rooney says. "Sometimes, elements from those rejected concepts can work their way into the direction I am trying to achieve. I see the process of designing as, first and foremost, being able to communicate clearly to readers while also being able to draw them in by conveying a feeling, whether it be humorous or sincere, plainspoken or evocative.

"Extraneous design experimentation sometimes can muddle what I am trying to communicate," Rooney explains. "Due to the lack of design constraints I was given with this invitation, I could have experimented in a number of ways. Yet, I choose not to, knowing that the invitation would follow the look of a vintage passport. Except for the RSVP postcard, I decided that all the pieces of the invitation would be letterpress printed in only two colors. I knew I would have to limit the way in which these two colors would interact with each other, especially because letterpress printing can be a bit tricky when it comes to registration. Fortunately, though, I used an experienced letterpress printer I've worked with in the past. In the end, budget constraints eliminated the letter-pressed gift bags that were to contain a Vietnamese coffee press and ground coffee beans for all the guests."

Despite his parting gift package getting nixed, Rooney's invitation was a big hit. The event was well attended, and recipients kept their invitations as keepsakes. Rooney was tapped to design the invitation for the 2003 event, but a more limited budget and a change of venue kept the invitation from being as lavish as the 2002 version. Hopefully, there will be another opportunity for Rooney to open his box of tricks.

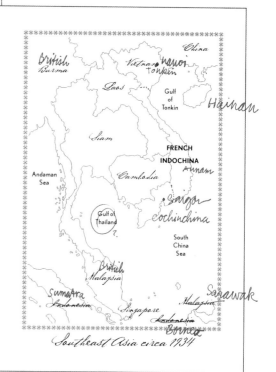

The designer found a circa-1930 map of French Indochina, which he used in order to keep the passport's look and feel authentic.

Rooney found inspiration in the art-deco Bakerscript and regal Avenir typefaces.

Southeast Asia: A Concise History
by Mary Somers Heidhues

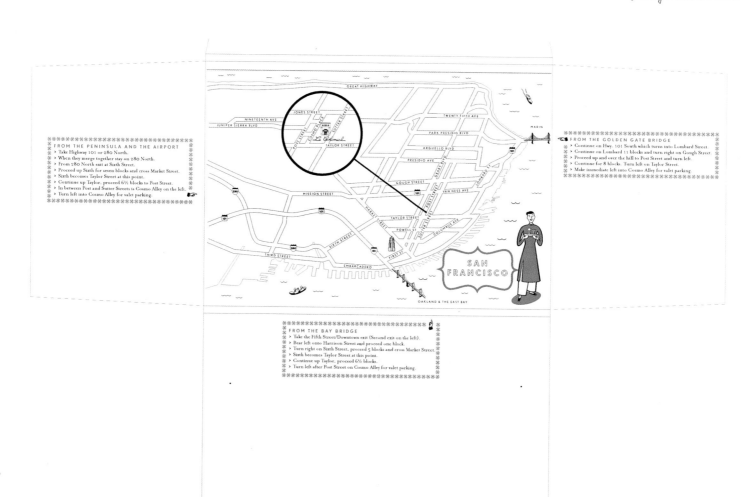

color palettes

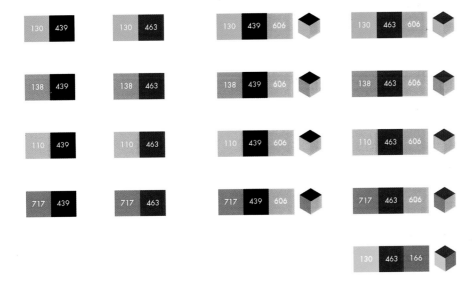

○ Rich colors were chosen for the passport and invitation to coincide with the overall look and feel of the event and its location.

○ Rooney luckily found authentic international passports on eBay, which he used for inspiration and for making the invitations feel as though they were straight out of the past.

directory of designers

1600ver90
121 Avenue of the Arts
Second Floor
Philadelphia, PA 19107 USA
(215) 732-3200
www.1600ver90.com
50

Alterpop
1001 Mariposa Street, #304
San Francisco, CA 94107 USA
(415) 558-1515
www.alterpop.com
54

BBK Studio
648 Monroe Avenue NW
Suite 212
Grand Rapids, MI 49503 USA
(616) 459-4444
www.bbkstudio.com
100, 112

Belyea
1809 Seventh Avenue
Suite 1250
Seattle WA 98101 USA
(206) 682-4895
www.belyea.com
80

Cahan & Associates
171 Second Street
Fifth Floor
San Francisco, CA 94105 USA
(415) 621-0915
www.cahanassociates.com
132

Chen Design Associates
589 Howard Street
Fourth Floor
San Francisco, CA 94105 USA
(415) 896-5338
www.chendesign.com
170

Crispin Porter + Bogusky
3390 Mary Street, Office 300
Miami, FL 33133 USA
(305) 646-7363
www.cpbgroup.com
124

dossiercreativeinc.
402-611 Alexander Street
Vancouver BC V6A 1E1 Canada
(604) 255-2077
(604) 255-2097 (fax)
www.dossiercreative.com
14

Douglas Joseph Partners
11812 San Vicente Boulevard
Suite 125
Los Angeles, CA 90049 USA
(310) 440-3100
www.djpartners.com
30, 70

Enspace, Inc.
3800 Lakeside Avenue
Suite 200
Cleveland, OH 44114 USA
(216) 431-2929
www.enspacedesign.com
166

envision+
Hirshbachstrasse 23
77830 Buhlertal, Germany
+49 7223 991802
www.envisionplus.com
152

Faust Associates
1322 South Wabash Avenue
Suite 109
Chicago, IL 60605 USA
(312) 922-9070
www.faustltd.com
190

Gauthier Associés Designers
131 rue de la Commune West
Montreal, Quebec H2Y 2C7 Canada
(514) 844-1159
ww.gauthierdesigners.com
174

Gensler Studio
30 West Monroe Street
Suite 400
Chicago, IL 60603 USA
(312) 456-0123
www.gensler.com
42

Hatch Creative
Studio 1
149 Chapel Street
St. Kilda, Victoria 3182 Australia
+61 03 9537 0608
www.hatchcreative.com.au
38

Henderson Bromstead Art Company
105 West Fourth Street
Sixth Floor
Winston-Salem, NC 27101 USA
(336) 748-1364
www.hendersonbromsteadart.com
96

Hornall Anderson Design Works, Inc.
1008 Western Avenue
Suite 600
Seattle, WA 98104 USA
(206) 467-5800
www.hadw.com
136, 144

Ideas On Purpose
27 West 20th Street
Suite 1001
New York, NY 10011 USA
(212) 366-6355
www.ideasonpurpose.com
140

iridium, a design agency
43 Eccles Street, Second Floor
Ottowa, Ontario K1R 6S3 Canada
(613) 748-3336
www.iridium192.com
84

The Jones Group
342 Marietta Street Northwest
Suite 3
Atlanta, GA 30313 USA
(404) 523-2606
www.thejonesgroup.com
88

Kolegram Design
37 St. Joseph Boulevard
Gatineau/Hull, Quebec J8Y 3V8 Canada
(819) 777-5538
www.kolegram.com
34, 58

Limb Design
1402 Caywood
Houston, TX 77055 USA
(713) 957-1117
www.limbdesign.com
116

Lowercase, Inc.
213 West Institute Place
Suite 311
Chicago, IL 60610 USA
(312) 274-0652
www.lowercaseinc.com
72, 198

Michael McDaniel
6804 North Capital of Texas Highway #812
Austin, TX 78731 USA
(512) 342-0022
www.michaelmcdaniel.com
46

Methodologie
808 Howell Street
Suite 600
Seattle, WA 98101 USA
(206) 623-1044
www.methodologie.com
148

Mimio Design
38 South Raymond Avenue
Pasadena, CA 91105 USA
(626) 449-1956
www.mimiodesign.com
108

Mires Brands
2345 Kettner Boulevard
San Diego, CA 92101 USA
(619) 234-6631
www.miresbrands.com
186

Nine Point Design
(780) 432-6118
www.ninepointdesign.com
156

Nolin Branding & Design
1610 rue Sainte-Catherine West
Bureau 500
Montreal, Quebec H3H 2S2 Canada
(514) 846-2542
www.nolin.ca
104

Ph.D
1524 A Cloverfield Boulevard
Santa Monica, CA 90404 USA
(310) 829-0900
www.phdla.com
62

Philographica, Inc.
1318 Beacon Street
Suite 12
Brookline, MA 02446 USA
(617) 738-5800
www.philographica.com
92

Pylon Design
445 Adelaide Street West
Toronto, ON M5V 1T1 Canada
(416) 504-4331
www.pylondesign.ca
164

Revolver Industries, Inc.
Cl 4ta Sur San Francisco
Chalet No. 15
Box 10701
El Dorado, Panama, Rep. de Panama
(507) 226-1272
www.elrevolver.com
66

Ringer Creative
5452 N. Sunland Drive
Virginia Beach, VA 23464-4066 USA
(757) 366-8947
www.ringercreative.com
194

Stefan Sagmeister
222 West 14th Street
New York, NY 10011 USA
(212) 647 1789
www.sagmeister.com
76

SamataMason
101 South First Street
West Dundee, IL 60118 USA
(847) 428-8600
www.samatamason.com
22

SETEZEROUM
R. da Constitução, 701
4200-200 Porto, Portugal
+351 225 509 685
www.setezeroum.com
18

Sussner Design Company
212 Third Avenue North
Suite 505
Minneapolis, MN 55401 USA
(612) 339-2886
www.sussner.com
10

Templin Brink Design
720 Tehama Street
San Francisco, CA 94103 USA
(415) 255-9295
www.tbd-sf.com
178

Tétro Design
464 Hargrave Street
Winnipeg, Manitoba R3A 0X5 Canada
(204) 942-0708
www.tetrodesign.com
182

Viva Dolan Communications & Design
99 Crown's Lane
Suite 500
Toronto, Ontario M5R 3P4 Canada
(416) 923-6335
www.vivadolan.com
26

Webb & Webb Design
16H Perseverance Works
38 Kingsland Road
London E2 8DD UK
+44 020 7739 7895
www.webbandwebb.co.uk
120

Werner Design Werks, Inc.
411 First Avenue North
Room 206
Minneapolis, MN 55401 USA
(612) 338-2550
www.wdw.com
128

The Young & Rubicam Group of Companies
303 Second Street
South Tower, Eighth Floor
San Francisco, CA 94107 USA
(415) 882-0766
www.yrsf.com
202

Zooom Productions
Felderstrasse 12
5330 Fuschl am See Austria
+43 6226 8848 0
www.zooom.at
160

about the author

Rodney J. Moore is an author, copywriter, and freelance journalist who has written more than 100 articles for such national publications as *Advertising Age, B-to-B Magazine,* and *HOW Magazine.* As founder of Moore Creative, a full-service editorial consulting company, he has worked with the Fortune 500 companies Xerox and Time-Life Inc., and also with nonprofit organizations such as the National Federation of Independent Business. For more information about Moore Creative, visit www.brandmoore.com.